Pragmatism and Social Hope

PRAGMATISM AND SOCIAL HOPE

Deepening Democracy in Global Contexts

Judith M. Green

 Columbia University Press *New York*

Columbia University Press

Publishers Since 1893

New York   Chichester, West Sussex

Copyright © 2008 Columbia University Press

Library of Congress Cataloging-in-Publication Data

Green, Judith M.

Pragmatism and social hope : deepening democracy in global contexts /
Judith M. Green

p.   cm.

Includes bibliograqphical references and index.

ISBN 978–0–231–14458–2 (cloth : alk. paper)—ISBN 978–0–231–51822–2
(e-book)

1. Social problems—United States 2. Social planning—United States.

3. Political science—Philosophy. 4. Pragmatism. I. Title.

HN57.G692 2009

36.10973—dc22

2008014177

Columbia University Press books are printed on permanent and durable
 acid-free paper.

This book is printed on paper with recycled content.

Printed in the United States of America

c 10 9 8 7 6 5 4 3 2 1

References to Internet Web sites (URLs) were accurate at the time of writing.

Neither the author nor Columbia University Press is responsible for URLs

that may have expired or changed since the manuscript was prepared.

CONTENTS

ACKNOWLEDGMENTS

I am grateful to Richard Rorty (1931–2007) for his contributions to the revival of pragmatism and to international academic freedom in times of adversity—and for "stinging" me so much in his role as a gadfly for democracy that I felt motivated to write this book.

I am deeply in the debt of Larry A. Hickman, director of the Center for Dewey Studies at Southern Illinois University, who has spoken tirelessly at universities around the world about how Dewey's kind of pragmatist philosophy can help us to meet the challenges we now face as world citizens in the twenty-first century, bringing me and other American pragmatists into conversation with scholars in other countries and helping many to establish Dewey Centers at their own universities. I learned a great deal by participating in conferences sponsored by the Dewey Center and the Center for Diversity Studies at Köln University in Germany during April 2005 and May 2007, where our kind hosts, Professors Kersten Reich and Stefan Neubert, and many other participants gave me helpful comments on my ideas about pragmatist metaphysics and cosmopolitanism. The experience of participating during May 2005 in the International Symposium on the Contemporary Significance of Dewey's Thought at Fudan University in Shanghai, China, where I presented "Hope's Progress," was life changing. I am grateful beyond words to our hosts, Professors Liu Fantong, Wang Tangjia, and Wei Hongzhong; to Ms. Mao Yan, who showed us great kindness and hospitality; and to Mr. Li Siqiang, who welcomed us to his home city of Xi'an, China's ancient capital. I am happy to thank Giuseppe Spadafora, Dean of Education at the Universities of Calabria and Basilicata in southern Italy, for inviting me to speak at an excellent international conference titled "John Dewey—Reconstructing Democracy" during May 2007. For earlier mind-expanding opportunities to learn from scholars in Poland and Slovakia, I am very grateful to Professors Beth J. Singer, Leszek Koczanowicz, Justyna Miklaszewska, Emil Visznovsky, and John Ryder. My future books, like this one, will reflect on what I learned at conferences with them in Karpacz, Krakow, and the High Tatras Mountains.

I am grateful to members of the Society for the Advancement of American Philosophy, who have listened to my ideas and taught me a great deal, both at their annual meetings and at the Summer Institute in American Philosophy. I am grateful as well to members of the American Philosophical Association, who have honored me by arguing with me about truth and philosophy. Many thanks to members of the Society for the Study of Africana Philosophy and the New York Pragmatist Forum for scholarly insights and personal support, especially to Alfred E. Prettyman, David E. McClean, and Hugh McDonald. I am deeply grateful for challenging comments on the entire manuscript from Carolyn Johnston, Alfred Prettyman, Howard McGary, John Lachs, William R. Caspary, John R. Shook, Jim Garrison, and Kersten Reich. My thanks to Fordham University for travel grants and a year-long faculty fellowship to work on this book, and to my colleagues and students for many helpful conversations, especially to Brian Henning and Mark Van Hollebeke, who first asked me to reply to *Achieving Our Country*. In shaping the final version of this book, David Anthony Wood offered me invaluable sympathy for its purposes and tough editing for its clarity.

I am grateful for their lifelong support to my parents Leo Green (1915–1992) and Helen O'Keefe Green (1907–2005), as well as to my brother and sister, James W. Green and Shannon L. Green, and to the other members of our Minnesota-based clan. Finally, I am grateful to my beloved life partner, David William Woods, who shares my deepest hopes and most of my best adventures, and who has generously commented on every draft.

New York City

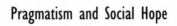

Pragmatism and Social Hope

Introduction

Pragmatism and Social Hope
Deepening Democracy in Global Contexts

Insistence in advance on coalitional "unity" as a goal assumes that solidarity, whatever the price, is a prerequisite for political action.

—Judith Butler, *Gender Trouble*

When it comes to political deliberation, philosophy is a good servant but a poor master. If one knows what one wants and has some hope of getting it, philosophy can be useful in formulating redescriptions of social phenomena. The appropriation of these redescriptions, and of the jargon in which they are formulated, may speed up the pace of social change. But I think we are now in a situation in which resentment and frustration have taken the place of hope among politically concerned intellectuals, and that the replacement of narrative by philosophy is a symptom of this unhappy situation.

—Richard Rorty, *Philosophy and Social Hope*

Insecurity has overtaken all habitats since 9/11 from Paris to Bali.

—Julia Kristeva, *Murder in Byzantium, a Novel*

Why America and the World Need Deeper Democracy and Widely Shared Social Hope

What America and the world need now is a multifaceted, context-sensitive, flexible, open-ended, constantly evolving, inquiry-guiding story, vision, and process of deepening democracy that can foster and educate widely shared social hope. We citizen-thinkers who have reawakened to our sense of democratic possibility and responsibility must think creatively and courageously about how to reestablish America's commitment to achieving the effective, democratic solidarity of mind and heart amid our diversity that Thomas Jefferson, Abraham Lincoln, Walt Whitman, William James, Jane Addams, John Dewey, Alain Locke, James Baldwin, Martin Luther King Jr., and other great thinkers of earlier generations affirmed as our peculiarly American goal and gift to the world. At the same time, we must reframe our country's imperfectly actualized democratic ideal in terms of a shared world citizenship that includes people of different cultures, in different life contexts, with different voices expressing compatible though not identical hopes, resolving our conflicts peacefully and to our mutual benefit, challenging one another to grow.

As Walt Whitman recognized nearly a century and a half ago in the wake of America's devastating Civil War, reenergizing shared social hope in the potentials of a democracy deeper than any nation or culture has yet achieved is the starting point of a world-transforming process in which America must play a leading part. As John Dewey pointed out in the fast-changing years between the twentieth century's terrible world wars, democracy is ultimately a quality of social living rather than a characteristic of institutions alone—a quality so attractive that, once people begin to see its potential, the longing for such a life in their own social context becomes contagious and yet frightening to those who feel that its expansion would cause them to lose wealth, power, or a truth they prize. However, as James Baldwin warned in the midst of the tumultuous 1960s, the cost of denying or deferring such democratic social hope, once aroused, is the desperate destruction of individuals and nations.

In this twenty-first-century era, which offers either continuous insecurity for all or peace with justice for all, deepening democracy in diverse global contexts is the key to what both Baldwin and Richard Rorty called "achieving our country," which I believe is now inseparable from the broader goal of "achieving our world"—a deeply democratic world. Like Samuel P. Huntington, Rorty believed that the deeply democratic world toward which I believe we must work is impossible—or at least, that there is no clear way to advance such a goal and no good reason to try. Rorty's reasons were philosophical: there is no common human nature to which we can appeal in seeking to bridge profound cultural gaps in our experiences, he said, and no common language in which to share those experiences with one another; there is no independent truth of history to which we can appeal when our values and our memories of painful events differ; and thus there is no basis for affirming a cross-difference human solidarity other than the fragile bonds that emerge when someone else cares about the stories we tell. We value what we do because that's who we are—a "Western bourgeois liberal," he called himself—with a particular set of inherited loyalties and aspirations for which we cannot argue or even offer reasons. We must forget sources of shame and division in our past, Rorty urged, because these will block the shared esteem of "our country" that may allow us to work together to fulfill its better potentials in a time of great dangers, without any "blessed assurance" about our future.

Huntington reached a similar conclusion, though he based it on his reading of the kind of empirical evidence that Rorty suggested carries no more weight than his own kind of "rhetoric." In *The Clash of Civilizations and the Remaking of World Order* (1996), Huntington argued that "culture and cultural identities, which at the broadest level are civilization identities, are shaping the patterns of cohesion, disintegration, and conflict in the post–cold war world."[1] Instead of "a universal civilization in any meaningful sense," Huntington argued, a seven-to-nine–sector "multipolar and multicivilizational" world order is emerging, in which the West's civilizational power is declining as Asian and Muslim civilizational powers are expanding, specific cultures are reaffirming themselves and cooperating along civilizational lines, and Western universalist claims tend to lead to conflict with other civilizations. Thus, to avoid devastating clashes, we must adopt a "hands-off" policy toward the affairs of other civilizations, limit our universal value claims, and cultivate whatever small areas of cross-civilizational agreement may be possible.

Moreover, Huntington argued, "the survival of the West" requires that Americans reaffirm our unique, now vulnerable Western cultural identity instead of claiming either a multicultural one or a universal one. We cannot hope to understand other civilizations in their "thickness," to share some of their nonmaterial as well as material interests, and to find or forge a common ground that we could advance together as what Jane Addams called a "universal motive"—an alternative to both civilization clash and mutual noninterference.[2] In dealing with other nations, we should "accept diversity," Huntington advised, while seeking to discover and to advance "thin" cross-cultural norms.[3] In America, however, the way to advance security and peace he recommended is to reclaim our founders' Anglo-Protestant culture, reaffirm their "American Creed," and reject both cosmopolitan and imperial identities in favor of a national one.[4]

Though their modes of thinking differ greatly, Rorty's and Huntington's shared conclusions grow out of at least two shared distortions that make their shared objections to my proposal less formidable than they might at first seem. Contrary to Rorty's and Huntington's underlying assumption, there are not now nor have there ever been pure and unchanging cultures, a basic anthropological fact that Alain Locke pointed out in 1917.[5] Instead, every culture that exists shows influences of other cultures, including some that are profoundly different. Thus, there is no way to firmly demarcate cultures and civilizations from one another or to protect them from multicultural-ism, whether to restore postcolonial cultures and civilizations to precolonial forms or to preserve them from future external influences. At the same time, the characteristics and impacts of globalization we now experience show that cross-cultural, even cross-civilizational mutuality already exists, and also that we must do more to acknowledge and to tend to the combination of material and nonmaterial interests this process is currently ill guided to positively transform and advance for most peoples. Even if cross-cultural influences are normal, and perhaps unavoidable, however, it would be preferable for such influences to be more reflectively chosen instead of imperially imposed or thoughtlessly adopted.[6] This is one of the meanings of and motives for deepening democracy in global contexts.

A second distortion in both Rorty's and Huntington's analyses is that both ignore real and important cultural, religious, regional, postcolonial, and economic *clashes within civilizations*, and even *within nation-states*. In his story of "achieving our country," Rorty treated the American people as ideally becoming a single political-cultural bloc, proposing that we simply "get over" all of our great historical differences and work together for equal opportunity and economic justice in the future. In a similar vein, Huntington's analysis treats cultures and civilizations as blocs, constituting these along lines of recent and ongoing international clashes in a way that is both theoretically arbitrary and methodically circular. Just what constitutes a distinctive culture or "civilization" in this age of globalization is unclear, especially after three centuries of colonization that have exported and imported cultural, religious, artistic, and linguistic elements as well as trade goods and whole families between subordinate nations and imperial centers. Moreover, Huntington has ignored the difference between typically eclectic cultural formations and the various cultural fundamentalisms on which Benjamin Barber has focused that have arisen in recent years in reaction to globalization and perceived American imperialism.[7]

Thus, how to ameliorate what Huntington calls "a clash of civilizations" is an empirical, conceptual, and aspirational question that I propose to respond to throughout this book, in the course of appreciatively and critically replying to Rorty's hope-spurring "new American story" of "achieving our country" and to the philosophical and historical claims on which it depends.

While I believe that Rorty and Huntington are wrong about these important matters, I must frame the central claim of this book by acknowledging the insightfulness of their key concern: Achieving America's democratic potential within a deeply democratic world that cooperatively interlinks diverse cultural, religious, economic, and political contexts will not be an easy process. It will be opposed by those "Islamic fundamentalists" who corrupt and blasphemously misuse the protodemocratic teachings of the Koran, thereby misleading countless citizens of desperately poor countries who lack the interpretive skills and historical perspective to challenge their misreading, intentionally inflaming a cadre of angry, patriotic, and religiously serious young men and women to sacrifice their lives in murderous terrorist acts the Koran expressly forbids because they see no other way to improve the bleak future of their peoples. It also will be opposed by those Jewish and Christian "fundamentalists" who believe that great differences in opportunity and in access to the basic means of living that currently divide the "haves" from the "have-nots" express the will of God, even though such a belief is contrary to Jewish and Christian scriptures.

Moreover, efforts to deepen democracy worldwide will be opposed by those "capitalist fundamentalists" who hope to benefit from economic inequalities in the present global order or believe that these promote the wealth of nations or leave everyone better off than they would otherwise be because they somehow reflect the operation of efficient and impersonal market forces. They will be opposed by those "democratic realists" who think of democracy and human rights as peculiarly Western ideals that we jeopardize when we try to share them more widely. They will be opposed by all those who believe that advancing their national interests, cultural integrity, religious purity, or the interests of multinational firms to which they have conjoined their destinies—or just facing "the way things are"—requires a hierarchical, adversarial approach to living that allows working with others only in temporary, shifting, limited coalitions within what Rorty called "campaigns."

Nonetheless, I will argue here that deepening democracy in America and in other global contexts is necessary for sustaining the great democratic achievements of the past and for fulfilling the present yearnings for a more secure, just, and life-affirming future that most Americans share with most of the world's citizens. Such yearnings were manifested in many generous, self-sacrificing, collaborative actions on and after September 11 that helped countless Americans and their friends in other nations to find an active way to express their love, concern, and deepest hopes for the future. Such yearnings have guided the successful transformation struggles of diverse peoples, of more than sixty nations who have reframed their countries as democracies since World War II, and continue to guide similar struggles today, even within the world's most repressive, authoritarian states.[8]

Such yearnings for deep democracy represent a positive potential for redirecting twenty-first-century processes of globalization that is not yet adequately expressed—and is even hindered in some ways—by the policies and procedures of the major international economic development organizations that were created during the last months of World War II in order to rebuild devastated nations and to peacefully interlink the world through trade: the World Bank, the International Monetary Fund, and the General Agreement on Tariffs and Trade (since replaced by the World Trade Organization). As a condition of receiving assistance from these powerful international economic development organizations, the "neoclassical" economists who have advised their appointed leaders typically have insisted that applicant states—whether postcolonial, postcommunist, or in crisis for some other reason—adopt Western-style capitalist economic institutions and property laws modeled on those of their wealthy, ethnocentric donor states. Usually, local cultures and customs have not been considered, and no provision has been made for the applicant nations' citizens to participate in the decision process.[9] In many cases, the advice of these economic "experts" about democratization and development has backfired. In postcommunist Russia and Eastern Europe, for example, it has led to national resource-grabbing by wealthy entrepreneurs, extortion by criminal syndicates, and government corruption. In many poor, postcolonial contexts in Africa, the Americas, and South Asia, it has led to unsustainable growth of impoverished "megacities," the emptying out of rural workforces, irremediable damage to forest lands as well as rare animal and plant species, and loss or profound distortion of unique local cultures with specific languages, lifeways, and local knowledge bases that were precious to their people and potentially valuable to the wider world.

Nonetheless, in spite of the many economic, environmental, and cultural obstacles to deepening global democracy that have come into being during the past sixty years through the intentional efforts of democracy's opponents as well as the unwise guidance of globalization processes by the dominant "experienced" democracies, countless people continue to yearn for and work for a more deeply democratic world. Foretastes of a deeper democracy's transformative power and joy already are being expressed in the different, culturally distinctive approaches to such globally shared projects as the composition and performance of jazz music, research in scientific fields like genetics and astrophysics, and the Internet-fostered international student movement of solidarity with those in diverse economic and geopolitical contexts who demand fair labor practices, respect for human rights, and respect for the Earth. What the world needs now is an inspiring general story, shared guiding vision, and effective process for expanding these networks of active, creative, energizing hope for deeply democratic living.

Ten years ago, Richard Rorty proposed one way to tell a hope-inspiring story of America's democratic future, *Achieving Our Country*, though he could not imagine how to tell it on a wider scale. Rorty was right to think we need such a story and right about many of its elements, even though he made some mistakes in its telling, and the scope of his story is too limited to guide the kinds of wider transformative efforts the world needs now. One of the world's best-known philosophical gadflies and democratic visionaries of the post–Vietnam War era, a broadly educated, creative, and iconoclastic thinker who shed a bright light on the value of many almost-forgotten contributions of the classical American pragmatists, Richard Rorty is gone now—he died on June 7, 2007—but the transformative challenge he threw down to citizen-thinkers everywhere remains. Taking up this challenge, with help from Jefferson, Lincoln, Whitman, James, Addams, Dewey, Locke, Baldwin, King, and many other still-living American thinkers, my purpose in this book is to critically reframe and expand Rorty's story in order to offer guidance for new hope-stirring, post-9/11 transformative efforts to deepen democracy in America and in diverse global contexts. Part of the meaning of 9/11 is that "achieving our country" now requires "achieving our world"—a more deeply democratic world, whose citizens can and must play active, reflective, competent, and mutually contributive roles in shaping a preferable future.

The Role of Public Philosophy in the Twenty-first Century?

On August 17, 2004, at meetings of the American Sociological Association in San Francisco on the theme of "Public Sociology," Richard Rorty and Judith Butler claimed that philosophy has no public role to play in the twenty-first century. Rising from the audience, I called upon them both to rethink that claim, especially in light of Rorty's effective invitation to intellectuals across the disciplines to reengage as leaders in the crucial project of "achieving our country."[10] I suggested that they accept the responsibilities and opportunities that their international fame as philosophers had given them to foster a broad, intercultural process of reflection and inquiry about the causes of our current global problem situation and about the kinds of transformations that would allow diverse citizen-thinkers to voice social hopes and work together to fulfill them.

Judith Butler responded fiercely on Rorty's behalf: "No one has spoken out more than Richard Rorty on the terrible events of our times—he has published op-ed pieces in newspapers throughout Europe—as have I, though we tend to publish in different places—and he also publishes in the *New York Times*. Of course, there may be another question about *who* gets published in these places." Rorty himself replied, "I tend to separate my voice as a philosopher from my voice as a citizen—I don't think I have anything important to say as a philosopher." He added later, in conversation with me, "No one listens to me, anyway." When I pointed out to him that his platform to speak as a world citizen grew out of his prominence as a philosopher and an insider-critic and that other philosophers as well as a wide audience of citizen-thinkers have read and found inspiration in his *Achieving Our Country*, Rorty thought for a moment and then replied that perhaps he had separated his two voices too much. As I thought about this conversation later, I wondered if 9/11 had undermined Rorty's confidence, as it had done to countless others. Maybe, like them, he was seeking a way to restore his hope, personal as well as social.

Rorty had explained in his public remarks that day that he and Butler had begun their careers as philosophers but had relocated to other disciplines because, in America and other English-speaking countries during the twentieth century, philosophy as an academic discipline had tried to model itself on the sciences instead of recognizing itself as one of the humanities. However, he argued, to be a science, philosophy would require a consensus about what is important, worth doing, respectable. Philosophy lacks such a consensus, Rorty rightly noted, which he thought suggests that it is actually more like literary criticism than like the sciences. Butler had begun her earlier remarks on the session topic, "Theoretical Cultures Across the Disciplines," by saying, "I don't actually engage in a metadiscourse on theory," though she immediately acknowledged that "theoretical assumptions are always in play—they're found everywhere—though they are difficult to treat as a specific phenomenon." Rorty reduced the theoretical issues about the possibility of a public philosophy that might have been raised by the conference theme to questions of democratic voice and its absence and then shifted into a reverie about a better time in philosophy, before the field was professionalized in the late nineteenth century by what William James in 1903 called "the Ph.D. octopus." Now, as then, Rorty suggested—telling a very different story about his philosophical purposes than James and the other classical American pragmatists told about their own—we philosophers should not aim to contribute to knowledge but instead should try, like "Mr. Chips," to hand down to the next generation the best that has been said in the past in order to produce "more sweetness and light." Periodically, perhaps a few iconoclastic "geniuses" or "gurus" will change the subject and style of philosophy for new generations of graduate students to grind to finer powder in their doctoral dissertations.

Of course, Rorty was vastly understating his influence that day, as I have since learned at philosophy conferences in California and New York and at the new Centers for Dewey Studies at Köln University in Germany, Fudan University in China, and the University of Calabria in Italy, at each of which Rorty's work was discussed with a combination of admiration and concern. Rorty was no "Mr. Chips"—rather, he was a "guru" to countless young philosophers and, ironically, he attracted them to philosophy just as he was decamping from it, to classical American pragmatism just as he was giving up its long-term projects, and to citizen participation in democracy just as he was consigning this vision to the junkyards of history and turning his attention to the roles of "geniuses" and "gurus." Rorty was a controversial figure among admirers of classical American pragmatism, both at home and abroad, because, over the course of his career, he did a great deal to return its methods and its democratic vision to philosophical influence, including his many favorable references to James, Whitman, and Dewey in *Achieving Our Country*. Yet he frequently misrepresented their views in arguing for his own, which were in some ways incompatible. Like these great American thinkers, whose work he clearly admired at least as much as that of his great European intellectual heroes—Hegel, Freud, Nietzsche, Yeats, Trotsky, Heidegger, and Wittgenstein—Rorty helped to revitalize the commitment of citizen-thinkers to the practical work of deepening and strengthening democracy.

However, Rorty differed greatly from James, Whitman, and Dewey in how he imagined the democratic ideal and in how he proposed to actualize it. For example, James urged us to consider all the available evidence on controversial and important matters before choosing provisionally—based on our own deepest sense of the matter, which he called "passional grounds"—between rival hypotheses to guide our belief and action, because that's the only way to get more evidence that will allow us to revise our hunches and eventually tell a more insightful story of what's really going on. James also urged us to make achieving the full meaning of democracy a lifelong cause to which we would bring the same kind of passionate, patriotic commitment that many in the past have brought to winning wars. In a related vein, Whitman imagined free individual people as naming and striving to fulfill their own highest and best potentials with the inspiration and support of a democratic nation that would help to give meaning and purpose to their life choices. In the same spirit, Dewey described a pragmatist process of collaborative, truth-seeking, intelligent inquiry—in science and in public life—that he believed would foster individuals' mutual growth within pluralistic, democracy-minded communities whose members would care about and be open to learning from others worldwide.

In contrast, Rorty argued as a self-described "neopragmatist" that James's talk about "what's really going on" doesn't make any sense, and he urged us to avoid causes and movements of all kinds. He recommended abandoning Dewey's truth-seeking collaborative inquiry, arguing that epistemology is a waste of time and that the concept of truth misleads us more than it helps us. Calling himself a "nominalist"—though he also said that metaphysics is a pointless philosophical pastime—Rorty denied that there is any human nature (innate or evolved) and that there are any real communities (human or otherwise) that amount to something more or different than a gathering of individuals. Thus, for him, the purpose of a democracy is to advance the private, self-chosen purposes of individuals; a nation cannot outlive its particular members or have meanings other than those they and other individuals give to it; and there is no human solidarity that arises from our species membership or from anything else, other than our active weaving of linguistic ties through what he called "persuasive rhetoric." Rorty replaced Whitman's piety toward divine sources of humanity's limitless, creative being with his own divinity-free, ethnocentric "ironism," recognizing only others' privacy and democracy's fragility in his "strong poet's" retelling of America's story, through which he aimed to inspire shared social hope and limited public campaigns for the "Western bourgeois liberal" reforms that make sense in a culture like ours and that he hoped would lead many to feelings of wider social solidarity.[11]

To this reader, Rorty proposed a poor trade—yet I have learned valuable lessons from him and am mindful that he opened up the resources of classical American pragmatism to a generation of readers worldwide who came to feel a certain piety toward him, though he would have made light of their attachment to him as their "guru." Moreover, I am mindful, as Judith Butler pointed out, that Rorty contributed his scholarly prestige to the liberatory struggles of fellow academics in Latin America and Eastern Europe when post-totalitarian democracy was a dangerous idea and a difficult project. Therefore, my own stance toward his memory and his legacy is both appreciative and critical. In this book, which derives its title from a collection of Rorty's essays, *Philosophy and Social Hope* (1999), I aim to show that his call to citizen-thinkers to take up again the active demands of working for democracy's fuller actualization was timely, even prophetic—and also to show that his specific proposals for deepening America's democracy must be reconstructed after 9/11 along lines that are closer to the classical pragmatists' original visions now expanded to include other global contexts, so that a new dream-story that grows out of his can become a feasible and desirable guide to deeply democratic transformative action in our troubled, hope-starved, twenty-first-century world.

In San Francisco, neither Rorty nor Butler answered my question about *why* and *how* public philosophers might serve as Socratic midwives to a wider public conversation of citizen-thinkers that is reflective, reconstructive, and deeply democratic. However, we might ask ourselves, if we took their advice, and all of us philosophers were to resign from the job of noticing, analyzing, critically challenging, and proposing alternatives to others' theoretical assumptions across the disciplines and in the conduct of our national and international life, would everyone be better off? Would scholars in other disciplines take up this work? Would "experienced democracies" find better ways of encouraging "democratic voice," or would they rely primarily on opinion polling and periodic voting? Would the "powers that be" listen more carefully to "persuasive rhetoric," or would they simply fight wars, erode hard-won civil rights and environmental protections, and advance the process of global economic reorganization more efficiently?

Public Philosophy, Pragmatism, and Social Hope

This book is grounded in a deep conviction about the role of public philosophers in the twenty-first century: we have important responsibilities to fulfill in helping our fellow citizens to come to a reflective, critical, and reconstructive voice in order to be heard by themselves, by one another, and by those who wield great undemocratic powers in our world—and we need to think carefully as public philosophers about how to fulfill this important democratic role effectively. "Public philosophers," as I understand this community of engaged citizen-thinkers, may include but is not limited to those who teach philosophy professionally at colleges and universities throughout America and the world. It also includes citizen-scholars in allied disciplines who are gifted in critical inquiry and synthetic reconstruction of prevailing methods, models, and guiding values, including sociologists, political scientists, historians, lawyers, urban planners, economists, and even theologians and literary critics. It includes leaders in community life who bring wide experience to the table and have gifts for bringing out others' voices. It includes wise citizen-thinkers of various social backgrounds and career fields who understand the importance of democratic values in the future-making struggles of our times and who are willing to speak out on their behalf. I believe that the kind of democratic theory that can grow out of and guide the collaborative reflection of such a community of "public philosophers" concerning recent, long-persisting, and possible future aspects of our shared and diverging experiences, illuminated and corrected by the work of the various arts and sciences, will help us to learn why and how we must do this public work inclusively, effectively, and toward the most desirable ends.

Creating a deeply democratic public philosophy must begin where we are in these early years of the twenty-first century, struggling with painful memories and searching for that social hope Rorty wrote about in that far-off, pre-9/11 context—a shared social hope that can inspire and guide our cross-difference transformative efforts to "achieve our country" and to "begin a new history of the world," as Baldwin prophetically framed our challenge even earlier. Stimulating realistic social hope in the simultaneous possibilities of deepening democracy in America and in other global contexts is a complex challenge that includes intertwined existential, practical, and theoretical aspects. We, as human beings now alive on Planet Earth and as members of diverse cultural streams of experience, must be able to find and to sustain the inner resources for such a hope in a difficult and dangerous time. To do this, we must be able to act in ways that seem likely to help our cause if, indeed, deepening democracy is to become the world's actual future-making process, rather than a sadly fleeting possibility. Though no guarantees are available, to be able to sustain belief that some particular course of transformative action can be both desirable and effective in deepening democracy in the face of significant obstacles, we need to find reliable, intelligent, theoretical guidance through a respectful, inclusive, collaborative process of thinking and acting together. This process must include multiple perspectives, the best information available, and a credible, shared story or set of stories about what's going on and how we can make things better. Many voices, many gifts, and many fields of study must contribute their tools and insights to the process of weaving together the combination of existential support, practical guidance, and intellectual clarity we need now.

Philosophy as an academic discipline can become a gathering place for such diverse voices, and it can make important contributions to the development of a deeply democratic "public philosophy"—if it is pursued in a way that critically interconnects many other fields and voices as a "liaison officer," in John Dewey's phrase, working to promote their "full and moving communication" as a key means and an important aspect of the goal of deepening democracy. With Dewey and others, I call such a way of understanding and pursuing the work of philosophy "pragmatism," though I recognize that this label has always confused a certain number of people into thinking that we who follow it mean to emphasize only "the rudely practical" in our focus on problem solving. However, for pragmatists, getting "the practical" right, so that we actually improve the problem situation on which we focus our attention, requires effectively interweaving a complex set of difficult intellectual and social actions, including:

- taking account of similar and differing felt qualities of our experiences in living;
- taking seriously our human concern with ideals, meanings, habits, and guiding values;
- connecting these with critical, reflective, and collaborative knowledge seeking;
- cultivating and actually employing shared social intelligence in transformative action.

In my view, philosophical pragmatism in this classical American stream offers good guidance to the emergence of a deeply democratic public philosophy for four important reasons. First, it frames inquiry in inclusive, pluralistic ways. Second, it works to remove some of the obstacles created by earlier theories that block the path of inquiry about our contemporary problems and their possible solutions. Third, it articulates the democratic ideal in ways that respect both cultural diversity and common humane values. And fourth, it insists on the importance of both individual fulfillments and vital communities in social living at many levels. Philosophical pragmatism so understood can effectively guide the development of a general theory and practice of democratic inquiry and collaborative transformative action while keeping our focus on the goal of crucial importance in these dangerous days of the early twenty-first century: deepening democracy in global contexts in ways that foster shared social hope by empowering creative, reconstructive responses to the great problems of our times from diverse individuals and peoples worldwide whose voices presently clash, pass each other, or remain unheard.

My own hope in writing this book is that my contributions to a pragmatist public philosophy, understood in this holistically practical way, can help to guide our rethinking about how to deepen democracy, both as the key to "achieving our country" and as a helpful prescription for healing our current global predicament. Therefore, in writing this book, I have drawn together wise voices of the past in conversation with diverse voices of contemporary world citizens and thinkers from various scholarly disciplines in an attempt to fulfill philosophy's role as a "liaison officer." In doing so, I have tried to reflect the depth of the pain and yearning in recent shared experiences while encouraging and educating our hopes for deepening democracy, drawing upon recent work in many fields of study to clarify some key aspects of a general but localizable transformative path that will be both feasible and desirable in diverse global contexts.

Why We Must Reconstruct Rorty's Dream-Story and Map to Achieving Our Country

Richard Rorty's philosophical best-seller reminded a wide American and international readership that our cross-generational dream of "achieving our country"—of actualizing the deeper potentials of America's guiding democratic ideal—is not yet completed, and if it is to be fulfilled in our times, it requires the best thinkers of our times, a broad coalition of actors, and widely shared social hopes. Though he wrote most of his works on democracy and social hope before September 11, Rorty's prophetic account of contemporary conditions and future possibilities offers us a rich combination of existential recognitions, theoretical analyses, wise voices from the past, and practical proposals for transformative action. Thus, Rorty's "inspiring story" offers a still helpful model and framework for thinking about now-crucial issues and for restarting our post-9/11 personal and social processes of vision questing and seeking a path to deeper actualizations of the democratic ideal than the world has ever known.

However, we must reconstruct Rorty's "new American story" to make it helpful as a general map to guide us in our efforts to deepen democracy now, not only because the world has changed since September 11 but also because his way of telling of our shared story is seriously flawed in a number of ways. For example, Rorty unwisely suggested in *Achieving Our Country*:

- that "achieving our country" is possible as a project for Americans in isolation from the rest of the world;
- that our cultural diversity and our memories of our nation's past injustices must be sacrificed—"melted away"—within a common dream-story that can guide our lives;
- that there are no truths about history, only differing stories that we tell in order to frame personal and national identities that help us decide what to do in the future;
- that academic intellectuals must be the principal leaders of "achieving our country";
- that to take on their new role as democratic leaders telling America a common dream-story, academic intellectuals must abandon their current scholarly projects and methods;

- that this common dream-story must assume no major change in America's current economic and political institutions, instead of imagining ways to make our economy more just and to expand roles for citizen participation in self-governance;
- that our story must limit our transformative efforts to campaign for specific economic and political reforms, instead of encouraging the emergence of broader, transgenerational movements like the civil rights movement;
- that our story must treat individual attitudes as well as the social practices of our labor unions, churches, fraternal organizations, and political parties with "hands-off" tolerance, guiding us to make "strange bedfellows" to advance our specific campaigns of reform instead of working to deepen democracy throughout our culture's shared ways of thinking and living, which Alexis de Tocqueville referred to as our "habits of the heart."[12]

In each of these elements of his new American story, Rorty's "neopragmatist" philosophical map diverges from those of a more ambitious yet potentially more fruitful public philosophy in the classical pragmatist stream—one that draws deeply on the electric charge of Whitman's democratic vision, is advanced by the philosophical methods and hard-won insights of James and Dewey, and is grounded by Baldwin's fierce wisdom about interconnections of memory and hope.

Therefore, drawing on the many strengths of Rorty's dream-story and transformative map while proposing alternatives to its specific, isolatable weaknesses, my purpose in this book is to reconstruct his American story of "achieving our country" in the wake of September 11, reframing it into a work of pragmatist public philosophy that can offer hope-sustaining guidance to the larger, now inseparable project of "achieving our world"—a more deeply democratic world. This will require me to employ a twenty-first-century pragmatist philosophical method of storytelling about recent events in dialogue with Rorty. However, unlike his solitary, "neopragmatist" approach, my pragmatist way of storytelling incorporates collaborative yet provisional historical and empirical knowledge claims that warrant the story's reasonableness (and also highlight its weaknesses) while energizing it into an ideal-guided, future-oriented general map for transformative actions that aim to further develop its desirable elements while counteracting its worrisome ones. As an additional check on its adequacy in light of the real risks that go with taking a story seriously, I filter my emerging, collaboratively correctable and extendable story map through an existential-phenomenological analysis in the classical American pragmatist vein that draws upon insights from Whitman, James, Dewey, Baldwin, and others, suggesting that "a higher rationality of the human spirit" should guide us in choosing the kinds of beliefs, hopes, and life practices that are necessary to and sustainable within an energetic, satisfying, deeply democratic life. Last, I conclude my part of telling our story by inviting others to join this project of pragmatist public philosophy in a spirit of "tragic meliorism," remembering Viktor Frankl's complementary, Holocaust-born insight that tragedy can stimulate a personal quest for meaning in living and is, in any case, deeply woven throughout the fabric of our lives.

Though I write as an American philosopher who shares Rorty's admiration of Whitman, James, Dewey, and Baldwin and who agrees with him that academics and other "intellectuals" have a great and urgent responsibility to work toward deepening democracy in our contemporary global situation, my own cultural location and generational commitments are very different from his. I am an American Midwesterner, a daughter of the fields and of the labor unions with whom Rorty called for renewed solidarity. I am a member of that student generation whose effective opposition to the Vietnam War he grudgingly praised and then forgot. Like Rorty's parents and grandparents, I am a critic of America's current "formally democratic" framework of limited representative democracy and global capitalism that he ultimately accepted, and I am a proponent of the processes of "participatory democracy" he seemed to fear. I am an ethnically conscious Irish American university professor, a multiculturalist who teaches courses in African American philosophy, Native American philosophies, feminist theory, and American pragmatism, and thus, apparently, a member of the "cultural Left" he castigated. I am a progressive Catholic activist immersed in faith-based causes of social and environmental justice, and thus a native speaker of one of the religious languages he proposed to ban from the public square. Clearly, my own hopes and fears are different in many ways from Rorty's and are sometimes adversarial to them. Yet I share his great hope that "achieving our country" is still possible, as well as his fear that the forces of globalization, fundamentalism, intolerance, and war may kill the dream of democracy.

In my earlier book, *Deep Democracy: Community, Diversity, and Transformation* (1999), I argued that formal, institutional democracies are not sustainable and may not even be desirable unless they are grounded in more deeply democratic habits, values, customs, and processes of daily living. In the absence of such a deep democracy, or in conditions of its erosion, I suggested, even Dahl's "experienced democracies" can fall prey to *a fourfold democratic disease* of *institutional subvertibility, ideological hollowness, individual nihilism, and cultural anomie* that now is common in the West. This is what I think happened to America in the years before 9/11: we as a people fell victim to this fourfold democratic disease, and our ability to respond to the terrible and tragic events of that day was badly damaged by it. This is why our nation faltered so badly in both its domestic and its international responsibilities in the years that followed. As an American people, we now are struggling to recover our national health, to revive our vision and our hopes for "achieving our country," and to take up our deeper democratic responsibilities to one another and to others on the world stage.

An American story, vision, and way forward that is feasible and desirable for us now must realistically reflect these current problems in our nation's state of democratic health and the complexities of our global context, factoring in the importantly *different* conditions and contexts in which other nations struggle for their own stories, visions, and ways forward, seeking sites at which we as diverse peoples can and must help one another. Our differing understandings of the meanings of and paths toward deepening democracy must converge at certain points, and we as their proponents must learn to collaborate effectively, if our hopes are to be achieved in this era of multifaceted, antidemocratic strife and poorly guided globalization. As public philosophers, we must draw guidance from, correct, and continuously contribute to an inquiry-based, context-sensitive, general story map of how to deepen democracy in diverse global contexts. In America, we will need this map's guidance to help us focus transformative attention on "democratic cultural revitalization" and "political reinhabitation." Let me explain.

The final chapter of *Deep Democracy* listed nine aspects of fully actualized deep democracies that emerge from reflecting on democratic transformation efforts in America and other contexts:

- respect for human rights understood as common humane values;
- democratic cultural revitalization (guiding cultural change by the democratic ideal);
- lifelong education within collaborative processes of rebuilding the public square;

- democratic political reinhabitation (active democratic participation as a way of life);
- shared community efficacy and commitment to mutual flourishing;
- democratic economic relocation;
- shared commitment to ecosystemic health;
- shared memories and hopes;
- an encompassing web of caring within a consciously shared community life.

I also listed six progressive stages that often recur within inclusive, collaborative transformation projects to rebuild what Cornel West calls "the public square" in more deeply democratic ways:[13]

- reenergizing of semiautonomous democratic cultural trajectories;
- critical multicultural education toward cosmopolitan unity amid valued diversity;
- cross-difference conversations to build shared understanding;
- trust and hope building, coalition-based transformative cooperation;
- gradual evolution of coalitions into diverse democratic communities;
- gradual deepening of diverse democratic communities into beloved communities.

My focus in this book is on how to make progress through these stages toward the two aspects of deep democracy that I think are central to transforming the American situation after 9/11: democratic cultural revitalization and democratic political reinhabitation. America's story, vision, and path forward is the center of my attention, both because this is my country and the context I know best and because I believe that deepening democracy here will have great significance for many other global contexts in which proponents of deep democracy are engaged in their own transformation struggles. This book includes examples from some of these other democratic transformation struggles that can teach important lessons to other public philosophers in America and worldwide. In future books, I will focus on other aspects of deep democracy, suggesting ways to advance these in specific global contexts while working together toward a more deeply democratic world.

My Pragmatist American Story and Map to Social Hope: Some Chapter Landmarks

In *Achieving Our Country*, Rorty mapped out one possible path for American cultural revitalization and democratic political reinhabitation—a path that begins with professional academics forgetting our old scholarly disagreements and our less imperative research projects in a shared impulse to reach out to our fellow citizens, to inspire them with a new American story, and to lead them in efforts to make it come true. In the following chapters, I will show why Rorty's American story is too limited and why the path he mapped in *Achieving Our Country* cannot lead us to deep democracy in this country and in our post-9/11 world. In the course of appreciative and critical conversations with Rorty's still-living texts, I will retrieve traces of an older map to America's more deeply democratic future that John Dewey outlined and Walt Whitman illustrated, adding field notes from William James, Josiah Royce, Jane Addams, George Herbert Mead, Alain Locke, and other classical American pragmatists, and improving the whole with some critical reminders and wise suggestions from James Baldwin, Martin Luther King Jr., and a group of our contemporary democratic pathbreakers. When Rorty's original dream-story and map is collaboratively reconstructed in this way, I believe the resulting story, vision, and general map can put us on a path toward deep democracy that will get us there someday, in America and in other global contexts—*if* we continuously revise it in light of subsequent experiences, events, and contributions from diverse public philosophers who reflect on and assist the transformative efforts and insights of democracy-minded world citizens.

Richard Rorty and I shared a belief in the importance of the stories that give direction and weight to democratic future-choosing processes, including their power to reframe our hopes and fears, and to transform these into shared motivations for collaborative struggle to achieve better life possibilities for all concerned. However, in contrast with Rorty, I believe that evidence and reasons also count, and that some stories show themselves to be better than others, not because of who tells them or the language in which they are expressed, but because they more inclusively and *truly* remember our shared history, more fully clarify our shared present, and more effectively guide our collaborative efforts to realize mutually desirable possibilities in the future. Stories, reasons, and evidence are related elements within the kind of productive, intelligent social inquiry in which I believe American public philosophers must reengage both our still-sleeping and our recently reawakened neighbors, while at the same time joining with a wider community of world citizens in processes of democratic deliberation and transformative action.

Because I need to show why it makes a difference whether we think about things in this way, I will interrupt my storytelling from time to time to talk about related philosophical issues on which I disagree with Richard Rorty. These include:

- the importance of memory;
- the role of forgiveness;
- the meaning of hope and how to revive it;
- the connections among individuals and nations and the world;
- how and why we need to know truths of history;
- how to do "reality checks" even if certainty is impossible;
- why democracy requires active forms of citizen participation;
- why we need to reconstruct philosophy's traditional fields of metaphysics and epistemology in pragmatist terms and use them (at least a little bit) within our democratic communication processes, our public policies, and our choices about how to live, instead of giving them up with one of Rorty's famous shrugs of the shoulders.

All of these issues actually play a role in whether we tell Rorty's more limited kind of story of "achieving our country" or my more ambitious story of "achieving our world," so I've used lots of examples in explaining them and why they matter to the story—including why they will make a difference to readers who are deciding whether to enter into the story in real time. However, sometimes it's possible to skip over them and come back later, so I've tried to suggest where this might be a good option if one is less interested in philosophy than in the story itself.

In chapter 1, "Achieving Our Country, Achieving Our World: Rorty, Baldwin, and Social Hope," I draw on insights from Whitman and Dewey, as well as from Baldwin and several contemporary American thinkers, to show why public philosophers working in the wake of 9/11 must approach the telling of a hope-reviving "new American story" somewhat differently than Richard Rorty in 1998. I suggest how a pragmatist approach can help us to understand and to address three of the most basic kinds of existential issues we now face:

- issues about memory and forgiveness;
- issues about democracy's meaning in a time of crisis;
- issues about how scholars and other citizen-thinkers can contribute to an inclusive process of public empowerment to achieve shared democratic ideals in diverse global contexts.

In contrast with both Samuel Huntington's proposal that we Americans turn our gaze backward seeking a common founding memory and Rorty's proposal that we erase our past differences in a common future-focused American dream, I propose that we acknowledge the unity of feelings and aspirations we felt on September 11 as well as the history-based, injustice-linked differences that still trouble our ability to work together to deepen democracy in "our country" and in other global contexts and thereby to begin, as Baldwin said, "a new history of the world." In contrast with Baldwin, however, I suggest that we can learn a valuable lesson from those African American ancestors who, without forgetting their suffering and loss, forgave those who had held them in bondage instead of seeking revenge, moving on with their lives while transforming a cycle of violence into a process of progressive stages of coexistence, mutual benefit, and democratic neighborliness. At the same time, I affirm Rorty's wisdom in suggesting that we need a new American dream-story that can ground a revival of social hope and shared pride in our country—not hope and pride based on the false presumption of economic, military, and cultural indomitability as the world's sole superpower, but on our active efforts as neighbors to repair the ravages of history, to create better opportunities for those who have been held back, and to model a democratic participatory approach to future making that can serve as a model to others worldwide. Though Rorty called upon "Left intellectuals" to tell this new American dream-story, I suggest that it must emerge from the voices and the actions of the American people themselves, with the wider group of "public philosophers" I described above acting as "liaison agents" who critically and creatively interconnect differing streams of research and of practical knowing, posing important questions, challenging some of the answers, and summing up for us as a people where we've been and how we're doing at advancing our shared social hopes.

In chapter 2, "American Dreaming: From Loss and Fear to Vision and Hope," I reflect appreciatively and critically on Rorty's brave and solitary telling of a pre-9/11 story about how our American universities changed after Vietnam into places of cynicism and quietism, which affected his own and many others' sense of meaning in living and hope for the future, as well as his vision of who is responsible for remedying this and how it may be possible to revive a widely shared social hope that can motivate campaigns of liberal reform to "achieve our country," in spite of the forces of globalization and backlash that now threaten our long-loved dream of democracy. My purpose in this chapter is twofold. First, I aim to appreciatively follow Rorty's example in using storytelling as a process of moving from fear and loss to vision and hope—a process through which many of us as individuals and all of us as a people still must pass in order to bring us to the stage of readiness for cooperative, democracy-deepening transformative action. Second, however, through a careful reading of Rorty's text, I aim to show that uncorrected errors in his telling of events that limit its usefulness, especially after 9/11, also show why our story-linked processes of grieving, naming, and vision seeking must be social and interactive rather than solitary. Moreover, in contrast with Rorty's narrowly "ethnocentric" vision, I argue that the vision-seeking process we need now must be both inclusively American and globally contextualized. Rorty's reformist "civic religion" and his "neopragmatist" philosophical methods offer some valuable suggestions about how to do this, but they must be distanced from his personal fears and nostalgic attachments to the past and corrected by using Dewey's pragmatist philosophical methods and related theoretical insights, which were born from struggles to deepen democracy during the first half of the twentieth century, including:

- context-sensitive employment of a "low-rise" democratic metaphysics;
- rethinking the meaning of truth processes within collaborative transformative inquiry;
- willingness to collaborate with those who disagree with us about many important matters.

In framing a more effective "American dreaming" process that respects the power of stories, we can draw on the continuing experience and long-established practices of many of our Native American neighbors, whose stories and elders have been guiding vision quests for generations and whose clans still send their representatives to deeply democratic future-choosing meetings.

Chapter 3, "Hope's Progress: Remembering Dewey's Pragmatist Social Epistemology in the Twenty-First Century," focuses on three key issues for our storytelling, visioning, and transformative map:

- what social hope is;
- why it matters so much to us, even though it is so difficult for us now;
- why truth properly understood matters so much in grounding and sustaining our hopes in living, which now and in the future will depend on experiences of effectiveness in deepening democracy in our own local and global contexts.

Hope's key question now for Americans and for others in diverse global contexts is this: *on what shall our future-shaping choices and actions be based?* Shall our hopes and the actions to which they give rise reflect narrow, ethnocentric loyalties and an exclusively national dream, as Rorty recommended? Or shall we risk larger hopes such as Dewey's and those of other pragmatist public philosophers, classical and contemporary—hopes of world-embracing local and national loyalties that can revive and sustain tragedy-chastened, knowledge-guided processes of recognizing and repairing past and continuing harms and shared efforts to achieve a global future in which each people's culture-specific dreams are conditioned by mutual commitments to every other people's well-being within a beloved human community? The latter course, which I favor, requires that we give up what Dewey called "the quest for certainty"—but not the pursuit of knowledge and truth as such, including the "truths of history" Baldwin said we must face but Rorty rejected as illusory. I draw insights from Dewey and James to suggest how we can create and correct the kind of fallible but useful, perspectively balanced, experience-warranted "well" of shared social knowledge we will need in order to guide our hope-sustaining collaborative projects of deepening democracy in diverse global contexts.

In chapter 4, "Choosing Our History, Choosing Our Hopes: Truth and Reconciliation Between Our Past and Our Future," I relate the kind of pragmatist social epistemology I think we need now to the process of telling an inclusive, truth-oriented, vision-guiding American story. I show how Rorty misread texts by Whitman and Dewey to support his general claim that knowledge of history is neither possible nor necessary and his more specific claim that Baldwin made a "category mistake" when he argued that telling the truth about America's history must guide our future-oriented pursuit of justice and national unity. Baldwin's wisdom on this point has become even clearer since 9/11—although the continuing costs of America's chattel slavery, seizure of indigenous people's lands, and social subordination of women, as well as the continuing legacy of the Holocaust and other tragic miscarriages of justice by other formally democratic nations, should have provided extensive reasons for concurring with Baldwin even before that awful day. Taken together, the evidence of these experiences shows that we need a collaborative, problem-focused method of social inquiry to guide cross-culturally inclusive efforts to learn the truth of history and to rectify outstanding debts from our shared past. In turn, such a truth-and-justice process will clarify our communications about the present and help to guide key aspects of our collaborations in future forging, including shaping and sharing our national and global story about our transgenerational pursuit of deep democracy.

Chapter 5, "Trying a Deeper Democracy: Pragmatist Lessons from the American Experience," offers a preliminary sketch of the kind of inclusive, truth-seeking American story and shared vision quest I think we need now to guide the pursuit of a deeper democracy in diverse global contexts. Part 1, "A Dialectical History of American Democratic Theory and Practice," highlights the ongoing struggle to express and experiment with a "second," deeper, Jeffersonian strand of democracy that calls for continuous and active citizen participation in self-governance, both within political institutions and within inseparably linked social institutions and all the aspects of our daily living. Proponents of the "first," formal, representative strand—and those who believe democracy is neither feasible nor desirable—have been working to erase this second, actively participatory, Jeffersonian strand of democratic theory and practice since America's beginning. This part of the chapter is my answer to the often-raised question, "If participatory democracy is such a good idea, why has it never been seriously tried?" I show here that this question rests on a false premise and that experiments in and institutionalizations of "second-strand" democracy have continued across the generations, expanding in scope and proving their worth as a companion to representative democracy in ways that we should take seriously in our present times of democratic emergency. Part 2 of this chapter, "Participatory Democracy:

Movements, Campaigns, and Democratic Living," shows why the limited, problem-focused kinds of campaigns Rorty called for cannot by themselves offer enough experienced citizen participants and enough transgenerational scope for the project of deepening democracy in diverse global contexts. I argue that American history should teach us that we also need movements that can interlink and sequence campaigns, that can carry on their work across generations if necessary until it is completed, and that can offer their citizen-participants a hope-sustaining sense of meaning and satisfaction in their life-framing democratic contributions.

Chapter 6, "The Continuously Planning City: Imperatives and Examples for Democratic Citizen Participation," brings my American and global story through the late twentieth century and into the twenty-first, focusing on a range of contemporary examples of "second-strand" democratic citizen participation, in the kinds of urban contexts in which most of the world's citizens now live. Strengthening this deeper, "republican" strand of democracy, to use Michael Sandel's term, is necessary if we are to achieve what Benjamin Barber calls "strong democracy" amid the destructive dialectic he traces between "Jihad" and "McWorld." Unless we more effectively interweave this second, more deeply democratic strand with the now dominant representative strand of democratic theory in our institutions, expectations, and habits of daily living, it may be impossible, as Robert Dahl fears, for "experienced democracies" to fulfill their potentials—or even, as Rorty feared, for America to withstand the cultural stresses of ongoing globalization processes. Fortunately, extensive evidence suggests that cities can become important sites for strengthening this second strand of democratic theory and practice by expanding four kinds of already existing, hard-won opportunities for active citizen participation shaping our shared future:

- within government, including well-established processes of urban planning;
- within nongovernmental organizations that influence government, the civic sphere, and democratic culture, as well as humanitarian relief and environmental protection;
- within gatherings of scholars and other citizen-thinkers to inquire together, to tell stories, to reconcile conflicts, and to seek guiding visions for our shared futures;

- within mass protests and reconstructive movements focused on peace, economic and social justice, democratic cultural inclusiveness, and environmental sustainability.

Through the process of participating in such "urban schools" of second-strand, Jeffersonian democracy while working to achieve Dewey's "continuously planning societies," citizen-thinkers can educate themselves in skills, knowledge bases, habits, and lifeways for deepening democracy in diverse global contexts; in the process, they may profoundly influence our future.

Finally, chapter 7, "The Hope of Democratic Living: Choosing Citizen Participation for Preferable Global Futures," explores how actively participating in such local and global efforts to deepen democracy can revive hope and guide ideal-directed living, even though we cannot know in advance with certainty that our efforts to deepen democracy will be successful. Reflecting on Dewey's hope for a worldwide rebirth of faith in democratic living, James's insight that the truths we most need to know sometimes cannot be warranted in advance, and Frankl's Holocaust-born insights about how to live a meaningful, even joyful life during tragic times, I advance a threefold, "tragically melioristic" hypothesis about the promising future of democratic citizen participation in creating continuously planning societies. It is this: good evidence of both empirical and existential kinds supports my provisional conclusion that these are times in which active democratic citizen participation may offer a feasible and desirable way to struggle against our own feelings of guilt and despair as well as against our various opponents, to refound social hope, to achieve something valuable over the course of our lives, and perhaps to weave some better, fairer pattern into the future of our nation and our world. Therefore, I suggest that framing our lives in terms of efforts to deepen democracy in local and global contexts is what James called a "genuine option" for many of us, in which Dewey's pragmatist "meliorism" can combine with Frankl's "tragic optimism" to warrant action from "a deeper rationality of the human spirit."

My part of this American and global story concludes with the suggestion that such an active, meaning-filled, even joyful life of mutual growth within collaborative democratic struggle can revive and sustain shared social hope while at the same time fittingly expressing appreciation of life and perhaps beginning a new history of the world. Whether my story will turn out to be true depends on what I and many others—including readers of this book—do and learn from one another and who we become in the future, as each of us manifests and continuously reframes our hopes in action, responding to the needs and events of our times.

Chapter 1

Achieving Our Country, Achieving Our World
Rorty, Baldwin, and Social Hope

Did you, too, O friend, suppose democracy was only for elections, for politics, and for a party name? I say democracy is only of use there that it may pass on and come to its flower and fruits in manners, in the highest forms of interaction between men, and their beliefs—in religion, literature, colleges, and schools—democracy in all public and private life.

> —Walt Whitman, *Democratic Vistas*

Democracy will come into its own, for democracy is a name for a life of free and enriching communion. It had its seer in Walt Whitman. It will have its consummation when free social inquiry is indissolubly wedded to the art of full and moving communication.

> —John Dewey, *The Public and Its Problems*

This is your home, my friend, do not be driven from it; great men have done great things here, and will again, and we can make America what America must become.

> —James Baldwin, *The Fire Next Time*

Nobody knows what it would be like to try to be objective when attempting to decide what one's country really is, what its history really means, any more than when answering the question of who one really is oneself, what one's individual past really adds up to. We raise questions about our individual or national identity as part of the

process of deciding what we will do next, what we will try
to become.

—Richard Rorty, *Achieving Our Country*

The Painful Beginnings of America's Twenty-first-Century Struggle for Social Hope

America and the world entered a new era in the always difficult struggle
for democracy on September 11, 2001, when three fuel-laden jet airliners
hijacked by criminals with an anti-Western ideological agenda slammed into
New York City's World Trade Center and the Pentagon, massive buildings
that represented America's economic, cultural, and military might to the
world. A fourth jet crashed in a field in rural western Pennsylvania after
courageous civilian passengers fought hand to hand with the hijackers to
prevent their plane, too, from being used as a weapon. As lower Manhattan's
schoolchildren watched in horror and a worldwide community stood trans-
fixed around televisions and radios, fellow human beings jumped to their
deaths from the skyscrapers' flaming top floors. Moments later, the World
Trade Center's seemingly indestructible Twin Towers collapsed, crushing
and burning thousands of workers as well as hundreds of police officers,
firefighters, and emergency medical technicians who had rushed in, hoping
to save others' lives.

More than three thousand ordinary citizens of the United States of America and many other countries died together that morning, their lives snuffed
out in intentional attacks on civilians and on symbolic targets by members
of a transnational organization who blasphemously claimed the sanction of
Islam for their plot to change the course of history. Their goal was to create a climate of terror within the most powerful nation in the world and
thereby demonstrate that no one anywhere would be safe ever again until
the cultural, political, and economic issues that motivated their attacks are
resolved. The final extent of the September 11 attackers' success or failure was
not determined by the events of that day nor those of the months and years
that have followed. Rather, the meaning of September 11 lies in the future,
in the responses not only of governments but of ordinary citizens here and
worldwide, as our lives demonstrate the meaning and the sustainability of
our hopes for achieving America's and other nations' highest potentials with-

in a shared process of shaping a more humane, life-respecting, and deeply democratic world.

One thing is clear already: a great chasm has opened between those worldviews and ways of living that seemed normal and reasonable before September 11 and those that have come to seem necessary and realistic since that awful day. It is a chasm born of the power of human evil, of the inspiration of heroism, and of the now unavoidable realization that even great oceans, incomparable military might, and the collective wealth of the American people are protective barriers no longer against the terrifying episodes of violence and the daily indignities that characterize twenty-first-century living in many other parts of the world. On September 11 and in the weeks that followed, as countless citizens of many nations grieved with us in a newfound unity—and a few danced in celebration of our pain—America irrevocably joined the rest of the world in facing a new predicament without parallel in our previous experience.

At first we Americans were stunned by such a massive, harsh violation of our deepest shared values, and we were uncertain how to proceed. Within weeks, however, President George W. Bush had decided for us, framing this new context of global living in terms of the old categories of war and vengeance and launching a war of reprisal against Afghanistan, the country that had sheltered the 9/11 terrorists and thus, he said, the country that deserved to be violently punished in the course of hunting them down. He proclaimed a "Bush Doctrine" concerning the practical meaning of justice, now and for the future, rhetorically dividing the world's nations into "us" versus "them," allowing no neutral noncombatants and rejecting the possibility of a measured, multilateral, and probably protracted judicial response to September 11 through the international courts. Instead, he demanded that other countries join the United States in prosecuting an open-ended "War on Terror" or be treated as supporters of the terrorists and expect to share their fate: death without trial, without recourse, as outlaws from the community of nations.

Immediately thereafter, with the aid of America's commercial news media, the Bush administration forcefully conveyed the message that American citizens who questioned the rightness and the efficacy of this response to September 11 would be treated as wartime traitors who must fear for their jobs and their lives. In subsequent weeks, the Bush administration argued with some success in American courts that the statutes, case law, and cultural consensus interpreting and protecting our civil liberties that had been so carefully built up through the struggles of generations would no longer apply to foreign visitors or even to American citizens—and certainly not to prisoners of war. Finally, the Bush administration convinced the vast majority in our American Congress that "homeland security" had become the issue that must dominate all others for the foreseeable future, its requirements to be determined secretly by the president in consultation with "experts."

Many shocked and grieving American citizens were swept up for a time in this rhetorical and practical framework of a great war against evil and vengeance as the meaning of justice. Many succumbed to depression, panic attacks, and pervasive feelings of insecurity that sapped their capacity for resistance to the sense of a world swept away and undermined their ability to think creatively and dream new dreams of the fulfillment of their deepest values. Our children were troubled by nightmares and by fears for their parents and older siblings; our elders struggled to sustain their hopes for the future. The dreadful waiting and working to retrieve bodies or even mementoes from the wreckage of the World Trade Center continued on and on for months. Filled with feelings of unity and of sadness, many of us flew the American flag, sang "God Bless America" as a new national anthem, drew closer to one another across our historic racial divides, and returned to the churches seeking comfort, protection, and answers.[1] Few spoke up to say that vengeance is of a very different spirit than justice. Few remembered that war—even when it seems necessary—seldom resolves underlying issues. Few recognized emerging threats to ongoing efforts to deepen democracy in diverse global contexts.

Making executive plans for our nation's and our world's future almost alone, without direct democratic communication among America's citizens or with our elected representatives, President Bush used his 2002 State of the Union Address to target an "Axis of Evil"—Iraq, Iran, and North Korea—as being uniquely responsible for destabilizing our twenty-first-century world. Later that year, as Americans began to express concerns about a flagging economy and the persisting problems of inadequate public education, racial injustice, and inequitable access to health care, all of which still cloud our dreams of democracy, President Bush announced that President Saddam Hussein's allegedly Al Qaeda–linked regime in Iraq had stockpiled hidden (never found) "weapons of mass destruction" that presented such a clear and present danger to the American people that it had become necessary to re-move him and his supporters from power by preemptive military means and to replace his dictatorship with a "democracy." George W. Bush did not men-tion—and perhaps did not recognize—that democracy is more than a struc-ture of government and cannot be imposed. In any case, he did not explain that, in the absence of support from the wider international community, such an invasion and coup d'etat would violate America's treaty obligations, in-cluding countless United Nations documents we had signed as a nation. Nor did he express or respond to concerns that such an invasion would violate the requirements of the "just war" doctrine that has evolved over the centuries through the contributions of philosophers, theologians, diplomats, and lead-ers of nations and armies as an effective and at least minimally moral way to limit military aggression and war's resultant chaos.[2] Nonetheless, fear-fueled patriotism combined with ignorance of our treaty obligations and of "just war" doctrine to persuade a majority of American voters to reaffirm President Bush's leadership in the 2002 midterm election, sending a majority from his party to the U.S. Congress, thereby assuring him constitutional legitimacy if he chose to declare war on Iraq.

Yet the Bush administration's determined preparations for war while using the mass media's drumbeat coverage to distract attention from other equally dangerous domestic and international policies and actions finally awakened many voices of loyal democratic opposition from their long months of shock and silence. The first in a series of courageous, very expensive, full-page news-paper advertisements challenging the morality, legality, and effectiveness of a preemptive war against Iraq without UN sanction appeared in the *New York Times* shortly after September 11's first anniversary. Ironically, those con-tributors who signed and paid for this advertisement were using this preemi-nent newspaper's commercial aspect to challenge it and the American news media in general to fulfill their constitutionally protected core responsibility: to provide balanced, accurate coverage of important events in order to inform the public, because this is a crucial prerequisite of the process of democratic citizen deliberation that America's founders understood from their own ex-perience of history. Lawn signs demanding "No War in Iraq" began to ap-pear throughout the country, in urban, suburban, and rural neighborhoods. A new, Internet-based antiwar organization, Move On, began to connect people of diverse backgrounds and political orientations who might have shared only one thing in common: opposition to President Bush's proposed invasion of Iraq. Move On even included prominent business leaders who were members of President Bush's Republican Party. Those economy-minded Republicans took out a full-page ad in the *Wall Street Journal* to express their judgment that America must not engage in a preemptive war that would undermine the United Nations' processes of investigation and deliberation at such a dangerous time in world history. Millions of Americans of all ages, races, religions, and political and economic backgrounds gathered in huge demonstrations in New York, Washington, San Francisco, and other cities to tell their elected representatives and a world audience: "We say NO to this war—we cherish a different dream of America and of a just, peaceful, more deeply democratic world."

However, the leaders of the Bush administration had already made up their minds, and they had already convinced Great Britain's Prime Minister Tony Blair to join them in invading Iraq without UN sanction and against strong opposition from the leaders of Germany and France. President Bush expressed pride in ignoring "public pressure" that contravened the judgment of his own "experts" and personal principles. America and Britain invaded Iraq in March 2003, and President Bush declared victory after three weeks, even though the devastation was spinning out of control in a multiplicity of rapidly changing forms, destroying countless lives, Iraq's urban landscape, America's reputation worldwide, and our national budget, making other good and necessary national priorities impossible to imagine, hope for, finance, and implement. Despite these terrible costs, George W. Bush was narrowly reelected in 2004 because his well-financed campaign succeeded in capitalizing on America's cultural divisions about "moral values" and on our fears about the consequences of failing to win this Iraq War and the wider "War on Terror."

However, by the time of the 2006 midterm elections, an ever-worsening war situation, combined with a stagnant domestic economy and a sense of impending crisis in many areas of our national life, led the majority of American voters to reject the Bush administration's framing of the imperatives our country faces at this moment in history. Instead, they elected a narrow majority from the rival Democratic Party to lead both houses of Congress, find a way to end the Iraq War, and resolve our increasingly worrisome domestic issues. For the first time, a woman would serve as Speaker of the House of Representatives; for the first time, a Muslim would serve in Congress. Coming together amid important differences in gender, religion, region, and race, as well as in their political, economic, and ethnic backgrounds, this newly empowered coalition of citizen-leaders sought a shared vision and an inclusive collaborative process that would allow them and our next president to fulfill the hopes of those who elected them: to revitalize our nation's democracy while fostering peace with justice in diverse, now troubled contexts worldwide. None of them knew how these necessary goods could be achieved—or even how to begin.

My purpose in this book, and especially in this chapter, is to suggest how to frame an American process of vision questing and transformative action to reclaim democracy as our guiding ideal, widen its inclusive reach, and deepen its meanings in our lives and in the public policies we devise to actualize its potentials in our troubled, post-9/11 world. I will propose that "public philosophers" drawn from diverse disciplines and backgrounds in community leadership begin to act as what John Dewey called "liaison agents" among the scholarly fields from which we will need to draw guidance and also within the various levels of gatherings at which citizens will need to talk directly with one another, with their elected representatives, and with other important decision makers. I will suggest that these "public philosophers" must first help us to address some existential issues that are hard but necessary to talk about before we can make real progress together on anything else:

- about memory and forgiveness;
- about democracy's meaning in a time of crisis;
- about the need to change some of our habits of feeling, thinking, and acting.

These must be addressed if we want to make a shared dream of deeply democratic, hospitable living together amid our differences the future shape of the world, as Seyla Benhabib recently imagined in *Another Cosmopolitanism* (2006), instead of facing the grim choices between civilization clash and noninterference, and between multiculturalism and our survival as an American people, which Samuel Huntington has claimed are our only options. These are issues about which the late Richard Rorty, an iconoclastic, democracy-loving philosopher and cultural critic who was a "guru" to many worldwide, had a great deal to say. His legacy of thoughtful insights and provocative spurs offers a good firing place from which to spark the kind of inclusive public conversation about deepening democracy in America and in other global contexts that we so greatly need now.

American Stories and American Hopes: Rorty Versus Baldwin

Three years before the tragic events of September 11, 2001, changed American history so profoundly, Richard Rorty performed a timely and valuable service by publishing *Achieving Our Country: Leftist Thought in Twentieth-Century America* (1998), a call to moral and political reengagement by American thinkers in the difficult yet urgent project of more fully realizing the meaning of democracy in twenty-first-century America. Originally presented in 1997 at Harvard University, these three lectures and the two essays that accompany them in their published form immediately became a nonfiction bestseller, finding a large audience among nonacademic American readers and professors and students in a wide range of disciplines. Clearly, Rorty touched something deep that many were feeling at that time in American history.

Claiming the moral and historical authority of Walt Whitman and John Dewey, Rorty transmuted their prophetic exhortations to fulfill the promise of America's shared democratic ideal into an inspiring, Freud-influenced "dream-story" of great reforms achieved by a coalition of intellectuals and grassroots activists. Rorty told this story in order to reawaken Americans' social hope in a common dream of economic justice and equality of opportunity that could motivate and guide new reform-focused campaigns to realize America's democratic potential in an imagined and feared twenty-first-century era of globalization. Now, in this time of national and global crisis on the far side of September 11's great historical divide, we must critically reconsider whether Rorty's American dream-story is as well-grounded—and as likely to be effective—as a very different kind of story of the continuing struggle to actualize our country's democratic ideal, guided by the hopeful yet historically attentive and world-conscious spirits of Whitman, Dewey, and James Baldwin, a critical opponent from the days of Rorty's youth in response to whom Rorty framed his tale.

The title of Rorty's book derives from a passage in Baldwin's *The Fire Next Time* (1963) that tells in a few words an American story Rorty ultimately rejected—a story of our country's unforgivable, continuing crime against the author and other black Americans: "This is the crime of which I accuse my country and my countrymen, and for which neither I nor time nor history will ever forgive them, that they have destroyed and are destroying hundreds of thousands of lives and do not know it and do not want to know it" (Baldwin, *The Fire Next Time*, 5). Writing in the turbulent middle years of the twentieth century, Baldwin reserved to himself and for history a refusal to forgive the larger social and institutional patterns of American racism and the self-centered obliviousness of so many of his fellow Americans who benefited from racism's fallout across the generations, while he and other descendents of the victims of chattel slavery continued to struggle in poverty and other legally and culturally entrenched forms of race-based inequality and cruelty. Yet despite his refusal to forgive this continuing crime, Baldwin, like his ancestors, claimed America as his country and called mature blacks and whites to work together in shaping a more democratic future. "If we—and now I mean the relatively conscious whites and the relatively conscious blacks, who must, like lovers, insist on, or create, the consciousness of the others—do not falter in our duty now, we may be able, handful that we are, to end the racial nightmare, and *achieve our country*, and change the history of the world" (105, emphasis mine). Rorty affirmed Baldwin's project of "achieving our country," as well as his recognition that this project would require a shared commitment from Americans now living on opposing sides of our great historical divides. However, to draw forth such a community of committed effort, Rorty argued, we must tell a very different kind of American story than the one Baldwin presented as true and motivating. In addition to claiming that knowing the truth about our history is impossible, Rorty rejected Baldwin's American story primarily because, he argued, such fierce, unforgiving criticism blocks the kind of hopeful, patriotic love for one's country that can motivate a person and a people to strive to fulfill a nation's highest potentials.

The questions we face now, as an American people awakened by September 11 to fierce and deadly international criticisms of our nation's recent history—but also to deep, cross-difference caring about us as fellow human beings expressed by unknown friends around the world—are these: How can we fulfill the aspirations for America's democracy that we still share with the generations who have gone before us? How can we "achieve" our country? Does a critical memory block shared social hope, as Rorty claimed? Or is Baldwin right that a painful, careful memory, even if it is unforgiving, actually anchors the kind of shared social hope we must find now: a chastened, clear-eyed hope that draws wisdom from hard experience—a realistic, empowering hope that can effectively guide us in these uncharted times to rethink our nation's story in order to understand and to fulfill what our long-shared American ideal of democracy demands from us now?

We can start to answer these urgent questions, as an American people now at war with multiple opponents, known and unknown, by considering whether we should affirm and act on or attempt to reframe some of the powerful moral emotions many of us now share: fear, anger, a desire for revenge, a longing for security. Would a fierce refusal to forgive, like Baldwin's, spur us on toward "achieving our country," or would it distort our perspectives and tie the meaning of our lives to a cycle of violence and vengeance that may rob us of a better, alternative future? Is Rorty right that forgetting, in spite of all that so many of us and our friends have lost and suffered, is the price for reclaiming more expansive social hopes?

Learning from the life stories of earlier generations of Americans who suffered enormous harms and losses yet succeeded in living satisfying and contributive lives can help us to understand two things we need to grasp before we can go further. First, our ability to tell a shared story of our country's future does not require forgetting the troubling aspects of our past. Second, forgiving those who have harmed us greatly without waiting for their repentance may well be the price we must pay for our spiritual freedom and the world's democratic future.

Social Hope and Forgiveness?

Thirty years after Baldwin wrote *The Fire Next Time*, another gifted African American thinker, Howard McGary, affirmed the truth of Baldwin's story as well as the importance of remembering the horrors of American chattel slavery and its racialized aftermath. However, McGary drew very different conclusions than Baldwin about the possibility, basis, and value of forgiving such unimaginable harms.[3] In an analysis that has gained even wider resonance since September 11, McGary argued that the autobiographical narratives of the lives of African Americans who were once chattel slaves—people whose humanity was denied under American law in the most minute and intimate aspects of daily living—show that, unlike Baldwin, many of these survivors *did* choose to forgive those who had so deeply harmed them. The key insight for our times that McGary derived from these slave narratives concerns the reasons that motivated many former slaves to forgive: while some forgave for religious reasons, the evidence of their narratives suggests that many forgave for what McGary called "self-regarding" reasons. That is, their choice to forgive was not based on their immediate persecutors' repentance, reform, and reparations—these were very rare. Nor was it based on an acknowledgment of moral and legal responsibility by the American nation that empowered and enforced their enslavement, an acknowledgment that is still not forthcoming. Rather, they forgave in order to break free from a cycle of violence and anger. Instead, without forgetting, they turned their energies toward reshaping their lives and transforming the nation that they and their forbears had helped to build—the place they called "home"—into a country that could fulfill the democratic ideals they shared.

All of us survivors of September 11 must reclaim the wisdom of these American ancestors to guide our hopes and actions in these hard times. Though some would say that our needs and choices as Americans today are very different than theirs were then, because we are powerful whereas they were powerless and because revenge is always sweeter than forgiveness, this is a dangerous delusion. September 11 should have taught us that even if we are the most powerful country the world has ever known, we cannot protect ourselves from the capacity of the seemingly powerless to destroy our lives and our illusions—if they themselves are willing to pay a very high price. Early in the nineteenth century, Gabriel Prosser, Denmark Vesey, Nat Turner, and their fellow slave revolutionaries taught a similarly shocking lesson to slave-holding America, rising up violently against those who held them in chains. And while these seemingly powerless ones eventually paid with their lives, they made it clear to their oppressors that their sweet dreams of luxurious injustice were over forever and must eventually yield to a more deeply democratic vision.[4] We must remember that *eventually* the cause of these antislavery revolutionaries prevailed, and we must reject the still-dangerous illusion that power protects forever. At the same time, we must remember that those whose resistance to chattel slavery took less violent forms *also* prevailed—especially those who achieved hopeful, history-transforming lives after their slavery ended by detaching their hearts and minds from a never-ending cycle of harm and vengeance, instead lending their energies to the realization of better possibilities for all.

Now, we must make these ancestors who remembered yet forgave and rebuilt their lives our guiding lights, instead of those who equated justice with vengeance or those who, like both Baldwin and Rorty, mistakenly linked forgiving with forgetting. Like these American ancestors, we survivors of September 11 may never hear repentance from those who perpetrated the great harms against us and ours, and we may never receive acknowledgment or reparations from those countries that made it possible for them to harm us.[5] It is *our choice now* whether we will deliver our hopes for the future into their control or instead draw on the best examples from our shared past in mapping a design for a better shared future. Though we will always live with a sobering sense of loss and sorrow, and we would lose our sense of meaning in living if we even tried to "just get over it," we must determinedly reinvest our hopes in a renewed struggle to actualize our country's best possibilities, taking this as the meaning of eventual victory and using these times of clarity to separate the wheat from the chaff in our complex American story.

This will require critically reframing some of Baldwin's best insights about remembering who we are, including his "black-white" racial logic, instead of succumbing to the historical amnesia Richard Rorty prescribed. When Baldwin described the American historical predicament, for which he called forth a diverse transformative community of "relatively conscious" whites and blacks, he acknowledged in passing the experiences of oppression and exclusion that diverse peoples of color, members of various religious minorities, and other "outcast" groups also had experienced in America. Perhaps he intended to include all these groups in some way within his oppositional category of "blacks," and perhaps such a bipolar racial logic had some justification when Baldwin wrote in 1963, based on certain "family resemblances" among these oppressed peoples' histories, their contemporary situations, and their group strategies for resistance and transformation.[6] Certainly Martin Luther King Jr. and other prophetic democratic leaders of the period employed such a bipolar racial logic and often intended to include other racial and religious minorities as well as poor people of all backgrounds in their advocacy.

However, to employ such "black-white" thinking in our post–September 11 context would be to hide the mixed-race, mixed-culture histories of increasing numbers of Americans that have not yet registered in popular conceptions of our national identity, here or abroad. This is Samuel P. Huntington's mistake when he says we **must** together reaffirm our founders' Anglo-Protestant lifeways and their American Creed or we will lose our national identity.[7] Such an overly simple racial and cultural logic also hides the emergence of Hispanics of diverse and mixed racial and ethnic backgrounds as the new "majority minority." It contributes to the near-invisibility of American Indians, Asian Americans, and other nonblack peoples of color in American public policy formation processes. It obscures the global significance of the widely publicized violent backlash by a handful of Americans against their neighbors of perceived Middle Eastern origin or Islamic religion that broke out in the early days after September 11, and finally, it may have contributed to the belief of many that the subsequent wars against Afghanistan and Iraq were justified defensive retributions against those who destroyed New York's World Trade Center.

Thus, in the wake of this second beginning of the twenty-first century, we must expand James Baldwin's proposal for a new kind of cooperative, mutually transformative, cross-difference reengagement in forging a deeper democracy than America or any other nation has ever known, pluralizing his "black-white" logic, expanding the membership in his called-for community of shared democratic struggle to a global scope, and, for "self-regarding reasons," forgiving one another and those who have harmed us all—without forgetting the painful history of America's racial struggle that framed Baldwin's initial call to "achieving our country." So reframed, Baldwin's is a visionary, forward-looking story of hard-won social hope, shared initially by a handful of members of America's historically adversarial groups who seek to redirect and thus to redeem a history of incalculable harms inflicted and borne. Their hope is to be wrought through painful remembering and the courage it stimulates to reach out to one another in knowledge and in determined love amid deep differences, seeking to forge a common struggle against enormous obstacles in order to awaken a still-divided American people and a diverse wider world to the attitudes, habits, and consequences that realizing deep democracy entails, thereby to begin a new, world-transforming way of living.

Social Hope, Forgetting, and National Pride?

In contrast with James Baldwin's story of painful memories of lived experience, courageous knowledge of who we have been and now are, and committed cross-difference love for each other as neighbors and for our nation's best possibilities, Richard Rorty's story employed Freud-influenced processes of forgetting, replacement, denial, and dream-inspiration to make room for a shared social hope grounded in national pride.[8] Rorty's story expressed faith in a new antiauthoritarian "civic religion of the Left" that would guide creation of social and economic conditions in America that could bring forth diverse, highly evolved, highly individualized realizations of what it is to be human, thereby showing the rest of the world how to achieve this greatest good. On the basis of the shared social hope his new American story would inspire, "Left intellectuals" were to make peace among themselves inside and outside the academy and then form an alliance with labor unions in order to articulate a "People's Charter" of specific legal reforms to create conditions of economic justice and equal opportunity for all. Guided by this "People's Charter," members of Rorty's resurrected "Left alliance" would commit themselves to achieving its goals together through determined, well-focused campaigns and thus would finally fulfill the end-meaning of the American story.

By his own account, Rorty derived the plot for his American story from his formative experiences within what he called the "Deweyan, pragmatic, participatory Left." Rorty's parents were anticommunist American socialists, New York–based contributors to journals of social and political criticism, and members of a network of politically active friends who talked together about books, great ideas, and what a wonderful country America could become if certain liberal economic and political reforms were finally adopted. His maternal grandfather was Walter Rauschenbush, the great "social gospel" theologian and religious leader of the Progressive Era. This reformist liberal *habitus* in which Rorty was raised was swept away in the late 1960s, he lamented, by a "spectatorial New Left" who rejected the older liberalism because they believed it had led America into the Vietnam War (Rorty, *Achieving Our Country*, 38).[9] However, the older "reformist Left" should once again be respected and imitated, Rorty argued, because it offered "the best model available" for the twenty-first century, with the potential for guiding the emergence of a Second Progressive Era (56). In his view, such a reconstructed "reformist Left" must accept America's existing institutional framework of constitutional democracy and market capitalism while steering clear of both of America's major political parties and the alternative processes and political formations of so-called participatory democracy. Instead, members of this "reformist Left" must dedicate themselves once again to a common dream of an American "melting pot" in which we no longer notice divisive group differences but instead foster enormous diversity in individual self-creations.

Like Baldwin's, the tone of Rorty's more detailed American story of "achieving our country" was more psychological than institutional. Perhaps because of this, whether one agreed or disagreed with its specific details, Rorty's story succeeded in re-calling many American academics and a wider reading audience to a commitment to actively participating in reshaping the terms and dynamics of our shared public life. It eloquently expressed many late twentieth-century hopes and fears—his own and those of others—while restarting a long-overdue discussion of the preconditions for processes of national and personal identity formation, self-respect, and individual human flourishing as the motivational and practical prerequisites to collaboratively achieving America's democratic potential.

However, a closer reading of Rorty's story with an eye to America's and the world's post–September 11 needs suggests to me that his analyses of each of these important topics, as well as his readings of others' texts and the transformative prescription he based in part upon them, are distorted by his unusual cultural location, his individualistic "neopragmatist" philosophical views, and his backward-looking generational commitments, including a nostalgic desire to have old battles come out differently in the future. These distortions matter because they block a more realistic awareness of the contemporary global situation within which he rightly called American intellectuals to work for a fuller actualization of America's democratic potentials. Thus, despite the renewed urgency of revitalizing our American democratic institutions and our overlapping cultural habits, as well as the importance of the questions Rorty raised and the insightfulness of many of his specific comments, I believe that a set of interlinked shortcomings in his dream-story of America suggests that a different kind of story with a more inclusive transformative strategy—one closer to Baldwin's earlier American story, revised with help from Whitman, Dewey, and others—can offer us better guidance for deepening democracy in the crucial years ahead. My criticisms and counterproposals concern seven aspects of Rorty's story:

(1) American dreaming: the processes and metaphysical undergirding of telling a common story that can revive common social hope and a shared vision to guide collaborative action to actualize the dream of democracy in America and other global contexts;

(2) democratic epistemology: the (in)compatibility of memory, knowledge, and social hope;

(3) participatory democracy: movements versus campaigns as required for democratic change;

(4) democratic political economy: the (in)compatibility of democracy and global capitalism;

(5) democratic diversity: "racial" and cultural differences as barriers to demo-cratic unity *or* as resources for deepening democracy in America and in other global contexts;

(6) democratizing academic cultures: the role of universities and those edu-cated citizens William James called "the college bred";

(7) democratizing the churches: banning the language and influence of church-es from "the public square" to make room for a shared American "civic re-ligion" *or* democratically reframing their internal processes and public roles to aid the rebirth of shared social hope.

Because these important topics are intertwined throughout Rorty's story of "achieving our country," and because I agree that they must be intertwined in any adequate American story, I will consider all of them in reassessing the value of Rorty's "achieving our country," focusing on the first three in this book and taking up others in later volumes of this three-part meditation.

Please remember, neither this nor any other philosophical project expresses "a view from nowhere." I experience the world and write these criticisms and counterproposals from my own social, historical, political, economic, and cultural location. My location overlaps with Rorty's in many ways, and we agree in our commitment to the ideal of democracy, to the American project of "achieving our country," and to American pragmatism as a philosophi-cal tradition worth advancing and tailoring to the needs of the twenty-first century. However, Rorty and I are members of different generations, differ-ent genders, different regional and economic groups, and different camps in some of the great social and political struggles of our overlapping lifetimes. Nonetheless, just as I believe that his views are well worth considering and that they have helpfully influenced the formation and expression of my own, I also believe that the views for which I argue here offer a helpful corrective to those for which Rorty argued in *Achieving Our Country*. Moreover, I sug-gest that the greater realism and potential fruitfulness of my way of telling America's story in a wider global context offers good reasons to take it seri-ously, both in rethinking theoretical issues about the democratic ideal and the realities we must reconsider post-9/11, and in acting to revitalize our hopes and redirect our lives in these unsettled times.

Running throughout my discussion in this and later books will be disagree-ments with Rorty about how to read Whitman, Dewey, and Baldwin; about what pragmatism means and implies; and about how the American struggle to "achieve our country" interconnects with similar struggles in other global contexts. If some of these discussions get "too deep," I advise my reader to skip them and come back later. Just a reminder: my thesis in this particular chapter is that a critically revised, world-embracing version of Baldwin's story of group-linked memory, shared social knowledge amid our differences, and loyalty-expanding and courageous love for our diverse neighbors and for other world citizens must reframe our way of reading and acting upon Rorty's admittedly "ethnocentric" story of reviving our social hope in democracy by restoring American national pride. In the wake of September 11 and the wars that have followed, a realistic social hope of "achieving our country" must include and depend upon a hope of "achieving our world"—a more deeply democratic world.

Rorty's Democracy: Patriotic Dream, Moving Image, Leading Story, Civic Religion

As I suggested earlier, in contrast with both the institutional focus of most of the economists and political scientists who have steered the world's economic globalization processes since World War II and the "democratization" processes in Central and Eastern Europe since the great day in 1989 when German citizens destroyed the Berlin Wall, Rorty's conception of democracy was more psychological than institutional, more uplifting than critical or directive. For Rorty, democracy in the visionary tradition of Whitman and Dewey—as read, we must note, through his idiosyncratic pair of Freudian and Nietzschean lenses—was "an inspiring story," "a dream," "an image" of America that stimulates faith in a "civic religion" that can guide campaigns of reform to achieve our nation's potential within our existing American constitutional and economic framework. Like many other readers of Whitman and Dewey, I too have been moved by their calls to a more deeply democratic quality of community living, which resonates within Whitman's definition of democracy as "a great word whose history remains unwritten" and within Dewey's explanation and advocacy of the democratic ideal as an imaginative extension of the most desirable experienced qualities of American community life, which he believed offers practical guidance for processes of deep social transformation. I also have been persuaded and guided by the various ways in which both of these great thinkers attempt to ground their claims about democracy in evidence and argument. In subtle contrast, Rorty read

Whitman and Dewey as telling a motivating "story" of America as the on-going pursuit of a new kind of individuality that requires achieving wider conditions of economic justice and equal opportunity. Through his lenses, this is a patriotic story that can inspire shared pride in America during all the stages of its continuing history of "self-creation" and, thus, that can stimulate future-oriented cooperative campaigns of transformative action in voluntary solidarity with others, guided by the desire to fulfill our story's meaning for us as individuals.

Continuing this story into the future, Rorty argued in 1997, requires American intellectuals to reject many shame-provoking accounts of our na-tion's meaning and trajectory since Dewey's death in 1952, especially those that ascribe to America an imperial role in the cold war and in Vietnam, those that highlight shameful treatment of our own racial and ethnic minori-ties, and those that criticize a coercive American role within the economic and cultural globalization processes that are changing the world today. In-stead, Rorty argued, effective public deliberation and collaborative action to "achieve our country" require that we as citizen-agents believe strongly in America's positive potentials.

> National pride is to countries what self-respect is to individuals: a necessary condition for self-improvement. . . . Emotional involvements with one's coun-try—feelings of intense shame or of growing pride aroused by various parts of its history, and by various present-day national policies—is necessary if political deliberation is to be imaginative and productive. Such deliberation will prob-ably not occur unless pride outweighs shame. (3)

However, even if Rorty was right about the importance of renewing our emo-tional commitment to our country, a realistic, desirable, and sustainable pride in America need not and must not exaggerate our nation's virtues, deny our serious shortcomings, or base its claims on demeaning or dismissing others' bases for proper pride in their own countries.

If another of Baldwin's intellectual inheritors, Derek Bell, is correct, achieving realistic and desirable pride in our country will be a more com-plex process than Rorty imagined.[10] It will require reconstructing existing processes of American national and personal identity formation that depend upon socially transmitted and enforced racial and gender hierarchies, which are expressed in widespread feelings, words, and actions that say it is "better" to be American than to be Mexican or African; "better" to be white than to be black, red, brown, or yellow; "better" to be male than to be female. Bell has insightfully argued that these hierarchies in our identity-formation processes serve as compensation and control mechanisms for economic inequality and for related anxieties about the difficulties many of us now face in meeting basic needs, maintaining self-respect, and attaining better opportunities in an increasingly precarious world.

If "achieving our country" means achieving a more deeply democratic American nation within a more deeply democratic world, we must challenge and change these now traditional, all-too-common hierarchies in our own and our neighbors' ways of thinking and living, which some of our fellow citizens see as part of "the American way of life" for which they are willing to fight and die. We must learn and we must acknowledge to others worldwide that proper pride in ourselves and in our country does not require feeling "better than" others, but rather fulfilling our diverse potentials and living humanly fitting lives. We must realize, however, that such a deeply democratic message is countered every day by "winner-takes-all" messages from other imaginatively potent realms, including business, politics, sports, and war.

Rorty's announced purpose in *Achieving Our Country*—to exhort American intellectuals to craft and tell a common, patriotic story that could guide transformative action to fulfill our nation's democratic potential—framed his choice of role models as well as his way of telling key events of American history. "Those who hope to persuade a nation to exert itself need to remind their country of what it can take pride in as well as what it should be ashamed of. They must tell inspiring stories about episodes and figures in the nation's past—episodes and figures to which the country should remain true. Nations rely on artists and intellectuals to create images of, and to tell stories about, the national past" (3–4). While Rorty acknowledged in passing here the importance of remembering what our nation should be ashamed of, he tended to forget this balancing insight in telling his own story of America, and to treat "truth" only as a kind of faithfulness, perhaps because of a belief that pride attracts more adherents than shame in the competition for dominance within political life: "Competition for political leadership," he said, "is in part a competition between differing stories about a nation's self-identity, and between differing symbols of its greatness" (3–4).

In the wake of September 11, Rorty's Nietzschean antirealist suggestion that rival American stories must be understood primarily in terms of a competition for political dominance seems both prescient and chilling. Clearly, a global struggle for narrative dominance helped to shape the events of those dreadful days and America's response to them. Yet Rorty's analysis offers no method or vantage point from which to assess the truth of rival American stories or to reframe them in terms of a larger story that includes other peoples' hopes. All that Rorty's "neopragmatism" allowed him to suggest in 1997 was that *if* Americans are to collectively recommit ourselves to fulfilling our nation's democratic potential, what he called "the intellectual Left" must gain the power to direct our nation's future by achieving dominance for its narrative about America's past. This includes establishing interpretive control over a set of symbols that express certain key national characteristics and their sources. Therefore, Rorty argued, changing the dominant American story must take precedence, at least strategically, over acknowledging, criticizing, and changing the undemocratic real circumstances in which we Americans have lived—and still live today.

Changing the dominant story gained such strategic prominence in Rorty's transformative prescription because he regarded America's greatest problem at the end of the twentieth century as a lack of "inspiring stories and images" (4). Instead, the national stories he assessed as most influential at that time offered only what he regarded as unacceptable choices among militaristic chauvinism, self-mockery, and self-disgust. He thought the first option was simple minded, though subsequent events have shown it to have tremendous imaginative and practical power in guiding a nation that has committed itself to an open-ended war against unknown and pervasive opponents who have already succeeded in wounding our oddly un-American sounding "homeland." The other two kinds of national stories, which were swept from the public scene as "unpatriotic" immediately after September 11—though the Iraq War revived them—seemed to Rorty to be impediments to the kind of shared social hope that once flowed from powerful, reform-guiding novels such as *The Jungle*, *An American Tragedy*, and *The Grapes of Wrath*. Those older, liberal, reformist national stories effectively challenged all Americans to work for economic justice and equality of opportunity for all (8).

Writing at the end of the twentieth century, Rorty argued that democracy-minded intellectuals must overcome all three kinds of discouraging and dangerous national stories with a reformist liberal "rhetoric" in which patriotism motivates action to finally achieve the long-shared American dream-story that Whitman and Dewey so eloquently expressed (9). In my own view, Rorty's kind of "persuasive rhetoric" will never be enough, and its resonances must always be tested against all the facts we can provisionally establish and against our deepest values and our most powerful experiences. Nonetheless, Rorty was prophetic in his insight about something really important: our need for a "new American story" to guide new generations of activists in transformative efforts to fulfill our country's moral and imaginative potential is even greater now than it was when Rorty wrote. However, an adequate American story for us now must express a wider, more inclusive, very different kind of dream of deeper democracy at home and abroad than Rorty dared to dream in 1997.

In Rorty's view, the contrast between the kind of active, engaged approach to political life he recommended and the political approach he believed typified "American Left intellectuals" from the late 1960s to the end of the twentieth century was the difference between "agents and spectators" (9). A century earlier, a similar contrast marked the difference between William James's engaged, activistic approach to public life and what Rorty called the "proto-Heideggerian cultural pessimism" of James's contemporary Henry Adams. According to Rorty, James regarded Adams' view as so "perverse . . . decadent and cowardly" that it contributed to the motivation for James's pragmatist conception of truth, which focuses in large part on the action-inspiring, world-changing significance of an idea as the test of its meaning and value.

Rorty argued that the significance for James of democracy as an idea is its role as a shared "civic religion" that calls citizens to hopeful transformative action to achieve its goals, even though the evidence that these goals are feasible is presently insufficient to compel belief.

> For James, disgust with American hypocrisy and self-deception was pointless unless accompanied by an effort to give America reason to be proud of itself in the future. . . . "Democracy," James wrote, "is a kind of religion, and we are bound not to admit its failure. Faiths and utopias are the noblest exercise of human reason, and no one with a spark of reason in him will sit down fatalistically before the croaker's picture." *(9)*

However, Rorty reported, only militaristic chauvinists claimed this sort of patriotic American "civic religion" at the end of the twentieth century. How did this happen? In his view, those James called the "college bred" had been systematically stripped both of faith in their country's future and of the agency that depends upon it, becoming spectators unable "to think of American citizenship as an opportunity for action" (11).

Clearly, this state of affairs changed dramatically in the weeks after September 11, when university students in New York City turned out in droves to give blood, make sandwiches for workers seeking survivors in the wreckage of the World Trade Center, and volunteer their services wherever they might be needed to help all of us move through our loss and fear toward hope and action. Their newly revived "civic religion" was further expressed in late 2002 and in the early months of 2003, as college students and their faculty members joined hundreds of thousands of their fellow Americans in cities throughout the country and millions of others in major cities worldwide in simultaneous mass protests against an anticipated war on Iraq. They listened in shock and horror to a "new American story" of global empire to maintain order and to impose democracy by force, as told by the "neoconservatives," whose narrative gained dominance within the Bush administration. The problem for them and for all of us since September 11 and since the Iraq War began has been how to find vision and to give voice to a rival "new American story" that can guide our way forward on the basis of a deeper and more realistic understanding of what justice, democracy, and security mean in this deeply unstable new world. In addition to imaginative power to attract support and guide action, an adequate "new American story" for these times must have critical qualities of humaneness, realistic depth, and historical truth that allow it to challenge and defeat the dominant story that led us into the Iraq War and that has undergirded all the official denials of its brutality and ineffectiveness.

Unfortunately, Rorty denied that humaneness, realistic depth, and historical truth are possible in a story—though I believe he was wrong on all these points and will try to show why this is so in order to support the process of collaboratively telling the kind of post-9/11 story of deepening democracy in America and other global contexts that we so desperately need now. For Rorty the "nominalist," as much as for Samuel Huntington, there are no common, cross-cultural ethical standards of humaneness—only how "we" see things as "Western bourgeois liberals" and how others see things, often differently, with no common human nature, and thus no Kantian universal rationality to serve as a common ground for the universal human rights on which Seyla Benhabib and other critical theorists have focused their democratic hopes for the future. There is no objective perspective on reality, said Rorty the "neopragmatist," and therefore no relative depth, distortion, or shallowness in our claims about it. There is no truth of history, said Rorty the "historicist," because there is no way to get out of the limits of our time and place, which are profoundly unlike other times and places. There is no divine plan to make sense of our present suffering and guarantee a better future, and this is a good thing, said Rorty the "ironist," because this is the prerequisite for the self-creative freedom of "strong poets" to shape personally meaningful individual lives as well as a nation unlike any the world has seen before—America—in which our democratic solidarity expresses and enhances our freedom.

All we can say about the process of narrative dominance, Rorty suggested, is that one story speaks to us more than another, engages our hopes, expresses our longings, and somehow triumphs over other stories on that basis. In explaining his choice of the word "image" to express the kind of common vision of America he urged intellectuals to strive to recreate, Rorty rejected the possibility of any "objective" account of our national identity. "Nobody knows what it would be like to try to be objective when attempting to decide what one's country really is, what its history really means," he wrote in 1997, "any more than when answering the question of who one really is oneself, what one's individual past really adds up to. We raise questions about our individual or national identity as part of the process of deciding what we will do next, what we will try to become" (11). Thus Rorty rejected not only objectivity per se, but any conception of truth or social knowledge that could trump or ought properly to guide individual judgments about what to do and who to become, other than a democratically achieved universal consensus. In his view, America's history, identity, and future are what "we" say they are, a reflection of "our" image of "our" country. It is the responsibility of American intellectuals to evoke a more desirable image through inspiring stories that attract action-guiding consensus—stories that reflect "our" fears and that inspire transformative action guided by "our" hopes.

Since September 11, even more than in 1997, Rorty's refusal to acknowledge any other basis or source of guidance for grounding and challenging our hopes and fears seems dangerous. James, Whitman, Dewey, and Baldwin all believed that there are ways of knowing that can undergird reliable tests of the insightfulness of our hopes and fears and serve as sources of wise guidance for framing a shared vision of community living that we would ignore at our peril. America and the wider world now greatly need such knowing, such reality tests, and such wise guidance in reframing what Alexis de

Tocqueville called our "habits of the heart" and our choices and visions of a shared future—especially if those of us who have gifts for words actually succeed in gaining a wider public for a rival "new American story," as Rorty rightly urged us to try to do.

Intellectual Self-Transformation in a Time of Democratic Emergency?

Instead of such ways of knowing, such truth tests, and such wise guidance from a common well of experience in living and from collaborative inquiries in the sciences and the arts, Rorty recommended that American academics and other citizen-thinkers give up all that in favor of a new way of thinking, valuing, and speaking that would allow us to arouse a large enough and a motivated enough constituency to actualize the rival "new American story" that it is our role and historical responsibility to tell. Instead of the loving collaboration of a small band of prophetic leaders across lines of racial-cultural differences to "achieve our country" and "change the history of the world" that Baldwin called forth in 1963, Rorty's call in 1997 was for a practical though not necessarily deep partnership across class lines, in which "reformist liberal" academics tell a motivating "new American story" that will wake up working people from their hopelessness, their apathy, and even their "values"-based attachment to the Republican Party. The point of telling this "new American story," Rorty said, was to engage the active commitment of labor unions as collaborators in a set of campaigns of limited reforms to advance our country's economic justice and equality of opportunity—interests not shared as directly by more privileged, ideal-motivated academics but that must be advanced in order to create the social basis for experiences of wider democratic solidarity that otherwise lack real support.

A further complexity of Rorty's proposal is that he assessed the "cultural Left" that he believed dominated the American academy as currently unfit for the crucial job of telling the right kind of "new American story." To deal effectively with the consequences of globalization, he argued, "the present cultural Left would have to transform itself by opening relations with the residue of the old reformist Left, and in particular with the labor unions" (91). However, the self-transformation Rorty actually called for would have to go much deeper than new patterns of association. Academics would have to change their self-understanding, the focus of their efforts, their language, and their current account of American history since World War II to fit the requirements of the unions and other remnants of the "Reformist Left." Philosophy is part of the problem, Rorty claimed, devoid of useful methods or insights, and for all its verbiage about rival theories of truth, knowledge, reality, and human nature, generally full of hot air. Thus, in order to "achieve our country," we should stop wasting time like this and get to work: "I have two suggestions about how to effect this transition. The first is that the Left should put a moratorium on theory. It should try to kick its philosophy habit. The second is that the Left should try to mobilize what remains of our pride in being Americans. It should ask the public to consider how the country of Lincoln and Whitman might be achieved" (91–92). Cheerleading must replace criticism, Rorty said; "rhetoric" must replace history, sociology, and philosophy. It is important to note that Baldwin's *The Fire Next Time* is not included on Rorty's list of imaginative guides to aid academic progressives in this process of self-reconstruction. Rorty recommended only Dewey's *Reconstruction in Philosophy* (1920) in his effort to re-call academics to "the problems of men," expressing exasperation about the kind of "sterile debate" now going on concerning "individualism versus communitarianism" and ridiculing the common belief among academics that "the higher your level of abstraction, the more subversive of the established order you can be" and "the more sweeping and novel your conceptual apparatus, the more radical your critique" (92–93).[11]

The academically fashionable intellectual practice of disengaged abstraction, Rorty argued, explains why a quasi-religious attachment to Michel Foucault's work has distracted so much of the academic Left's time and attention from its real and pressing practical responsibilities to lead democratic political processes of economic reform in America. "Disengagement from practice produces theoretical hallucinations. . . . The cultural Left is haunted by ubiquitous specters, the most frightening of which is called 'power,' which Mark Edmundson calls 'Foucault's haunting agency, which is everywhere and nowhere, as evanescent and insistent as a resourceful spook'" (94). In being everywhere and inescapable, Rorty argued, Foucauldian power is like original sin. In the academic "Left's" commitment to abstract theory, it has "gotten something which is entirely too much like religion . . . within a vast quasi-cosmological perspective" (95). In such a Gothic world, "democratic politics has become a farce" (95). Like traditional religions, he claimed, disengaged, abstracted, spectatorial philosophies and the social sciences that build on them confuse and obstruct public deliberation about urgent practical problems.

This kind of "philosophy," like religion, should be regarded as a private indulgence, Rorty argued, because neither has a public role to play in addressing the problems of achieving our country.

> [Such] quasi-religious form[s] of spiritual pathos. . . . should be relegated to private life and not taken as guides to political deliberation. . . . When we take up our public responsibilities . . . the infinite and the unrepresentable are merely nuisances. Thinking of our responsibilities in these terms is as much of a stumbling block to effective political organization as is the sense of sin . . . For purposes of thinking about how to achieve our country . . . we can give both religion and philosophy a pass. We can just get on with trying to solve what Dewey called "the problems of men." (96–97)

Whether Rorty's criticisms of "postmodernist" philosophy were well taken or merely reflect careless reading, his proposal to get on with solving Dewey's "problems of men" did not tell us *which* practical problems—and *whose*—should become the focus of our transformative efforts toward "achieving our country."[12] In the absence of Baldwin's painful memory, quotations from Lincoln and Whitman are easily employed as tools of a dangerous erasure and forgetting that would misguide our social hopes and our transformative action.

Moreover, in addition to requiring whole disciplines to give up their current practices, the intellectual self-reconstruction Rorty called for seems to require a fundamental reorientation in the sources of personal identity of the "academic Left," in their beliefs about the present, and in their hopes for the future. It would require rejecting the widely shared conviction that nation-states are in some ways obsolete, as Benhabib argues, and, instead, "deriving our moral identity, at least in part, from our citizenship in a democratic nation-state, and from leftist attempts to fulfill the promise of that nation" (97). Such a change is necessary for academic progressives to effectively reengage as transformative leaders, he argued, because "the government of our nation-state will be, for the foreseeable future, the only agent capable of making any real difference in the amount of selfishness and sadism inflicted on Americans" (98). Thus, the academy must shed "its semi-conscious anti-Americanism" and instead "construct inspiring images of the country" that will allow it to "form alliances with people outside the academy—and specifically, with the labor unions," which are essential if the academic "Left" is to significantly influence our country's laws (98–99).

Within this new "reformist liberal" alliance, Rorty called for agreement on "a concrete political platform, a People's Charter, a list of specific reforms" that "might revitalize leftist politics" (99). Such a transformative agenda should focus mostly on problems that stem from "selfishness rather than sadism," Rorty argued, apparently because he believed that economic issues would be the core concerns of his prospective nonacademic allies. Or perhaps Rorty emphasized economic justice because, having forgotten his own acknowledgment both of the "New Left's" correctness in opposing the Vietnam War and of the "cultural" Left's insight that sadism has a different mechanism than selfishness, he still believed that economic inequalities were more fundamental than other injustices and that they caused or at least could somehow be separated from racism, sexism, and traditional prejudices against other cultures and religions and the social harms to which these lead. To assume leadership in organizing this new progressive alliance and in guiding the articulation of such a People's Charter, the academy would have to "change the tone" in which it talks about sadism, Rorty argued, including its rejection of the "melting-pot" metaphor that he, like Huntington, thought we should reclaim (100).

This was no small concession Rorty called for—as his contemporary Nathan Glazer, a sociologist, commented in explaining his own abandonment of the "melting-pot" metaphor: "We are all multiculturalists now."[13] Glazer argued that even reformist liberals like himself, who would prefer to think of America as a place in which racial, ethnic, and gender differences no longer impede equal opportunities, must recognize that we are not yet that America and that "color-blind" strategies inspired by the "melting-pot" metaphor have failed to rectify still radically unequal opportunities, especially for African Americans. This is why purely voluntary, individualistic affiliation strategies inspired by a "postracial," "postethnic" perspective within a common culture are premature, if our transformative concern for justice is to be effectively grounded in descriptive accuracy and honesty about how we now live. Instead, we must work through multicultural strategies in the school curriculum and in the larger culture, as Glazer wisely argued, in order eventually to move beyond them.

Rorty's proposal that academic progressives reconstruct their own self-understandings by embracing the "melting-pot" metaphor once again would require Glazer and other progressive social scientists to forget more than thirty years' worth of data and theoretical struggle about how to frame recommendations to guide democratic reforms in public policy. Why should honest scholars deny and forget such collective evidence of their hard and careful work and of our nation's growth of experience? Wouldn't this require abandoning their integrity in the process of abandoning their disciplines' methods and guiding paradigms? How could such deep changes be justified? Are they even possible without electric shock or brain transplants, or at least without cultivating habits of deep denial? Wouldn't such an abandonment of the still-evolving theoretical processes of the social sciences simply fuel cultural conservatives' attacks on scientific truths and on the growth of a common fund of knowledge?

As repressive and inauthentic as Rorty's "embrace the melting pot" recommendation sounded, his sense of the urgency of the times may have driven his demand that progressive academics abandon many of our disciplinary and personal commitments in order to meet, on common ground, the expectations of our other partners in his projected "Left" alliance. Such a self-transformation process might be made more palatable, he suggested, if we also could bring ourselves to give up other incompatible ideas, such as our metaphysical notions of self-continuity and our epistemological commitments to the growth of knowledge, in order to make room for free self-creation and joyous social hope. (More about this later.) We need "common dreams," Rorty insisted, and fulfilling our responsibility to forge them requires that we "cease noticing . . . differences" (100–101).

However, as James Baldwin reminded us, it is impossible for at least some of us Americans to cease noticing at least some of our differences. Race, gender, economic background, region, religion, and profession still matter when they count against or in favor of a person in daily life and when they represent different angles of vision that can contribute to deepening our democracy and making it a more effective "cosmopolitan bridge" in the process of achieving our world.[14] Therefore, contributing what our gifts most fit us to offer to the urgent project of "achieving our country" requires us as progressive citizen-thinkers to remember all that these differences have cost us while reaching out to others in Baldwin's "courageous love" and in a more realistic hope for a better, collaboratively forged, more deeply democratic future. This process of realistically and hopefully remembering and then mutually transforming our American differences can be the key to our effective participation in a wider project of global inquiry, reconciliation, and justice-guided transformation, as we absorb the losses and lessons of September 11 and commit ourselves to ending war and terrorism and to replacing destructive and divisive processes of globalization with better ones that foster diverse, interlinked efforts to deepen democracy worldwide. How we may be able to do these great things is the focus of the last chapter of this book—but first, I must explain in more detail why truths of history, hope, and even some of the moss-encrusted areas of philosophy still matter, if we are to launch an inclusive enough, effective enough, and ambitious enough democracy-deepening process.

The Better Party for American Progressives to Join: Whitman, Dewey, Baldwin

I have argued throughout this chapter that a pragmatist approach offers us better guidance than Rorty's neopragmatism in understanding and addressing three of the most basic kinds of existential issues we now face as Americans and as world citizens: issues about memory and forgiveness, issues about democracy's meaning in a time of crisis, and issues about how scholars and other citizen-thinkers can contribute to an inclusive process of public empowerment to achieve shared democratic ideals in diverse global contexts. Even before September 11, Rorty rightly urged us not to take the viewpoint of detached, economistic, shallowly cosmopolitan spectators when assessing our country's past and prospects.[15] Instead, he urged us to substitute shared utopian dreams for knowledge claims and to rejoin Whitman's and Dewey's—and, we must add, Baldwin's—American party of democratic hope (106–107).

Theirs is the right party for American progressives to join now, though it was not really Rorty's party when he wrote *Achieving Our Country*. His nostalgic attachment to winning old battles, his suspicions of old opponents and their inheritors, and his willingness to read abstract theories but not works of contemporary "public philosophy" grounded in participatory democratic practice distorted the way he told his story and even led him to try to tell it alone. Nonetheless, Rorty's American "dream-story" has been a spur to many of us readers to do better, to get going, to wait no longer. This will be his great and lasting legacy.

In contrast with both Huntington's proposal that we Americans turn our gaze backward in search of a common founding memory and Rorty's proposal that we erase our past differences in a common, future-focused American dream, I propose that public philosophers working in the wake of September 11 must approach the telling of a hope-reviving "new American story" differently than Richard Rorty did in 1998. We must remember the unity of our feelings and aspirations on September 11 as well as the history-based, injustice-linked differences that still trouble our ability to work together to deepen democracy in "our country" and in other global contexts and thereby to begin, as Baldwin said, "a new history of the world." In contrast with Baldwin's refusal to forgive, however, I believe we can learn a valuable lesson from those African American ancestors who—without forgetting their suffering and loss—forgave those who had held them in bondage instead of seeking revenge, moving on with their lives while transforming a cycle of violence into a process of progressive stages of coexistence, mutual benefit, and democratic neighborliness.

Rorty's prescription for guiding democratic transformation is too limited to meet our needs now, in large part because it lacks the kind of revisable democratic ideal Dewey favored as a motivator and guideline for the long-term practical processes of deepening democracy to which Rorty rightly recalled American academics and other citizen-thinkers. As a place to start, Rorty's advice is very wise:

> I think that the Left should get back into the business of piecemeal reform within the framework of a market economy. . . . Someday, perhaps, cumulative piecemeal reforms will be found to have brought about revolutionary change. . . . But in the meantime, we should not let the abstractly described best be the enemy of the better. We should not let speculation about a totally changed system, and a totally different way of thinking about human life and human affairs, replace step-by-step reform of the system we presently have.   (105)

Rorty was right that we can't wait to begin our transformative efforts until we have a complete picture of what we're trying to achieve—we must do our best to reform obvious problems and to meet basic needs, using the ideal of deep democracy as our guide. We will have to experiment in deepening democracy in ways that meet the challenges and work with the opportunities we find in particular contexts, understanding that democracy evolves locally and within networks of relations rather than by following a uniform pattern that we can successfully impose or import.

Nonetheless, establishing a realistic grounding for our hopes as we work toward particular reforms requires that we discover and interrelate the series of successive reforms our country and the world now need with directional guidance from a revisable democratic ideal. Sustaining our hopes amid real dangers and manifold uncertainties over the uneven course of a long-term collaborative struggle requires employing a practical process of mutually adjusting our strategies and our guiding ideals to one another, as we gain understanding and practical capability through active participation in democracy-deepening transformative practice. After all, how would a revived "reformist Left" know *which* reforms to strive for, *how* to organize our efforts, and *how to assess them* without such a democratic ideal and the experience of using it within the kinds of collaborative, practically focused, mutually educational transactions that Dewey and others have called for and that many are now testing and learning to generalize in action?

As the next chapter will show, we can revise Rorty's very personal story with the help of Whitman, Dewey, and Baldwin, and we can start the process of telling an American "we-story" and seeking a common vision, with experienced guidance from our Native American neighbors, reaching out to include many of the groups who are active now in pursuing democratic reforms in America and in other countries worldwide. In starting up and encouraging this "American Dreaming" process, public philosophers can act as "liaison agents" to bring in all the disciplines and to help smaller "publics" form and start talking, until a great "Public" emerges with a story it knows to be true and a shared vision that can serve as an inspiring guide for our future transformative efforts. If the dispersed knowledge of all these participants, their particular experiences in struggles for democracy in their own contexts, their unique voices, and their differing but potentially converging social hopes for the future are conjoined within shared stories and visions to guide the ambitious transformative project of "achieving our world," we would have good grounds for a shared social hope that "achieving our country" *is possible.*

Chapter 2

American Dreaming
From Loss and Fear to Vision and Hope

Democracy . . . is a kind of religion, and we are bound not to admit its failure. Faiths and utopias are the noblest exercise of human reason, and no one with a spark of reason in him will sit down fatalistically before the croaker's picture.

—William James, "The Social Value of the College Bred"

Songs are thoughts, sung out with the breath when people are moved by great forces and ordinary speech no longer suffices. Man is moved just like the ice floe sailing here and there in the current. His thoughts are driven by a flowing force when he feels joy, when he feels fear, when he feels sorrow. Thoughts can wash over him like a flood, making his breath come in gasps and his heart throb. Something, like an abatement in the weather, will keep him thawed up. And then it will happen that we, who always think we are small, will feel still smaller. And we will fear to use words. But it will happen that the words we need will come of themselves. When the words we want to use shoot up of themselves, we get a new song.

—Orpingalik, Netsilik Shaman, in Joseph Brown and Emily Cousins, *Teaching Spirits*

Linguists have long suggested that we are determined by our native language, that language defines and confines us. It may be so. The definition and confinement do not concern me beyond a certain point, for I believe that language in general is practically without limits. We are not in danger of exceeding the boundaries of language, nor are we prisoners of language in any dire way. I am much more concerned with my place within the context of my language. This, I think, must be a principle of storytelling. And the story-teller's place within the context of his language must include both a geographical and mythic frame of reference. Within that frame of reference is the freedom of infinite possibility. The place of infinite possibility is where the storyteller belongs.

—N. Scott Momaday, *The Man Made of Words*

From Stories of Loss and Fear to Vision, Hope, and Action

For us now, as for Richard Rorty when he composed *Achieving Our Country* (1998), losses and fears deeply influence the kind of guiding vision we are able to hope for and the actions we are able to take toward fulfilling its meanings. Writing and speaking bravely from his personal experience, Rorty told a pre-9/11 story of how our American universities changed after Vietnam into places of cynicism and quietism—a loss of their institutional purpose that so damaged his sense of meaning in living and his hope for the future that he greatly feared that America's long-loved dream of democracy might be destroyed by the forces of globalization and backlash. Out of his story of loss and fear, Rorty brought forth a guiding transformative vision of academic intellectuals shaking themselves out of less important preoccupations and taking up their civic responsibility to tell a "new American story" that could change the future by reviving widely shared social hope, expressed in coalition-based campaigns of liberal reforms to "achieve our country." In the following pages of this chapter, I aim to appreciatively follow Rorty's example of using storytelling as a process that can help us move through loss and fear to vision and social hope—a process through which many of us as individuals and all of us as an American people scarred by 9/11 still must pass in order to bring us to full readiness for democracy-deepening transformative action. Through a close, interactive reading of Rorty's text, however, I also aim to show that unchallenged mistakes in his telling of earlier events and in his background philosophical claims limit the usefulness of his story and vision to us now. These faults show us why the processes of storytelling and vision seeking we need to undertake must be social and interactive, rather than the solitary work of a "strong poet," if they are to help us move through loss and fear to widely shared future-visions, democratic hopes, and transformative actions for our country and our world.

Many of us who endured profound losses and a great birth of fear on September 11—the sudden destruction of previously unchallenged images of the meaning of America's past and the deflation of confidence in our personal and national future—still struggle with deep feelings of grief, anxiety, nostalgia, defiance, and longing for justice like those Rorty expressed in 1997. To fittingly acknowledge what we have lost and what we now fear while moving through and beyond these deep feelings, we need a collaborative process of "American dreaming"—storytelling and vision seeking with others, grounded in realistic insights about what brought this new era of our nation's history into being, through which we can seek together a wise guiding path for our future that can motivate personal and cooperative commitments to transformative action. In contrast with Rorty's narrowly "ethnocentric" story and vision, however, the process of storytelling and vision seeking we need now must be both inclusively American and global in inspiration and implications. We need *a wide-awake American dream* that can evoke feelings of shared pride in actively contributing to transgenerational efforts to fulfill our country's potentials—one that can foster wider, global loyalties that lead us to open-mindedly respect both our cross-cultural commonalities and our democratically tolerable differences, and one that can guide us in working open-heartedly and open-handedly with others to achieve local and global conditions that support fully human living and deeply democratic mutual flourishing.

In framing such a collaborative process of post-9/11 American dreaming, Rorty's reformist "civic religion" and his "neopragmatist" transformative vision offer us valuable suggestions. However, these must be distanced from his personal fears and nostalgic attachments to the past. They must be corrected by some of John Dewey's classical pragmatist philosophical methods and theoretical insights born from struggles to deepen democracy in the twentieth century, including a context-sensitive employment of a "low-rise" democratic metaphysics, a sensible rethinking of the meaning of truth processes within collaborative transformative inquiry, and an openness to collaborating with diverse intellectual competitors. Finally, our reconstruction of Rorty's contribution to "achieving our country" must reflect lessons from our Native American neighbors about how to work wisely with the power of stories to guide our vision questing, as many of their elders have been doing for generations, and how to work together in local and national, deeply democratic future-choosing gatherings, as many of their communities still do.

American Civic Religion and Its Opponents: Rorty's Losses, Fears, Vision, and Hope

What were the great losses and fears that motivated Rorty's storytelling and vision questing in 1997? Both are suggested by his scorn for what he called "the academic Left," because of its failure to tell a motivating American story: "The academic Left has no projects to propose to America, no vision of a country to be achieved by building a consensus on the need for specific reforms" (Rorty, *Achieving Our Country*, 15). As Rorty told his own American dream-story, there was a time when "the American Left" was an active and effective alliance between intellectuals and labor unions. However, he explained, this alliance broke down in the 1960s over the Vietnam War—and also, we add, over the civil rights movement, because some of Rorty's favorite leaders of "the American Left" believed that race issues were secondary in importance and resolvable purely in terms of economic issues, because some labor union members resisted racial integration, and because Martin Luther King Jr. spoke out against the Vietnam War, which many labor union members supported on patriotic grounds.

In any case, Rorty charged, after seizing intellectual leadership of "the American Left" in the late 1960s, "the academic Left" sank into "an attitude like Henry Adams'" cultural pessimism that his contemporary, William James, regarded as "perverse . . . decadent and cowardly"—even into unintended collaboration with the Right—allowing "cultural politics" to replace "real politics" (9). Such a harsh criticism suggests that in 1997, Rorty's greatest fear was that America's "academic Left" would betray his intellectual legacy and the dreams of his youth. Or perhaps he was expressing a hard-to-name sense that his youthful vision of America already had lost its imaginative power—that it had been replaced irretrievably with something less. Perhaps this is why his analysis of what had gone wrong with America has an oddly spectatorial and retrospective quality of the kind he himself argued is incompatible with the responsibility of "the Left" (14). Perhaps this also is why Rorty's transformative prescription seems to express a nostalgic longing for a long-lost struggle and an unrealistic hope like that of Kierkegaard's unhappiest man: that the past will come out differently in the future.

In 1997, Rorty's transformative vision called for a revival of what William James described as America's "civic religion." During Rorty's youth, such a secular faith had motivated effective action by his family's anticommunist, liberal, reformist branch of the pre-1960s "American Left." Though always opposed by "the American Right," Rorty tells us, this "civic religion" attracted enough popular support before the Vietnam War to motivate real progress, while sustaining for its partisans a sense of meaningful, engaged living by supporting their vision of someday achieving economic justice and equal opportunity for all. In describing the complex times during which this American civic faith was lost by so many, Rorty admitted that the rival "New Left" did the right thing in forcing an end to the Vietnam War, which he called a necessary task, yet an impossible one for his own liberal reformist branch of "the Left" (67–68). Rorty devoted many more pages, however, to criticizing "the New Left" for its failure of democratic leadership after the Vietnam War, when it turned our nation's attention to "cultural politics"—issues of race, culture, and gender identity—instead of renewing the great pre–Vietnam War struggle for economic justice and equal opportunity.

There is some truth in Rorty's harsh criticisms of "the academic Left" during this period: the cultural critiques of some influential French "postmodernists," especially as interpreted by their American disciples, did indeed tend to change the subject of ethical and political debate at many American universities for twenty-five years, taking up time, attention, and opportunities that might have been devoted to democratic transformative theory and practice both inside and outside the academy. Thus, the works of these French "postmodernists," widely interpreted in American universities as apolitical or even antipolitical, became intellectual impediments to the embattled and internally divided project of "achieving our country" during a crucial period. Rorty himself was deeply influenced by these thinkers, as he frankly admitted in autobiographical writings and as his later works showed. In retrospect, the divisive and distracting effects these "postmodernist" works had may actually reveal a lack of careful reading by both their partisans and their critics.[1] For example, Jacques Derrida, an influential French thinker who often was labeled "postmodernist" and whose work greatly influenced Rorty, argued in *Spectres of Marx* (1994)—to the horror of some of his American disciples—that the larger point of his work always had been to unmask and to remove barriers to the achievement of social and economic justice worldwide.

However, "postmodernist" theorists were only a part of what Rorty branded as "the academic American Left" in the twenty-five years after the Vietnam War. The thinkers Rorty seemed to fear even more are those who pursued a culturally more inclusive vision of America, such as those of Elizabeth Cady Stanton, Jane Addams, James Baldwin, and Martin Luther King Jr., and who achieved some practical and theoretical successes in the process. Many new ethnic studies and women's studies departments, as well as new courses, specializations, and research focuses within traditional academic disciplines like philosophy, sociology, psychology, English literature, and history, have emerged since the early 1970s in response to concerns these intellectuals shared with many other citizens about American culture's race and gender hierarchies. Though Rorty regarded these efforts as distractions from his liberal reform agenda, these new departments and their partisans in the traditional disciplines actually have had some practical, democratic impact on matters of economic justice and equal opportunity in America, including who gets educational opportunities, who holds what jobs, who makes government decisions, and on what these focus. In fact, beating back their effectiveness has become a major focus of conservative political activists, who have used executive orders, legislation, and appointments to the U.S. Supreme Court to widen the income gap between rich and poor, limit the effectiveness of labor unions, and once again limit admission to desirable educational and professional opportunities to those who can pay for them or can show they "deserve" them according to standard, elite-favoring measures, including "legacy" admissions of children of alumni to their parents' universities and social network–based influence in hiring decisions.[2] "Traditional values" became the conservatives' political code phrase for advocating against feminism, multiculturalism, and recognition of the rights of gays and lesbians and on behalf of war, capital punishment, fundamentalist Christianity, fundamentalist capitalism, standardized test–focused education, and limited assistance to poor people facing socioeconomic disasters, including hurricane-ravaged New Orleans.

Moreover, contrary to Rorty's nostalgic hopes and despite the continuing efforts of these same conservatives, Marxists have not disappeared from the American academy, even after the fall of the Berlin Wall and the collapse of the Soviet Union. As Robert Heilbroner and Jacques Derrida predicted, the Marxists' call for social and economic justice has continued to resonate in our era of poorly guided processes of economic and cultural globalization.[3] In

coalition with professors in the new women's studies and ethnic studies departments, diverse cultural critics, Deweyan pragmatists, proponents of participatory democracy, and a revived "religious Left," American Marxists now
advance influential critiques of capital punishment, the American prison-in-
dustrial complex, local and international failures to respect and to enforce
workers' rights, and other antidemocratic aspects of the emerging global economic and cultural order. This raises a practical question about Rorty's story:
how could his way of framing a liberal reformist "civic religion" guide us now
in revitalizing America's "intellectual Left," when it retrospectively opposes
all of its actual component groups, the goals they advocate, and the methods
they employ?

The vehemence of Rorty's determination to erase Marxism from America's
story as he anticipated the beginning of the twenty-first century suggests that
past-grounded losses and fears permeated his nostalgic hopes for a fuller vin-
dication of the struggles during his youth of the old "reformist Left" that he
described in a moving autobiographical essay, "Trotsky and the Wild Orchids," blurring his ability to recognize new opponents and to envision more
realistic, forward-looking hopes.[4] Of course, as Rorty rightly pointed out, social democracy and economic justice, the ideals that guide his American "civic
religion," are much older ideals than Marxism. In Rorty's view, the "achievement" of these ideals actually was impeded by Marxism-Leninism—a view
with which many Central and Eastern Europeans who lived through the Iron
Curtain years and the ongoing political, economic, and cultural transformative struggles that have followed would agree. Marxism was, he asserted, "not
only a catastrophe for all the countries in which Marxists took power, but a
disaster for the reformist Left in all the countries in which they did not" (41).
To move beyond Marxism's failure, Rorty argued, "the American Left" must
repudiate the Marxist claim that "capitalism must be overthrown" (41–42).
He did not explain why: whether because capitalism as we know it is desirable or at least acceptable (a claim with which his parents would have disagreed) or because he believed its revolutionary overthrow is neither feasible
nor desirable as a means of democratic transformation (a claim Dewey actually made when recommending other transformative means).

In order to move us all through the particular losses and fears he named in
his own American dream-story so that we can find a new vision and regain
social hope, Rorty proposed that we undergo an odd kind of backward-looking "talk therapy." We must change the language we use when we refer to the

twentieth-century "American Left's" adversarial groups and key actors, he said, in order to change what people think of them now. We should abandon the Marxist "leftist versus liberal" distinction, for example, and we should use the term "Reformist Left" (instead of "Old Left") to refer to those self-described American "socialists" who "struggled within the framework of constitutional democracy to protect the weak from the strong" during the years after World War II and before Vietnam. We should use the term "New Left" to refer to post-1964 "American Leftists" who rejected the possibility of working for social justice within our existing political and economic system. He even suggested the odd phrase "part-time Leftist" to categorize democratic reformers such as Woodrow Wilson and Franklin Delano Roosevelt, who were hated by both "the Right" and their Marxist contemporaries (43–45).

Can changing our language in this way magically change the past and the future? While Rorty's proposed linguistic reforms better express and honor his own experience, they clearly center some actors in our American story of "achieving our country" while decentering and even erasing others. Moreover, contrary to my own experience, the political analysis with which Rorty backed his linguistic-reform proposal suggested that there has been no "reformist Left" since 1964 and that no self-described "New Leftists" became intrasystem reformers. However, many of my friends and I who were activists during our college years in what we still call "the Movement" would disagree, having earned graduate and professional degrees and then having invested our adult lives in working to open up democratic dialogue within the academy and within our larger society, empower new generations of democratic activists, and deepen democracy in our country's institutional infrastructure beyond our schools and universities: in our churches, the mass media, business and the economy, government and law, urban planning and philanthropy, and through the arts, social research, and service within nongovernmental organizations. So what was Rorty getting at in erasing our efforts from his own American story?

Perhaps the linguistic-reform proposal that was most important to Rorty gives us a clue by suggesting how he hoped his story would end: this was his call for American intellectuals to give up the sentimental self-designation as "Marxists" that appalls many Poles, Hungarians, and Chinese dissidents, especially because the only thing these American intellectuals meant to express by it, in Rorty's view, was their belief that the rich exploit the poor and retain control of the system (46). But surely there is more than this involved in these contemporary American thinkers' self-designation as "Marxists"—it also expresses their moral judgment rejecting the justice of the global situation Rorty himself sketched and their active commitment to liberatory transformation including by "revolutionary" means. Rorty may have been right that most American academics who adopt the Marxist label today are somewhat self-deceived, because they have no intention to "mount the barricades" in a revolutionary attempt to overthrow our government as the first phase in a profound transformation of American politics, economics, and society. Instead, they may be wishfully dreaming of a more effectively engaged life—one quite different from that writer's world of armchair experiences Rorty surprisingly praised as preferable to change-movement activism in the fourth essay of *Achieving Our Country* and quite different also from typical academic existences of repetitious teaching and narrow, "expert" research within institutionally constricted domains driven by a "publish-or-perish" imperative.[5] Despite Rorty's concern, the impulse such scholars feel toward a more actively engaged, contributive life may fittingly express the meaning of America's "civic religion" now.

Of course, Rorty could have agreed with the gist of all of these criticisms, because the main point of the future-vision he derived from his story of our country's recent past was neither his anti-Marxist historical revisionism nor his proposed linguistic reforms but rather his call to American intellectuals to recommit themselves to "achieving" America as what he called "the cooperative commonwealth." The dividing line between "the Left" and "the Right" in American politics, Rorty claimed, was always whether the state must take responsibility for a morally and socially desirable redistribution of wealth (48). His own transformative vision of intellectuals and labor unions cooperating to harness the powers of government to the task of creating "the cooperative commonwealth" through campaigns of liberal reforms, Rorty claimed, was what the pre-1960s Deweyan "Reformist Left" had in mind when they advocated their own version of "socialism." In using this term in the particular way they did, he said, they were expressing the criticisms of "individualism" they had learned from progressive "social scientists" such as Richard Ely and "social workers" such as Jane Addams who, Rorty noted, had supported the first great labor strikes and had advocated turning American universities into "something like a national 'church.'"[6]

Regrettably, Rorty's choice of a label for Jane Addams obscured her contribution as a public philosopher whose writing and activism greatly influenced

William James, John Dewey, George Herbert Mead, and other pragmatist thinkers and Progressive social reformers worldwide who read her books and, in Dewey's and Mead's cases, actively assisted her work of democratic hospitality at Hull-House, Chicago's pioneering "settlement house" for new immigrants to America, which Addams and a collective of women friends founded, financed, and operated. Addams employed Hull-House as a philosophical laboratory for discovering deeper meanings and methods of advancing what she called "social democracy" through serving and learning with a diverse community of people in need, bringing her the wisdom and fame she later invested as hard-won social capital to advocate for economic justice and international peace. Her widely read *Democracy and Social Ethics* (1902) impressed James as "among the best books we have produced," and it so deeply influenced Dewey that he quoted it in explaining his own view in the 1932 revised version of the *Ethics* he wrote with James Hayden Tufts. [7]

This small linguistic flaw in Rorty's otherwise laudatory description of Jane Addams's work in this passage from *Achieving Our Country* reveals two other aspects of his story and vision that need reconstruction. First, we need to reframe his story in terms of a more accurate account of the factions and fissures in America's political history and present tendencies. And second, we need to reclaim the Progressives' understanding of "socialism" as both a deeply democratic political and economic program and as a related *metaphysical tool* for critiquing and imaginatively transforming our cultural habits and social institutions. Concerning the first point, this may be the best place to correct Rorty's retelling of America's political history, taking seriously his concern that language matters: there is not now, nor has there ever been, a mainstream American "Left" and "Right" in the European ideological sense of that dichotomy, and it would not be useful to attempt to introduce it here in the wake of September 11, just when Europe seems to be abandoning it. Instead, there have always been shifting, issue-focused coalitions of individuals and groups, united in some ways by what Samuel Huntington has called a broad "American Creed" and by a certain piety toward "the Founders" but divided in many other ways—by region, race, gender, religion, economic location, profession, educational attainments, social status, and more personal "habits of the heart" such as open-mindedness, compassion, and a sense of connection to a wider world, or the lack of these qualities—which neither Huntington nor Rorty recognized adequately in telling their American stories and in projecting their future-visions.[8] Americans' beliefs about what kinds of roles government should play in shaping the shared conditions of our national life, and what levels of government should play these roles, have been closely tied to specific issues and have changed in different eras of our political history, except for small numbers of ideology-minded citizen-thinkers who have represented a range of views. For example, small rival parties of Marxists, conservatives, and Rorty's own liberal anticommunists struggled in small journals with one another during the mid-twentieth century, and each occasionally had some limited influence in shaping issues and policies within the wider American political discussion, but very few Americans knew anything about them. On the whole, mainstream American politics has always been a piecemeal, patchwork affair of persuasion, perspective, and temporary alliances of people constantly repacking their political baggage so as to retain at least some of their cherished old political symbols while making room for new treasures and new tools for responding to emergent needs.

Attaching ideological labels like those Rorty employed to these complex, shifting alliances tends to oversimplify them in ways that even their most thoughtful members may reject. For example, Rorty referred to the "New Left" as if it embraced a single, tightly interconnected set of issues and solutions. However, in my experience and that of many others, "the Movement" in its ten-year lifespan was a tense coalition of groups with overlapping but sometimes rival agendas. It emerged in part out of the civil rights movement, and it embraced many children of the American labor union movement like me, agreeing in general in our opposition to the Vietnam War but disagreeing in our views about how American society must be transformed in order to accommodate more liberatory understandings of race, gender, and economic justice. As I pointed out earlier, we have not disappeared from the American political scene. Instead, we have continued to develop our understandings of what democracy requires and our transformative strategies for achieving it. Some of us have discovered Dewey and the other Progressives and added them to our lists of American heroes, while realizing that what I call "pragmatist piety" requires continuously reframing their best insights and loyally rejecting what would mislead us now. Rorty was an obvious ally for us, as shown by many aspects of his story of "achieving our country" and his generous democratic practice of lending his presence as a megaphone to scholars taking real risks in democratization struggles worldwide, even though his ideological "purity" tests made it hard for him to ally himself with people who had friends like some of ours.

In the wake of September 11 and the wars that have followed, those of us who are committed to rescuing our shared social hope in democracy from its powerful opponents foreign and domestic need all the allies we can find, and an overly refined, backward-looking system of political labels that aims to show who was right thirty years ago would be counterproductive. Therefore, let us call ourselves "thinkers" and "active citizens" rather than "intellectuals," a term most Americans regard as elitist and therefore alienating. Instead of signing on as members of Rorty's invented, carefully delimited, non-Marxist, nonreligious, "reformist Left," let us call ourselves *democrats*, or even *progressives*, if we wish to honor James, Dewey, Addams, Mead, Baldwin, and others who found this a useful banner in the past. More importantly, let us learn wisdom from them if we can. Part of that wisdom includes learning from their understanding of "socialism" as in some sense "metaphysical," going deeper than the political and economic levels on which the late, great American liberal philosopher John Rawls thought it would be possible to achieve sufficient "overlapping public consensus" to revive and expand the project of achieving democracy in our times, despite disagreements in our deeper, faith-linked views.

Do We Need a "Socialist" Metaphysics and Pragmatist Philosophical Methods?

I think this part of my discussion of Rorty's *Achieving Our Country* is very important for showing how we can tell a better "American story" that gives birth to a trustworthy guiding vision and that maps a feasible and desirable plan of action, but you can skip over it and come back later if the labels "metaphysics" and "philosophical methods" make it too scary for you to read now. You see, despite Rorty's celebration of Dewey and his fellow Progressives as philosophical and political role models for the twenty-first century, his American dream-story and the philosophical views it reflected actually downplayed the value of the "socialist" metaphysical analysis they employed so seriously. In fact, *Achieving Our Country* implicitly advocated an *individualist* metaphysics— Rorty called it "nominalism"—and it employed a post-Freudian understanding of the individual psyche that rejects important aspects of the pragmatists' social psychology. In fact, the psychic power of Rorty's American dream-story to motivate transformative action depended on forgetting important lessons from our shared past while denying powerful elements of our present national and global situation. Whether Dewey's pragmatism or Rorty's neopragmatism offers better guidance in reviving and expanding shared social hopes of "achieving our country" may seem like an overly technical question, or maybe just a matter of family rivalries, but its answer makes a great difference for how we imagine public philosophy's role in contributing to the urgent project of deepening democracy in global contexts and for how desirable and effective that contribution is likely to be.

In writing *Achieving Our Country*, Rorty seemed to have had difficulty making up his mind about whether explaining the meaning and importance of this project to a wide "intellectual" audience requires plunging into the currently unpopular depths of metaphysics, a cold bath Dewey frequently found helpful in clarifying his thinking and never gave up, although it required him to swim against strong currents in Western philosophy and contemporary political life. On the one hand, against the kind of deliberative democratic process proposed by John Rawls, who famously claimed in a 1985 essay that issues of justice, including the preferability of democratic forms of living, can be understood entirely in terms of political procedures without metaphysical implications, Rorty quoted Dewey's argument that the meaning of democracy is not reducible to a set of political forms and processes because it is ultimately, in some sense, metaphysical: "Democracy is neither a form of government nor a social expediency," Dewey wrote, "but a metaphysic of the relation of man and his experience in nature."[9] Almost immediately after quoting this passage, however, Rorty in *Achieving Our Country* apologetically called Dewey's language of metaphysics "a bit unfortunate" and misleadingly suggested that all Dewey meant was that, contra Nietzsche, "democracy is the principal means by which a more evolved form of humanity will come into existence" (142).

Surprisingly, despite this move to lighten the conversation-stopping weightiness of talking about a democratic "metaphysics," Rorty went on to say, using Kenneth Burke's language, that the human persons who emerge from the kinds of deeply democratic processes of living for which Dewey called will have "more being" than predemocratic humanity: "The citizens of a democratic, Whitmanesque society are able to create new, hitherto unimagined roles and goals for themselves. So a greater variety of perspectives, and of descriptive terms, becomes available to them, and can with justice be used to account for them" (143). Rorty's phrase "with justice" carries a great deal of weight in grounding the application of his "descriptive terms," evoking as it does older cords of shared meaning that suggest a divine perspective, directive forces within nature, or at least some common standards of judgment within a still-vital cultural tradition. Yet Rorty explicitly attempted to cut away each of these kinds of metaphysical tethers to the past, leaving only a slim linguistic thread: what it is possible for us to say in a common language that appeals for the liberation of individuals. How such appeals could work, and why anyone would or should hear them, are things Rorty left unsaid.

These are dangerous silences for a therapeutic and transformative dream-story that aims to revive our shared commitment to the democratic change process of "achieving our country." Such a process requires that we be able to explain ourselves to other democracy-minded thinkers and to those in various global contexts who do not share our "form of life" and may even feel antagonistic toward it. We will need their assent, or at least their tolerance, if we are to create together the sustainable peace that allows us to invest time and treasure in deepening democracy instead of prosecuting wars and defending our "homeland" from foreign and domestic terrorists.

Rorty has failed to answer two key questions in the linguistically "lite," individualistic metaphysics with which he undergirds his dream-story and transformative vision. First, how should we understand the process of transforming a whole culture's internal social relations and transactional practices, which Dewey rightly regarded as inseparable from the liberation of individuals? And second, how should we understand the processes that shape and guide transactions among the communities, nations, and international associations that structure the relations of individuals with one another? The answers to these questions are missing from *Achieving Our Country* because Rorty threw overboard the "socialist" dimension of the pragmatists' and Progressives' democratic metaphysics that concerns the grounding, quality, and equity of our relations with one another and with the larger whole of nature locally, nationally, and globally. Contrary to the claims of Huntington and Rawls, the importance of a shared understanding of these dimensions of reality as something *to be developed* is increasingly clear since 9/11; we certainly cannot treat it as *already universal and operative within human rationality as such*, as Seyla Benhabib suggests, following Kant, but we also cannot pretend now that individual, national, and cultural differences on these points don't matter or can't be helped without making matters worse.[10]

Contrary to the advice of Rorty, Rawls, Habermas, Heidegger, and some of my pragmatist friends who think we should give up on metaphysics entirely, I believe it is wiser to reengage in the Progressives' project of reconstructing metaphysics.[11] Of course, it would not be helpful to think of such a reconstructed, democratic, pragmatist metaphysics as a "first philosophy" that somehow "precedes experience," as the great medieval metaphysicians framed this field; instead, we should think of metaphysics as a reflective, even a therapeutic dimension of later thinking that can spur critical insights about our own and others' particular intellectual habits and cultural assumptions that helped to construct our "first take" on experience and that can help us to see that none of these is necessary and some of them are quite misleading.[12] As Larry Hickman has pointed out, such a context-sensitive, "low-rise" metaphysics can play a valuable role in challenging the common assumption that "the facts" with which the sciences engage simply reflect "the way the world is," apart from the structures of our thinking about it and the modes of experimental transacting with it that these modes of thinking prompt.[13] In addition to this critical dimension, such a democratic "socialist" metaphysics also may spur imaginative insights about how we might think and live differently in our transactions with one another as humans, as well as those transactions with the wider world in which our lives participate.

A Deweyan "socialist" metaphysics also can help us to realize that the hypothetical "atomic individuals" who populate the worlds of neoclassical economics and liberal social choice theory—each seeking to advance their own competitive interests against one another in pursuit of ever-larger bundles of consumer goods and personal power—do not describe human nature as such, nor do they function merely as placeholders within data-driven, prediction-focused theorizing. The imaginative power of this misleading metaphysical model has leaked into our larger culture, in part through the multitudes of undergraduate college courses in which countless students have been taught these economic and political ideas uncritically, and even as models for thinking about themselves and the world of their future striving. To undo the damage such unwarranted, counterfactual "individualist" thinking has wrought in Western societies and in the larger world in which these countries now wield unprecedented power, we need to reframe the work of the social and natural sciences in terms of a low-rise pragmatist "socialist" metaphysics that challenges the now dominant "individualist" one. We need to use such a pragmatist "socialist" metaphysics as a transformative intellectual tool that frames our evolved nature and our preferable future possibilities in terms of a better-warranted account of long human processes of development, acculturation, language acquisition, identity formation, and ideal orientation, and in terms of our perennial need for intimate and communal bonds with human and nonhuman others within well-functioning social and biotic systems.

Moreover, we need to employ such a pragmatist "socialist" metaphysics as a tool for argumentation and a "democratic apologetics" in those academic and cultural contexts—still widespread in America—in which the older, "grand metaphysical tradition" still lingers on, serving as a source of justification for conservative forms of religious discourse and related aspects of our political and economic life that assume or assert their own version of "individualism" in combination with an otherworldliness the original Progressives sought to challenge. It is as practically necessary for us as it was for them to engage in metaphysical critique and reconstruction, if we are to highlight the background problems in thinking that underlie the intuitions, allegiances, habits, and institutions that structure currently problematic patterns of social living. To direct attention to this level of background thinking for the purpose of critical and reconstructive analysis, we must use some term or other. Many of those philosophers and social theorists who are uncomfortable with the term "metaphysics" still use the term "ontology" for this purpose. However, ontology always was and still is one of the divisions of the old-style, otherworldly metaphysics they reject, so they have not succeeded in distancing themselves from that larger project simply by employing a label for one of its branches, nor do they engage enough of the problematic terrain by restricting their concerns to ontology alone.

There is, of course, the alternative philosophical strategy of inventing a new name instead of "metaphysics" for expressing general (even if never eternal, culture-free, context-independent) insights about how time, nature, relations, persons, minds, processes of growth, change, choice, and individuation, as well as sources of great power James sought to evoke with the label "the divine" weave deep patterns in our lives and in the larger framework of personal and transpersonal experience, within which we seek to gain some meaning-making understanding and some modicum of control. However, simply inventing new names for referring to overlooked or misunderstood features of this dangerous yet unavoidable stretch of intellectual terrain, instead of clarifying the meanings of old terms that mark others' maps, runs the risk of Whitehead's choice: that the name-inventor may never be understood except by a few, because so much effort is required to learn an entirely new vocabulary for describing what initially may seem alien territory. Therefore, I think the wiser course is frankly to reengage the larger battle: to reconstruct metaphysics as pragmatists.

For those pragmatist philosophers who are willing and able to do the heavy lifting, this means arguing that a process metaphysics is preferable to a substance metaphysics. It means arguing on behalf of a "socialist" ontology that treats relations with others as constitutive of all beings within nature, including human beings, while democratically attributing value and contributive power to each of the dispersed elements within relational networks of humans and other-than-humans, and to their networks as such. At the same time, it means arguing against an individualist ontology that problematizes relations while divorcing values from nature or attributing them only to humans. In general, it means arguing, with Dewey, that metaphysics must not be understood as a systematic "first philosophy" that somehow stands outside and prior to experience, but as a "second" or "last" philosophical activity that can assist us in critically reconstructing our experience within nature in context-sensitive, problem-specific ways.

Interestingly enough, in arguing for his own vision of how a historical-change process of "achieving our country" could bring more evolved, "self-created" democratic individuals into being, Rorty abandoned his own linguistically "lite," nominalist-individualist reconstruction of Dewey's pragmatist "socialist" metaphysics in favor of a much more ambitious, quasi-Hegelian analysis of America's political history as a dialectical struggle between "the Left" and "the Right." In this aspect of his story, Rorty's "neopragmatist" metaphysics ironically went too far, offering an overly weighty analysis that oversimplified America's political history and tendencies while fostering dangerous delusions about how and by whom a democratic change process could be guided.[14] Within his historicist analysis of the dialectic in American political history, Rorty's *Achieving Our Country* treated "the Left"—by which he meant the now dwindled labor unions working in concert with the revitalized cadre of reform-minded "Western bourgeois liberal" intellectuals he hoped to inspire—as "the party of hope" (14). Why would a "neopragmatist" philosopher who felt the need to explain away Dewey's much less theory-freighted metaphysical approach import Hegel's elaborate and historically ill-fitting metaphysical machinery at this point? The answer once again seems to be the ghosts of the past.

Rorty's continuing obsession with defeating even the remnants of Marxism misled his thinking about past and future American realities. Rorty read Marx as having erred in treating Hegel's dialectic as useful for predicting the future, unwarrantably exceeding the limited "inspirational purposes" for which Hegel and his more careful readers like Whitman, Dewey, and Rorty himself employ it (19). By his own account, Rorty's purpose in using the language of dialectic within his own American story was to reclaim it from rival Marxists, as well as to draw attention to a struggle of ideas he believes does real work in the world. This may explain why Rorty's account of "the Left's" hopeful role in American history highlighted labor unions' campaigns of reform in pursuit of social justice and equal opportunity while at the same time oddly erasing the harsh, Marxist-sounding criticisms of America's capitalist economic system and related social structures and political processes that once were forcefully voiced by Eugene Debs, Joe Hill, and other radical labor organizers. Instead, Rorty's "Left" is hopeful about creating better life possibilities by working within America's existing economic and political institutions while refusing to accept an unjust status quo; its dreamed-of members are determined to achieve only limited, particular reforms that will stimulate Americans' national pride and the confident individual self-creations that depend upon it.

Strangely enough, despite evoking an unceasing dialectical movement within America's history—a potentially important insight for a more adequate American story to which I will try to do justice in chapters 5 and 6 of this book—Rorty seemed to express his own greatest fear in attributing to Dewey a fear of "*stasis*: a time in which everybody would take for granted that the purpose of history had been accomplished, an age of spectators rather than agents, a country in which arguments between Left and Right would no longer be heard" (20). I know of no passage in Dewey's writings that supports Rorty's attribution of such a fear to him. Nor is it clear why Rorty himself feared this situation, which he seemed to think had already come to pass in 1997, or was on the verge of coming to pass. Perhaps what Rorty feared was a loss of the kind of meaning-giving vision of America he claimed as our principal inheritance from Whitman, Dewey, and others. This is the image of an exceptional America, the fruit and "the vanguard" of human history, a collaborative creation that makes individual self-creation possible exactly because "we put ourselves in the place of God: our essence is our existence, and our existence is in the future" (22).

Many aspects of this startling claim about our common, transgenerational American dream that supposedly finds its prophetic sources in Whitman and Dewey call for critical challenge, but perhaps the most important one here is Rorty's oddly Leninist-sounding suggestion that "intellectuals" who have neither a divinity to guide them nor a set of broad, cross-cultural checkpoints in experience and nature can and should lead an American "vanguard," and with it, the world, into the future. Unfortunately, Rorty calmly noted, "the price of temporalization"—of seeing the events of history as grouped into eras that have their own inner dynamics, instead of reflecting eternal processes or some larger purpose—"is contingency," because with no larger laws of nature at work, and no guiding hand, there are enormous risks in the choices we make at any moment in time: America, "the vanguard of humanity," may "lead our species over a cliff" (23). However, instead of offering even minimal criteria for determining whether he and the other "intellectual" leaders of his vanguard seemed to be on the right track, Rorty simply evoked Whitman and Dewey as companion spirits on the journey, announcing that this very lack of assurance about where we've been, where we are going, and how to get there makes room for "pure, joyous hope" (23). As *Mad Magazine*'s fictional hero Alfred E. Newman famously declared, "What me, worry?" Rorty's kind of pure, joyous social hope has no grounding; it is possible, he said, exactly because any grounding for our choices is impossible.

In our real world in the twenty-first century, such supreme self-confidence is no longer possible for most thoughtful Americans; September 11 stripped away any residual belief in America's invulnerability and removed also any well-insulated assumption that the world at large will accept America's unilateral leadership in forging a new, entirely desirable, globalized way of living. A common social hope adequate to our experience of our recent past, the present, and the foreseeable future must now be more chastened, more collaboratively transactional, more experience grounded, more susceptible to criticism and also to validation. In contrast with Rorty's "joyful because groundless" social hope, ours must be more akin to Dewey's cautious, contingent hope for a better, more deeply democratic future, which he grounded and directed into the future—though also without guarantees—in two ways. First, Dewey traced a hypothetically irreversible historical process of real, deeply felt human desire to live in conditions of mutual growth and flourishing, expressed in increasing practical commitment to the democratic ideal. Second, Dewey proposed a self-correcting method for framing and guiding active, inclusive, collaborative efforts toward democratic social transformation.[15]

Such a faith in the eventual triumph of democracy was not easy in Dewey's last years, when Stalin and Hitler rode the crest of history during a long, murderous, hope-devastating era that must have seemed interminable. Such a faith in democracy is not easy now, when America and many other countries that have evolved their own approaches to democratic cultural, political, and economic transformation find themselves locked in global struggle with those who fiercely oppose democracy. Many of our elected officials on whom we rely for democracy's defense do not seem to understand its metaphysical, cultural, and historical depths. They do not understand what they ask us and others to sacrifice when they propose to immolate its evolved rights and protections on the altar of an all-consuming "homeland security."

When Rorty wrote, in a now distant, pre–September 11 context, in celebration of the kind of unchecked national self-confidence that once made it possible for many Americans to ignore the fate of other nations and cultures, he characterized Dewey's conception of democracy as "the only form of moral and social faith" that does not try to subject experience to some form of external control or authority. "Antiauthoritarianism," he wrote in *Achieving Our Country*, was the main motive behind Dewey's objection to "Platonic and theocentric metaphysics" as well as to the correspondence theory of truth (29). However, a more careful reading of what Dewey himself wrote shows that there always was much more at stake for him than a perhaps adolescent-sounding "antiauthoritarianism." Instead, Dewey's commitment to democracy expressed his piety to the sources of value it serves, including gratitude and caring for nature, for those who have made one's own way of life possible, and for the sense of gift within oneself and others that we can maintain, develop, and express only within mutually respectful and growth-evoking transactions.

It was against Rorty's metaphysical principles to express Dewey's kind of pragmatist piety, because he thought it involved sneaking in the Christian God, or pantheism, or some kind of ancestor worship by the back door, which would have been dishonest for him as a philosophical "atheist" or "ironist." This latter, Nietzschean label Rorty used for himself evokes those heroes in ancient Greek dramas who followed their own paths without worrying about whether the gods might smite them for exceeding the limits of human autonomy and thereby violating divine laws and prerogatives—

which they usually did.[16] This is what people who would be free and "self-creating" must do, Rorty believed. Furthermore, he argued, God-talk tends to make trouble in what Cornel West calls "the public square," both because people worship different deities and because reliance on any divinity diminishes self-reliance and democratic reliance on one another within self-chosen social solidarities.[17] In later years, in dialogue with Gianni Vattimo, Rorty wrote that he had come to realize that he had always been "religiously unmusical"—that is, he had had no religious upbringing and religion had never mattered to him, in the way music doesn't matter as much to someone who is tone deaf as it does to someone who really hears it. Therefore, he wished he had described himself as an "anticlericalist" instead of an "atheist," because the former is a political view whereas the latter is an epistemological or metaphysical one, and the whole issue of God's existence just was not a "living" one for him in James's sense. It was churches he opposed, he said, as dangerous to a democratic society.[18]

America's "poetic self-creation," Rorty argued in *Achieving Our Country*, requires breaking through previous frames of reference to become "the paradigmatic democracy . . . in which governments and social institutions exist only for the purpose of making a new sort of individual possible, one who will take nothing as authoritative save free consensus between as diverse a variety of citizens as can possibly be produced," rejecting castes and classes as incompatible with the self-respect required for "free participation in democratic deliberation" (29–30).

However, Rorty's "self-creative" neopragmatist metaphysics now reads as a prescription for disaster, an invitation to think that there is only one possible democratic way of living—the American way, because it is "our" way—and that such a way of living must reject *all* claims of piety as illegitimate intrusions on individual liberty, attending to no other sources of guidance than those interactively corrected ideas of free individuals that might emerge from "democratic deliberation." What kind of transformative role beyond the now underutilized franchise such "democratic deliberation" is to play is unclear, given Rorty's clear objections to what he labeled "participatory democracy." Rorty made two claims in defense of the kind of individualistic, "Western bourgeois liberal" society he advocated: that it would produce "less unnecessary suffering than any other"—though again, how is unclear—and that it offers the best means to achieving democracy's greatest goal: "the creation of a greater diversity of individuals—larger, fuller, more imaginative and daring individuals" (30).

Because it has not yet been achieved, Rorty argued, once again employing his quasi-Hegelian metaphysical framework, "this conception of the purpose of social organization is a specifically leftist one," opposed by most supporters of "the American Right" because they are unwitting pawns of the rich and powerful, who exploit a convergence in their desires to prevent social and economic change (30–31). Such a divisive metaphysical analysis may cheer the hearts of those who identify themselves with Rorty's "Left" because it links them with a better future, while at the same time it seems almost prescient in light of the peculiar coalition that narrowly achieved George W. Bush's reelection in 2004. However, this combination of context-insensitive metaphysical abstraction and argument by insult offers no guidance on the wide range of issues that might form an operative agenda for deepening democracy in America and other global contexts today.

To remedy this lack, Rorty offered another worrisome neopragmatist claim: later "American Leftists" have offered no advance over what he claimed was Dewey's belief that "the only point of society is to construct subjects capable of ever more novel, ever richer, forms of human happiness" (31). This ultimate metaphysical goal, Rorty argued in 1997, offers good and sufficient guidance for a transformative democratic politics for the twenty-first century. However, we must ask ourselves, in light of the tragedy-tinged process of individual, national, and international soul-searching that September 11 has inspired, what do we mean by "human happiness"? What would it mean to pluralize its forms and to increase the real opportunities for diverse peoples to achieve it in the kinds of global contexts in which we now live? What reply might we offer to those many voices in our world today who would disagree with Rorty about the point of society? Answers to these questions are among the real-world demands on a pragmatist metaphysics today—demands a public philosophy drawing more deeply on Dewey's methods and insights than does Rorty's neopragmatism can help us to fulfill—demands for which "postmetaphysical thinking" lacks critical, reconstructive, and argumentative resources.

Rorty's Transformative Vision:
Intellectuals Rejoin the Reformist Left

As I explained earlier, Rorty's vision in *Achieving Our Country* for reviving social hope, and thereby continuing the story of "achieving our country," casts intellectuals as a vanguard within "the American Left," leading a democratic partnership with labor union members whose ways of thinking and living are presumed to be very different from their own: "In democratic countries you get things done by compromising your principles in order to form alliances with groups about whom you have grave doubts" (52). Until the fateful breakdown of this "reformist Liberal" partnership in the late 1960s, Rorty claimed that it achieved real progress by using America's political institutions of constitutional democracy in effective campaigns to correct vast inequalities in American society: "The history of leftist politics in America is a story of how top-down initiatives and bottom-up initiatives have interlocked" (53–55). Looking to this precedent, Rorty argued for replacing the "anti-American" story of "the New Left" with which C. Wright Mills and Christopher Lasch influenced student generations during and after the late 1960s with his new American story, which "gives the reformers their due, and thereby leaves more room for national pride and national hope" (56). Instead of magnifying differences between rival democratic reformers' visions, Rorty argued, we should emphasize continuities in the views and reformist campaigns of Herbert Croly and Lyndon Johnson, John Dewey and Martin Luther King Jr., Eugene Debs and Walter Reuther. This approach would help us to respectfully remember all of them as participating in a diverse but unified "reformist Left," a model that can guide our transformative efforts in the twenty-first century.

This was the main transformative thesis of Rorty's future-vision in 1997: "If the intellectuals and the unions could ever get back together again, and could reconstitute the kind of Left which existed in the Forties and Fifties, the first decade of the twenty-first century might conceivably be a Second Progressive Era" (56). Though it distorts the role of "intellectuals" in suggesting too much leading and too little listening, this vision was insightful in its stress on continuing efforts toward democratic reform achieved through a mutually committed partnership among diverse groups amid significant differences in their ways of living, thinking, communicating, and imagining the good life. However, Rorty's vision ignored many important developments, such as the radical decline in America's percentage of union workers, which would be even more profound except for the growth of unions in the lower-paid service sector. It also ignored problems American unions have had about race and gender since their origins in the early nineteenth century that have always complicated more egalitarian citizen-thinkers' support. Its feasibility for us now is further complicated by recent decisions by the Teamsters Union and others to pursue "a bipartisan approach" to advancing their political agenda. Moreover, Rorty's transformative thesis ignored the practical gains that other citizen-activists working for the kind of "participatory democracy" Rorty scorned have continued to achieve since the late 1960s, especially at local levels. Last but not least, Rorty's transformative thesis was overly influenced by the writings of elite "Left intellectuals" who did not speak to or for the vast majority of Americans—and perhaps also, to be fair, by still-repeated anti-American comments from certain civil rights activists and antiwar activists in the late 1960s, which even at the time misrepresented the beliefs of many others in these movements, who always believed that America means more and deserves better than the injustices against which we protested.

These factors—both the "intellectual" influences to which Rorty gave too much attention and the social developments he ignored—may explain why his transformative prescription seems oddly detached from post-1960s reality, ironically expressing a nostalgic, spectatorial quality. Of course, like the author of this book, Rorty was not "a voice from nowhere." He was a child of New York–based "reformist Left intellectuals" who grew up proud of their committed struggle, shaping his personal identity around his determination to carry it forward, perhaps in the process overstating the extent to which they and any other American "intellectuals" have influenced the course of our history. In contrast, Whitman, Dewey, and Baldwin knew that the most important contributions American thinkers make to "achieving our country" are their gifts for hearing acutely what others are saying, for understanding what it means, and, on their best days, warning, celebrating, and exhorting in tones that others can hear and consider in deciding what to do.

A final factor that distorted Rorty's solitary vision of a contextually appropriate democratic transformation process for America's present and future was a generational hang-up about whether the cold war should have been fought, given that it entailed the atrocity of Vietnam (56–57). Many liberation-seeking leftists in Central and Eastern Europe supported his view that the cold war was necessary, Rorty pointed out, though he acknowledged that many leftists in Latin America and Asia agreed with Frederic Jameson and other opponents of the cold war. Why does this matter now? Rorty answered this question and explained his own stance autobiographically: he was a "red-diaper anticommunist baby" (58). When he was growing up, most American leftist writers did not doubt that America was "a great, noble, progressive country in which justice would eventually triumph," by which they meant "decent wages and working conditions, and the end of racial prejudice" (59). This is a hopeful future-vision that I and many others still share. However, the cold war is over. In the global context in which we must do our "American dreaming" now, the cold war paradigm of struggle and the old team loyalties that framed and fostered it would distort our analysis of our current situation and drain imaginative energies that we need to reemploy in deepening democracy in our own country and other global contexts.

Nonetheless, if Rorty's transformative thesis is revised in light of later developments and some he ignored in 1997, and if it is reframed to include language and partisans he feared—other voices of the poor; various groups who continue to struggle against oppression linked to race, ethnicity, and gender; environmental activists; and the progressive, justice-focused churches he wanted to exclude from "the public square"—it could become a useful prescription for drawing upon our vast American and global legacy of past reformers' historical achievements as partial guides for sustaining and realizing our democratic social hopes in this time of great need. What Rorty hopefully called a "Second Progressive Era" will not emerge in the coming years from strategies that were only partially successful for the original Progressives or from those that "reformist Leftists" employed with mixed results during the cold war. Rather, the prospects for success of this revised transformative prescription will depend on America's citizen-thinkers serving as public philosophers in partnership with labor unions and many other "progressive" groups, all of them telling stories together that can critically and imaginatively influence one another's personal transformations in order to achieve the kind of democratically well-informed collaborative "unity amid diversity" that the critical pragmatist Alain Locke called for, on the basis of which they can give rise to a shared vision to reshape the processes of globalization and war that now unevadably contextualize the project of "achieving our country." Moreover, as both the international character of the list of September 11's immediate victims and the continuing international support for finding and punishing its perpetrators clearly show, the project of "achieving our country" is both too important to the rest of the world and too narrow a focus for democratic transformative efforts in a time of locality-penetrating global interactions to exclude other countries from participating as partners in this collaborative process. For us and for other peoples, "achieving our country" requires "achieving our world"—a more deeply democratic world that welcomes "democratically tolerable" national, cultural, and religious differences as well as individual ones, and whose citizens collaboratively shape its future with mutual respect and to achieve mutual flourishing.

Recentering the Economic Issues: Rorty's Nightmare and the Dream Beyond

The corollary to Rorty's transformative prescription also deserves our attention now: the "Left intellectuals" who formed his audience when he presented the first three chapters of *Achieving Our Country* as a lecture series in 1997 must reconcile themselves with one another if they are to engage in effective transformative leadership to recenter the economic issues that now threaten the American dream. Rorty attempted to begin this process of reconciliation within the "American Left" by acknowledging, as a member of the older Reformist Left generation, that my New Left generation "may have saved us from losing our moral identity" by forcing an end to the Vietnam War (67–68). Moreover, Rorty conceded, his older "Reformist Left" was wrong to focus solely on nationwide economic reforms, rather than on more directly addressing the needs of oppressed groups, because they incorrectly believed that overcoming economic inequalities would eliminate racial and other forms of discrimination: "In retrospect this belief that ending selfishness would eliminate sadism seems misguided. . . . Sadism [has] deeper roots than economic insecurity" (76). This is why, Rorty suggested, Freud has partially replaced Marx as a source of social theory, as sadism became the principal target of those members of the "academic Left" to whom his own ears were so closely attuned in the twenty-five years after the Vietnam War ended.

However, the "cultural Left" that emerged into academic leadership after Vietnam made an enormous mistake, Rorty charged, by focusing on a politics of difference, identity, and recognition while ignoring economics. American intellectuals' shift away from fighting for economic justice, he suggested, may have been due in part to resentment toward the labor unions for failing to support George McGovern for president in 1972 and also due in part to a migration of the center of "leftist ferment" from the social sciences to the humanities. However it came to pass, the "cultural Left" Rorty criticized in 1997 had few ties to the pre-1960s "reformist Left," except for what he regarded as a "saving remnant" that thought more about passing laws than about changing the culture (76–78). While the "cultural Left" generally approved of reformist activities, Rorty noted, its own work was too abstract to guide particular political initiatives. In any case, Rorty wrote, the dominant view within the "cultural Left" was that "the system, not just the laws, must be changed. Reformism is not good enough" (78). Yet the "cultural Left" proposed no alternative: "When the Right proclaims that socialism has failed, and that capitalism is the only alternative, the cultural Left has little to say in reply. . . . Its principal enemy is a mindset rather than a set of economic arrangements" (79).

This enemy mindset against which the "cultural Left" struggled, Rorty noted, was variously called "cold war ideology," "technocratic rationality," and "phallogocentrism." Such a mindset could be subverted, its critics argued, by teaching Americans to "recognize otherness" and "to help victims of socially acceptable forms of sadism by making such sadism no longer acceptable" (79–80). In Rorty's view, the "cultural Left" was successful in this, and this was a good thing: "The change in the way we treat one another has been enormous" (80–81). Conservative critics may decry this "politicizing of the universities," he noted, but such "outrage against cruelty" is part of the history and role of universities.

Moreover, charged Rorty the gadfly, "conservative intellectual" is an oxymoron, because "intellectuals are supposed to be aware of, and speak to, issues of social justice" (82). Of course, such a quick *ad hominem* dismissal of those whose vision has governed America since the end of the cold war, guiding the advance of economic globalization and associated processes of "democratization," is not an argument against their views, nor is it a countervision. Nonetheless, these comments show that it was not the "cultural Left's" work against "socially acceptable forms of sadism" to which he objected but rather their lack of comparable effort to develop a much-needed economic critique and liberal counterproposal.

Though Rorty overstated American academics' preoccupation with cultural issues since the Vietnam War, given that our efforts to advance economic justice and to increase equality of opportunity have drawn the fierce conservative counterattack I described above, he was right to note that during this same period economic inequality and economic insecurity "steadily increased" in America without effective opposition from progressives. This left the fomenting of "a bottom-up populist revolt" to "scurrilous demagogues" like Patrick Buchanan, the one-time Republican presidential candidate (83). On a global scale, this same process of American-led economic antiequalization in the name of "democracy" was giving credence to the anti-American and antidemocratic claims of violent nationalists and transnational revolutionaries, some of whom included religious references in their recruiting justifications. As Rorty rightly pointed out, an important factor in Americans' increasing sense of insecurity was "the globalization of the labor market—a trend which can reasonably be expected to accelerate indefinitely . . . a problem Dewey and Croly never envisaged" (84–85).

In his insightful diagnosis, the world economy was becoming "owned" by "a cosmopolitan upper class which has no more sense of community with workers anywhere than the great American capitalists of the year 1900 had with the immigrants who manned their enterprises." Moreover, "this frightening economic cosmopolitanism has [had], as a by-product, an agreeable cultural cosmopolitanism" limited to the richest 25 percent of Americans, which has added to its allure and its danger (84–85). In the twenty-five years before 9/11, the trend toward antiegalitarian patterns of ownership and elite consciousness was already leading to "an America divided into hereditary social castes," run by what Michael Lind called "the overclass," as suburbanites raised their communal drawbridges against the poor, thereby initiating what Robert Reich called "the secession of the successful" (86). Sometime in the 1970s, Rorty reminded us, America's once-progressive Democratic Party started moving to "the center," distanced the unions, and stopped talking about redistribution of income and wealth. Thus, he harshly charged, by the 1990s, the two major political parties offered a choice only between "cynical lies and terrified silence" (86–87).

In this Orwellian world, as Rorty wrote, academics are expected to ensure that the decisions of "the Inner Party—namely, the international, cosmopolitan super-rich . . . are carried out smoothly and efficiently" (87). This could be and has been achieved by turning attention away from economic issues and toward "ethnic and religious hostilities, and . . . debates about sexual mores" (88). In the 2004 presidential and congressional elections, for example, as the economy and the Iraq War were failing simultaneously, conservatives achieved reelection by distracting voters' attention with claims about the threats to "traditional values" posed by abortion and gay marriage. Even before September 11, as Rorty pointed out, American progressives had become divided over whether to focus on combating globalization's selfish, antidemocratic process of upward redistribution of power and wealth by calling for mitigation of inequalities between nations or to focus on the needs of our own nation's least-advantaged citizens, rival responses that attracted different constituencies and divided "intellectuals" from unions and the marginally employed (88).

At some point, Rorty's nightmare future-vision continued, economic anxiety could motivate urban working people to refuse further cooperation with this erosion of their security and their future hopes and to seek a "strongman" to lead their resistance to globalization (89–90). When this happened, Rorty prophetically warned, the antisadist gains of the past forty years could be wiped out. Security, not civil rights, would come to dominate their concerns. What even Rorty could not foresee, however, is how effectively such a "strongman" might pursue economic globalization after 9/11 while convincing American working people to sacrifice civil rights for the sake of "homeland security" in a war against transnational enemies who were willing to use terrorism to overcome enormous disparities in conventional power by attacking civilians and symbolic targets that left their real opponents invisible and unscathed.

Rorty's prophetic nightmare shows that, in spite of his forgetful dream-image of America before the Vietnam War, by 1997, he was wide awake to the fact that economic globalization had created a sense of peril within America's working and middle classes, to which both major American political parties responded by lying to voters about their intentions while pandering to our increasingly powerful economistic, "cosmopolitan" minority. Rorty rightly saw America's universities as complicit in this, training the rising members of this "econo-cosmo" minority while distracting attention from key economic issues by focusing attention on cultural issues and failing to theorize transformatively about the kinds of government-led, socioeconomic reforms that a democratic understanding of justice requires.

Thus, Rorty's greatest fear was not "*stasis*" any more than it was Dewey's; it was rather the end to the dream of democracy. In what he rightly recognized as a time of democratic emergency, Rorty called upon progressives, and especially those fellow academics he so fiercely criticized, *to wake up*, to focus on the economic heart of the problem, to develop an economic countervision, and to take a leadership role in efforts to achieve it. Reframed as a call to collaborative leadership with others who are already working for global economic democracy, Rorty's prophetic summons is even more on target after September 11. Whether he is right about what we should aim to achieve and how we can best achieve it is another matter.

Participatory Democracy and the End of Capitalism: "Useless" Ideals?

In advising us to forget our differences in order to "achieve our country," Rorty implicitly rejected Baldwin's insightful analysis of the inextricable interconnections between the nature and consequences of past failures of America's democracy and an effective transformative path toward a preferable future. Instead, Rorty designated a surprising candidate as the great problem to be overcome in restarting the democratic reform process: it is not racism, or sexism, or poverty, or any other deeply entrenched social formation that blocks our path, but rather a now habitual expectation among American "intellectuals" that someone else will come to our rescue. "The Left" has had trouble dreaming the common dream we have needed in such perilous times, Rorty argued, because it still awaits rescue "by an angelic power called 'the people' . . . a force whose demonic counterpart is named 'power' or 'the system.' The cultural Left inherited the slogan 'Power to the people' from the 1960s Left, whose members rarely asked about how the transference of power was supposed to work. This question still goes unasked" (102). Rorty's memory was faulty here, perhaps because he continued to fight old battles in the hope that they would come out differently in the future. As I will outline in some detail in chapter 5 of this book, American citizen-thinkers' intellectual reliance on the democratic power of the people goes back to America's founding, and even earlier. Its prophets are also Rorty's prophets: Jefferson, Emerson, Lincoln, Whitman, Dewey, and the other Progressives.

Like Robert Westbrook, Rorty was right to express concern that these great American citizen-thinkers' shared dream of participatory democratic self-governance was in many areas short on details about how it was to be actualized. However, this shows the need to develop those details, not a deficiency in the dream, whose power within their shared intellectual inheritance explains to a great extent why the "New Left" so passionately invoked the slogan "Power to the People." This was not, as Rorty implied, some alien, foreign phrase reflecting a lack of national self-respect at the deepest layers of these late-1960s Americans' personal identities. Rather, it was an affirmation of our distinctively American intellectual inheritance. Moreover, its attractiveness abroad as a democratic transformation-guiding slogan ever since America's founding days shows that there are aspects of American "exceptionalism" that we are right to value—when this is taken to mean that our county is a moral and political experiment for the world rather than a nation apart.

Plunging into the Freudian language field he attributed to a supposedly monolithic "cultural Left," Rorty confused together a *power-wary* Foucauldian social analysis—which suggests a *power-defusing* transformative prescription—with the "New Left's" generally *power-affirming* social analysis and *power-redistributing* transformative prescription. The Foucauldian "cultural Left" helped to produce a "politically useless" national collective unconscious, Rorty claimed, one that "dreams not of political reforms but of inexplicable, magical transformation," not only through its talk of power as "an invisible, ubiquitous, and malevolent presence" but also "by adopting ideals [from the 'New Left'] which nobody is yet able to imagine being actualized. Among these ideals are participatory democracy and the end of capitalism" (102).

Rorty's analysis of Foucault's influence on America's "collective unconscious" included three important mistakes. First, contrary to fact, it suggested that Foucault's analysis of power *has* widespread currency within American society, whereas most Americans know nothing of Foucault and actually tend to regard power as *a good thing* in their nation, in the groups to which they belong, in individuals like themselves, and even among deserving others whom many of them might gladly agree to help "empower." Second, Foucauldians do not tend to advocate participatory democracy; they tend to be wary of it. In contrast, Jeffersonians and most Deweyan pragmatists favor it. Third, many Foucauldians join Marxists, Christian socialists, and most Deweyan pragmatists in calling for and peering beyond the progressive transformation of "capitalism as we know it" into something better, though these strange bedfellows engage in continuous, heated battles about *how* to transform capitalism and *toward what goals*. None of them regard "the end of capitalism as we know it" as an ideal *per se*. Instead, they treat it as an objective, a midrange goal, or an "end-in-view," to use Dewey's language—one that progressively unfolding meanings of the democratic ideal they favor indicate must be achieved.

Guiding ideals like participatory democracy cannot be, Dewey reminded us, "cookbook recipes" for actualizing final outcomes. Instead, they are directional indicators we must continuously throw before ourselves and retrospectively redetail as we reflect on the active processes of transformative experience they help to guide. Thus, careful readers of Dewey should not be surprised that, as Rorty pointed out, "nobody is yet able to imagine" just how such guiding ideals would be actualized. Deweyan pragmatists do not expect that we would or could know this, because this is not the function of ideals within democratic change processes. Instead, at best, our ideal-guided, fallibilistic, gradually evolving, self-correcting, experience-based process of knowing contingently guides actions that, in turn, make it possible to expand our reflection-inclusive experience in the course of shaping new contexts for our future actions. We give ourselves continuous, though not unchanging, directional guidance in new contexts by relating the projected consequences of alternative courses of choice and action to our always incomplete, historically unfolding, location-specific, yet imaginatively extended ideals.

Rorty tripped on his own theoretical coattails by paying too much attention to the theorists he himself castigated and too little to others we would do well to take seriously. His Freudian language of "collective unconscious," "magical transformation," "malevolent presence," and "dream ideals" unconnected to practical experience expressed a self-insulating thought-world that Rorty sometimes mistook for reality. At the same time, he dismissed out of hand—"nobody knows," he said—various promising suggestions that have actually been offered, some of which already are being tested in Deweyan experimental practice, about how to actualize participatory democracy, including how to progressively transform "global capitalism as we are coming to know it" into a better economic system, one that fosters democracy instead of undercutting it.

For example, Rorty simply rejected practical proposals about how to use citizen participation to democratically transform our American economy, such as those by David McClean, a New York–based contemporary Deweyan pragmatist thinker and Wall Street ethics consultant, to pass greater power within corporations to shareholders and to require that managers complete social audits as part of fulfilling shareholders' expectations. Please remember, shareholders are no longer just the truly wealthy; most Americans now own shares in corporations, many of these through their retirement funds. As a result of such changes, practices of entrepreneurship and economic markets would no longer play their present roles. This may be part of what it means to say that "capitalism as we know it" will have ended, having been progressively transformed into a more democratic economic process and institutional framework.[19] Rorty would have been wise to think in such practical, progressive, transformative terms about the meaning of economic democracy, instead of unnecessarily frightening himself and others who recognize the need for change by saying, "What this new thing will be, nobody knows" and "they never told us how 'the people' would learn how to handle this" (103).

To become a "political Left," the "cultural Left" will have to confront impossible questions, Rorty insisted, including how the public will gain the know-how to fulfill the roles these thinkers propose to assign to such unprepared citizen-actors (104). Deweyan progressives must, and in fact *are*, confronting such questions. However, they are framing them with the advantage that, unlike Rorty, they believe it is possible to "know" in some sense what we will need to know, and also to teach ordinary citizens how to fulfill many different kinds of roles. Rorty could not hear the experience-based, provisional, partial solutions that twenty-first-century progressives were already proposing, perhaps in large part because his long-term rivalry with Marxists who advocated "participatory democracy" made him suspicious that anyone who advocates it really could be, as Dewey argued, deriving an ideal to guide democracy-deepening transformative practice from valuable, already-experienced realities within community life.

Collaborative Storytelling and Shared Vision Questing: Lessons from Native America

The discussion in this chapter has aimed to show what we can learn from the important contribution and also from the mistakes Rorty made in telling a dream-story and a future-vision of "achieving our country," including his metaphysical "nominalism," his preoccupation with academia, his nostalgic hope to have old battles come out differently in the future, and his "ironist" belief that one person alone can tell a hope-reviving, nation-redirecting American dream-story, unchecked by others' conflicting memories and uninformed by their differing experiences and aspirations. Drawing on Dewey and his Progressive friends, as well as some of my own Deweyan pragmatist friends, I have tried to show *why* we must learn to do better. In this concluding section, I will suggest *how* we can learn from the experiences of some of our Native American neighbors to frame the kinds of local, national, and transnational storytelling and vision-questing processes we need now to help us move through 9/11-linked losses and fears to shared visions and social hopes of deepening democracy in America and other global contexts.

Of course, it would be absurd to even try to summarize and to differentiate among the storytelling and vision-questing practices of the hundreds of diverse, still-living Native American cultures, so I am glad to assure you, Reader, that I will not try to do that here. What I will do is to suggest some of their convergent insights that can help us to understand some key points for beginning the kinds of large-scale, cross-difference, collaborative processes I think we need. In my essay "Philosophical Windows on Native American Spiritualities" (2003), I outlined some of the convergent insights among diverse traditions of Native American metaphysics, epistemology, philosophy of language, ethics, and aesthetics helpful for this purpose. Some of the sources on which I drew in writing that essay, and that I usually assign for my course on Native American philosophies, are Robert Bunge's *An American Urphilosophie* (1984); Roger Dunsmore's *Earth's Mind: Essays in Native American Literature* (1997); Bruce Wilshire's *The Primal Roots of American Philosophy: Pragmatism, Phenomenology, and Native American Thought* (2000); and Scott L. Pratt's *Native Pragmatism: Rethinking the Roots of American Philosophy* (2002). All four of these books are cross-cultural reflections on ideas from diverse Native American traditions, with excellent bibliographies for further reading. Various Native American thinkers also have worked in cross-cultural philosophy in recent years, including Vine Deloria Jr., the late Dakota theologian and legal scholar, and Thurman Lee Hester Jr., a Choctaw philosopher who also is trained in Western analytic philosophy. Thus, as Thomas Alexander argued in "The Fourth World of American Philosophy" (1996), "if there is not yet a Native American philosophy [recognizable to Western thinkers], there soon will be."

Native American philosophies are closely related to the processes of storytelling and vision questing, both in these recently emerging cross-cultural forms that speak to a wider audience in the languages of other world philosophies and also in traditional forms that speak directly to their communities of origin in their native languages. This is a little hard for some Western thinkers to get used to, especially if they're looking for a thesis statement, an argument, a main conclusion, or at least an explicit reference to some other philosophical thinker from the past. In his foreword to Dunsmore's 1997 book, Vine Deloria Jr. offered this advice for those from other cultural traditions who are encountering Native American philosophy for the first time: "It is not enough . . . to read the thoughts of Indians. Our task is to take the ideas, bring them to our inner selves, make them our own, and then see if they have applicability in our lives and in the lives and values of the people around us."

This may be made easier by realizing that in Native American thought there is not just one meaning that a story, vision, dream, or ritual is assumed to have. Instead, the process of interpretation is a process of imaginative entry into the story world that involves self-discovery, collaborative choice, and, eventually, community decision and action—a process of respectfully working out meanings that do not "belong" to the storyteller or visionary but have a larger origin, a larger life, and a larger purpose.

So understood, stories "tell" us as much as we tell them. They are long-lived strands of cultural experience symbolically coded in language that carries information and aspiration from the past, social complements to the internal DNA that suggests our biological future, together helping to shape us and send us on our way. When we tell or interpret another's telling of a story, we enter into this powerful creative process, influencing and being influenced by these long-lived strands of meaning, which not only report the past and predict the future but also help to shape the world through us, while at the same time showing us aspects of the world that will always exceed human reach. Stories do not tell us our "fate" any more than DNA does, because we can learn to live with their power, make wise choices in relation to them, sometimes "beat the odds," and sometimes change their future course within and beyond our individual lives and the particular times in which we live.

Rorty made the mistake of thinking we could or even would really want to be self-creating, one of a kind, isolated in a moment in time, instead of what we are: "patients" as well as "agents" within the life process, to use Dewey's terms, in our psyches as much as in our social relationships and our always changing embodiments within an always changing cosmos. This living world passes through our dreams, aspirations, loves and losses, hopes and fears, reflective judging, dancing, mythmaking, and storytelling, as much as it does through our eating, drinking, inhaling, suntanning, giving birth, aging, toning up, exercising to get the endorphins going, and unconsciously undergoing DNA "swerves" in the wind of cosmic rays. The very idea of the kind of autonomy Rorty and other "Western bourgeois liberals" have aspired to is kind of crazy—but it is no wonder he wanted to distance his philosophy from the older story of science that Kant learned from Newton, which made *him* so crazy for freedom that he tried to split the world in two, or at least to wall off some corner as a sanctuary where our thinking and choices really matter, as we humans have always hoped they do.

But we no longer need to fear Newton and the self-appointed death squad of philosophical freedom-killers who still say choice is illusory within a mechanical, deterministic cosmos, as they stuff their fingers in their ears to keep from hearing that contemporary scientists at the leading edges of physics and biology now fight for the other team. These new scientists tell us how profoundly intertwined everything is around and within us—and yet that new things happen all the time in this living and communicating cosmos and that small things can bring about big changes, even across enormous distances. The stories of these "poet warriors" are very like those told by the most whole, healthy, and visionary of Native American thinkers, whose strong "spirit medicine" has helped their peoples to outwit and outlast genocide. This is why Brian Greene's latest work on the successors to string theory sounds a lot like *Blackfoot Physics*.[20]

We who are so immersed in this more-than-mechanical cosmos, in which "we are all related," as the Lakotas say and in which everything works together nondeterministically at multiple levels and in more than one way, need not fear the loss of a valuable individuality we have not yet discovered as our hidden potential and have not yet heard named by the "power voices" of others in a world that actually needs and calls us to become fully ourselves. To say this is to suggest a kind of *telos* for human personalities, but it's a "vague" one in James's helpful sense, not a one-size-fits-all, least-common-denominator goal or purpose, and it's neither fully detailed nor inevitable. We must grow into our individuality, as Dewey said, if we're to become what we will find our fullest, most satisfying experiences in being. This requires our affirmation and the development of supportive habits, as well as the cooperation of our social milieu, the major events of our times, and our whole biotic reality, including our own bodies. This also is true of the subunits and elements within our lives, as much as it is true of us as whole individuals; of the families, the social networks, the communities, and the nations of which we are parts; and of the whole human species in which all these levels of humanity participate within our largest community of life and within our even larger, still changing, unfinished cosmos. We only think we must be utterly self-creating, solitary, and private in order to be free because we are still in the grip of an older story whose power in our lives we don't even notice.

To get free—to find our individual, national, and cosmopolitan purposes as human beings and citizens of Planet Earth, and to live these in chosen, creative, responsive ways—we must learn to understand, respect, and work with the great power of stories. This includes learning to work with stories within vision questing, in which we speak to the larger world, and the world speaks back through the story-beings who also test and reshape the story, and test and reshape us, because the deeper powers of the world are at work within them. In Native American traditions, one tells stories with care and respect, acknowledging that they are older, powerful, living streams of information, imagination, and inspiration while recognizing that they are new and different each time because of the distinctive "life breath" of the one who tells them. That is, one does not "create" stories, one "receives" them, and yet who one is as a person trusted to tell a story always enters into its stream and affects how it "comes out." Traditional and contemporary vision quests to help a young adult "come into power," or to help a confused adult get back on track, are guided by stories that are both told orally and embodied within rituals, through which at least one elder takes responsibility to protect the safety of the vision quester in the midst of all that story-power and nature-power, and to help that individual bring forth the meaning of the vision, for him or her, and also for the larger community affected and guided by it.

Storytelling and vision questing have always enlivened and redirected larger communities, cultures, and multicultural nations, as well as individual human beings' lives. The most sacred story of the Haudenosaunee, also known as the Iroquois Confederacy, is the story of their founding as a unified, multicultural people out of five (later six) warring nations who had been causing one another to live for too long in loss and fear. A great Peacemaker came to them out of the northwest from another place across the waters, proposing new stories and rituals that would offer them mutual opportunities to learn from one another, grow as individuals and as peoples, and stand strongly together against opponents of their peace. At first they would not listen to him because they could not understand his way of speaking, but then he found a respected leader, Hiawatha, who had gone off into the woods by himself in deep grief and near despair after his family had been slaughtered by one of the rival nations in another round of revenge violence. Hiawatha really "got" the Peacemaker's vision, and at the same time, he had learned from mourning within nature about the stages of grieving and recovery a person must go through after a great loss.

Together, the Peacemaker and Hiawatha could be heard, they could heal, and their vision could guide the beginning of a new history of their world—especially after it had been improved even further through negotiations with their most powerful opponent, who was so profoundly changed by this process that he could serve effectively as what we might think of as the first "Secretary-General" of these newly formed "United Nations." They ritually "buried their hatchets" under a great white pine tree, which became their symbol and daily reminder of how they had chosen, and still choose, to live in peace. Their union, with its deeply democratic arrangements for representatives to consult back and forth directly with their home communities, whose consent was required for any decision proposed, negotiated, and provisionally affirmed by them around the cross-cultural campfire, has endured for over five hundred years, despite all adversity. There's a lot more to this sacred story of how loss and grief gave birth to vision and hope, but I don't know it all—I've heard Jake Swamp, a trusted storyteller and subchief of the Mohawks, tell a one-hour version as part of a tree-planting ceremony for Earth Day, and he said there are also nine-hour versions, three-day versions, and so on, some of which he uses in working with men in his community who are struggling with grief, alcohol, and violence.

Many contemporary Americans are unaware that our nation's founders "caught" this story and vision from the Iroquois Confederacy, as Scott Pratt and his sources convincingly document. Benjamin Franklin, Thomas Jefferson, and their collaborators were searching for a new American story and vision that could help our diverse states and far-flung local communities to become "One out of Many" through a way of living together democratically and a process of making decisions cooperatively that were very different from the dominant ways and processes of the European cultures out of which their families and other recent immigrants had come. They traveled to meet with Haudenosaunee elders and leaders because they had learned from a frontier government official that these people had such a story and vision—and that it really worked. The story that Franklin, Jefferson, and the others sought, caught, and retold (with additions from old European stories, from the sciences of the times in which they were active participants, and from their own experience-based creative imaginations) was old and new, distinctive, multicultural, cosmopolitan, incomplete, and deeply flawed. Yet they were hopeful that the future generations who would revise it in the retelling would make it better and better and that it would guide a new, democratic nation that would offer hope to the world that other peoples, too, can bring forth peaceful, growth-productive, and mutually beneficial ways of living in their own global contexts.

We must "catch" this story from them and from those who have told it even better since them, keeping it alive by being both old and new, as powerful stories always are. We must seek the guidance of our own council of elders about how to make peace, do justice, and include everyone in a process of "achieving our country," "achieving our world," and "saving our beautiful blue-green Planet Earth," perhaps the largest story we can all tell together, as Al Gore's excellent first efforts in *An Inconvenient Truth* have persuaded many of us to believe in recent years.

Our Native American neighbors' collaborative processes of storytelling and vision questing that were used to frame the great American story that our founders "caught" from them, and that their successors have retold in new ways ever since, can help us move through loss and fear to vision and hope, if we refresh and reempower this story with imaginative new materials, new knowledges, and the new technologies that have emerged in our local and global experiences in recent years. Here are a few ideas for getting started:

- we can create more storytelling classes and "contests"—some already exist;
- we can organize gatherings of representative American Vision Questers, with consultants from the various scholarly disciplines and "public philosophers" (such as those I described in the introduction to this book) acting as Deweyan "liaison officers" and facilitators among them: helping them talk to, listen to, and learn from one another's stories, reframing questions and comments, summarizing, criticizing, and encouraging the visioning process;
- we can organize great storytelling gatherings of poets of all kinds, perhaps headlined by some of the really great ones, such as J. K. Rowling, whose Harry Potter books have motivated millions of children to read, and Sherman Alexie, who in addition to being a successful novelist is also a very funny Native American (Spokane) storyteller and winner of many extemporaneous poetry slams;
- we can get schools, churches, community centers, youth clubs, elder homes, labor unions, and firehouses involved, all of them telling American stories both old and new, with winners of in-house storytelling contests taking them "on the road" to these other kinds of locations;
- we can use the existing legal framework and developed processes of urban planning I describe in chapter 6 of this book to make storytelling part of the visioning element of land-use decisions and comprehensive planning;

- we can ask candidates for public office to tell us their own American stories and to listen to and reflect on those told by some of our best community representatives when they come seeking our votes;
- beyond protest and policy advocacy, we can make storytelling and vision sharing part of the mass communicative events that movements organize in order to get their messages out;
- we can use the Internet, webcams, Web sites, blogs, chat rooms, and listservs, as well as television, radio, movies, newspapers, magazines, books, and personal letters to tell our stories to whomever will listen;
- we can let the best stories emerge, share them with others, celebrate them, and try them out in action, letting shared standards of judgment emerge as the world responds;
- we can draw on a Council of Elders, not as judges, but as commentators, wise guides, and roving ambassadors for a process of telling true, humane, imaginative, and hope-inspiring stories that motivate people to want to work actively toward "achieving our country," "achieving our world," "saving our beautiful blue-green Planet Earth," and becoming their best selves in the process.

Such storytelling and vision-questing processes can start small and locally. Some are already underway and have been going on for hundreds of years, contributing powerful, well-tested strands of information, imagination, and aspiration from the American past, such as those I describe in chapter 5 of this book. They can help us to revive and advance our shared social hopes now, locally and globally—if we learn how and why to tell true, humane, and realistic stories. This is why we need what I call a "pragmatist social epistemology," as I explain in chapters 3 and 4. Reader, please read on.

Chapter 3

Hope's Progress
Remembering Dewey's Pragmatist
Social Epistemology in the Twenty-first Century

Given a world like that in which we live, a world in which environing changes are partly favorable and partly callously indifferent . . . any control attainable by the living creature depends upon what is done to alter the state of things. Success and failure are the primary "categories" of life: achieving of good and averting of ill are its supreme interests; *hope* and *anxiety* (which are not self-enclosed states of feeling, but active attitudes of welcome and wariness) are dominant qualities of experience.

—John Dewey, "The Need for a Recovery of Philosophy"

Those who wish to reduce objectivity to solidarity—call them "pragmatists"—do not require either a metaphysics or an epistemology. They view truth as, in William James's phrase, what it is good for *us* to believe. So they do not need an account of a relation between beliefs and objects called "correspondence," nor an account of human cognitive abilities which ensures that our species is capable of entering into that relation. They see the gap between truth and justification not as something to be bridged by isolating a natural and transcultural sort of rationality which can be used to criticize certain cultures and praise others, but simply as the gap between the actual good and the possible better.

—Richard Rorty, "Solidarity or Objectivity"

Why We Need Well-Grounded Social Hopes Now

Since ancient times, many of the world's great philosophies and religions have stressed the importance of hope, understanding it as the connective center of all transactions in our human emotional systems—as the future-focused nexus of "embodied feelings" that generate and in turn are framed by those aspirational ideals that give faith and love their capacity and direction for action. Hope draws upon yet exceeds evidence and previous experience.[1] As John Dewey taught us, our hopes also include the stirrings of creative imagination in projecting a future in which the best possibilities within our past-to-present trajectory in living will be actualized. Hope's presence allows us to endure shock, heartbreak, and temporary defeat. Hope's absence or malformation can destroy our lives and the complex edifices of our civilizations. Thus, hope is a crucially important moral emotion in the lives of individuals, communities, and nations, because our hopes reflect and affect our levels and sources of "ontological security"—that is, our deep sense of whether our world is a safe, trustworthy place for us and for those we love, a place capable of supporting a future in which our longings for some kind of peace, for satisfying relationships, and for meaning in living will be fulfilled.[2]

Like some of "hope's" customary uses in daily conversation, the philosophical literature over the centuries sometimes treats hope as if it were primarily a matter of cognitive belief states concerning the future that are insufficiently warranted by evidence and thus somewhat disreputable for reasonable people to entertain. However, this tinge of disreputability rests on two mistakes. The first is confusing hope with faith, a closely related aspect of human openness to the future that concerns what we believe is likely to happen, and also a wider picture or story of what we think or sense at some deep level has been going on in the world, even though there is insufficient evidence available now to fully warrant such beliefs. The second mistake is thinking that there is no place for faith in a life guided by reason, intelligence, or common sense; as James argued in his famous and widely misunderstood essay, "The Will to Believe" (1896), learning the truth about some complex and disputed matters requires a belief hypothetically on "passional grounds"—faith—in order to act in ways that contribute to finding out the truth about how things are or could be with our help. Faith and truth are topics for the next chapter—hope, the attitude of "welcome" to an anticipated or "dreamed"-of future

Dewey wrote about, is my topic here. Hope is closely related to love, under-stood not in a romantic sense but as a passionate concern for some other's life (that of one's children, one's neighbor, or someone who lives in a different part of our shared planet)—a transpersonal commitment to achieving a pos-sible and preferred quality of future living that is not yet actual. Hope, faith, and love are all deeply rooted in us:

- in our biological nature as long-developing, intensely communal beings;
- in our communicative nature as social beings who inherit through a shared language a set of powerful concepts that initially shape our minds;
- in our system of moral sentiments as deeply felt motivations that reflect both biological and communicative aspects of our constitution;
- in our imaginative powers as collaboratively "minding" beings (to use Dew-ey's term) who project a future that we "build out" conceptually in complex ways, as we continuously become individuals within collaborative social pro-cesses that seek to enhance our shared meanings, our common safety, and our transactional experience of mutual flourishing.[3]

Our hopes as a whole, interactive nexus of embodied and cognitive moral emotions involve many intentional objects and aspects of our future lives, within which our specifically *social* hopes concern future stages of social liv-ing in which we or those we love in both intimate and communal senses will have opportunities to fulfill important needs, to achieve individuality-en-hancing and community-enhancing recognitions, and to play out our most cherished and enduring ideals in living. Because we humans are social beings, as Aristotle noted, our experienced capacity to formulate and sustain *social* hope affects the content and strength of all our other kinds of hope. At the same time, as Dewey pointed out in rejecting the ancient biblical claim that "there is nothing new under the sun," we experience ourselves as living within a not entirely hospitable world—a world that changes deeply at times in its ongoing processes of becoming, as it did on September 11, 2001, for many Americans and other world citizens. Such a cosmological "earthquake" dam-ages our basic sense of ontological security and breaks some strands of the complex web of beliefs that supports our guiding faith in what's going on and our hopes concerning what good may come of it.

At such a time of upheaval, we question how much and what we *do* know and *can* know about the world, and we rely on our creative, faith-linked hopes to motivate and guide our efforts to "regain our footing," so that we can deal effectively with present threats and with the project of world-remaking for ourselves and for those we love. If we think of knowledge in terms of the old "correspondence theory of truth," that is, as a set of uncontestable, timelessly true, context-independent beliefs signaled by a shareable personal certainty—a set of beliefs that accurately map permanent, unchanging underpinnings of this world of our experience—it seems clear that *there is little we do or can know in this sense about this world* on which we can reground our hopes. *This world* has been too freshly broken up by human hands for those still shaking from its continuing tremors to believe that the profound change process we are experiencing now is somehow grounded in a hidden, unchanging reality. And if this world itself changes profoundly, then it seems clear that there can be no certain, unchanging *knowledge* of *this*, our only world.

However, we need not, and most of us generally do not, think of the world and of knowledge in this way. We live in an era of everyday evolutionary thinking, in which most Americans take real change to be ongoing and sometimes productive of good. We expect that our thinking will have to change with the times, especially if we are to regain any semblance of control over the future we both long for and dread. Moreover, like William James, John Dewey, and the other classical American pragmatists, most modern people tend to believe that *there are some practical certainties and well-supported generalizations of experience* that we can and do share with many others, while recognizing that even *these could be wrong or not quite right*. In addition, we may notice that there are at least some existential truths on which we would "bet our lives," such as the truth that my beloved loves me, that my life is a remarkable gift if I can keep it in a certain kind of perspective, and that at least *some* other people have important things to teach me. Such valuable "knowledges" that we need to gain from and about others are marked not by uncontestable epistemological certainty but by deep, action-guiding, experientially warranted though fallible convictions that reflect our particular social locations within those open-ended historical processes of world-becoming that frame our faiths, hopes, and loves.

Combining such provisional, fallible "knowledges" and existential truths in living is possible, revisable, and necessary as a basis for active, effective social hoping—but we must notice the partial, perspectival character and purpose of such "knowledges" when we seek to reground shared social hopes.

That is, "knowledges" so understood must flow into a common well where they can influence, correct, and rebalance each others' alkalinity or acidity in creating what William James called a reliable "fund of experience." Moreover, these diverse "knowledges" also must contribute to and gain critical correction within common projects of developing always uncertain though nonetheless well-supported generalizations about past events of the kinds that the various sciences strive to offer as a resource for what Dewey called "social intelligence" in living. We need such inclusive, open-ended social and natural sciences to aid us if we are to regain *some* degree of shared, democratic control in influencing the shape of a common future that will certainly be different from our recent and more remote past in many ways but that we *hope* to make as secure and humanly fulfilling as possible. Finding good grounds, locations, and processes into which these many "knowledges" can flow effectively is a crucially important project for our times, because we need the outflows of these recombinant wells of future-focused "knowledges" to revive and fulfill our shared social hopes during our downstream interactions with a world that will test their viability. This is the meaning and the value of *a democratic social epistemology*: a project and a process for creating reliable, mutually corrective wells of "knowledges" that can revive our social hopes and correct our related faiths within those complex economies of the moral emotions that motivate and guide our collaborative employments of social intelligence in shaping a shared world future.

An important lesson of September 11 and its aftermath is that John Dewey told the truth when he told us that we must collaboratively focus reflective social intelligence on our nation's future in order to attend effectively to our own individual lives. In addition, however, these recent years of shock, mourning, and struggling to reframe and reground our hopes also should make us realize that we cannot fulfill our nation's democratic potential in ways that will allow us to live secure, free, and flourishing lives as individuals and as an American people unless we at the same time bring a sustainable, richly diverse, transformatively energetic, deeply democratic global community into being. Without a wider democratic commitment to aid other world citizens in their projects of transforming their own local contexts, Richard Rorty's proposed campaign in *Achieving Our Country* to assure economic justice for all Americans sets too low a horizon of hope to be feasible now.

In order to revive Americans' hopes for living in our post-9/11 era, we must recontextualize them, with the guidance of Dewey's inclusive, creative democratic ideal and within the wider currents of now mutual global influences. Attempting to ignore other global contexts of human hoping, or to protect our nation from the reflux power of global currents through military and economic might—ethically grounded only by an uncritical patriotism that cheers "our way" and castigates other peoples as evil—will prove to be as futile as the apocryphal efforts of the old woman to brush back the sea with her broom. Instead, we must recognize that powerful cross-cultural currents of influence carry within them differing historical standpoints, rival memories, differing needs, and deep challenges to some of America's customary ways of thinking and living that had become so *normal* to most Americans before September 11 as to be almost invisible to us, because they seemed so obvious, so universal, so unalterable, so right.[4] Now, however, world events of human making are rushing toward a "perfect storm" that will destroy all values and lifeways in its path—unless human choices and actions can somehow turn events in a different direction.

Thus, *hope's key question* for Americans and for other peoples at this moment of historical divergence between very different paths of future-making effort must be this: *on what* shall our future-shaping choices and actions be based? Shall we base them on narrow, "ethnocentric" loyalties directing more concerted efforts to fulfill an exclusively American dream, as Richard Rorty recommended at the end of the last century? Or shall we cultivate wider, still-to-be-achieved global loyalties like those Walt Whitman, William James, Josiah Royce, John Dewey, Jane Addams, George Herbert Mead, and Alain Locke envisioned and fostered at the last century's beginning? These would be utopian, world-embracing, "cosmopolitan" loyalties that are at the same time locality-born and proudly "provincial" in the best pragmatist sense of the word. These would be loyalties that can sustain tragedy-chastened, knowledge-guided processes of recognizing and repairing harms and neglect from the past while reviving and guiding shared hopes for a global future in which the contents of every people's dreams are mutually conditioned by commitment to the opportunities of other peoples to actualize their hopes, too, as long as these are democratically tolerable.

If we are prepared to risk our future on the former, more parochial choice, we may choose to accept Rorty's verdict that we no longer need historical knowledge, careful memory, and a sense of the divine acting within our world, because these block the creative processes of "joyous social hope." If we choose this path, however, we must also hope against reason and evidence that an "invisible hand" will somehow reconcile the seemingly incompatible hopes of rival peoples in the world today, some of which have fermented into a heady brew of frustration and wrath exactly because other peoples' powerful dream-nectars, including America's, have led to ignoring and to forgetting their neighbors' equally great need for life-sustaining hope. This is the epistemological and moral risk of Rorty's American "ethnocentrism," which grew out of his own late-twentieth-century reading of history, his own sense of the urgency of reviving Americans' hopes for our country, and his own Nietzschean "neo-pragmatist" philosophical sensibilities, which led him to distrust any quest for the kinds of social knowledge that could effectively and critically guide and sustain cross-cultural loyalties and globally shared social hopes.[5]

Like the classical American pragmatists before him, Rorty was right to reject the tempting vision of a complete, timeless, and unchanging Super-Truth somehow grounded in a fixed and unchanging moral, natural, and supernatural reality and graspable with certainty as such. Claims of possessing such a Super-Truth have been used again and again historically in attempts to defeat and silence rival absolutisms of nation, culture, and religion in ways that still keep the world churning in what Alain Locke called "value strife." In our own times, such value strife has flared into devastating wars and acts of terrorism that have kept us as differing human peoples from collaborating effectively to end many forms of unnecessary human misery, to open up the possibilities of more desirable lives for more people, and to find ways of living more gracefully and sustainably within our ecosystem. With Rorty, I believe that we twenty-first-century people must give up what Dewey called "the quest for certainty" for three reasons. First, it makes us monsters to others when we think we have it and they lack it. Second, it gets in the way of working together to improve the real conditions we and our fellows live in. And third, it always was based on beliefs about the way the world is and about our role within it that we have increasingly good reasons to regard as false—and not just harmlessly false, but dangerous. However, Rorty went "too far," as Pascal Engel justly suggested, in concluding that we should "give up on truth." [6] This compelling set of reasons for rejecting "the quest for certainty" about the Super-Truth does not mean that we do not need truth per se, and that we do not already know many truths that matter. We *do* know many such truths, and we have the means of learning many more truths that can guide our process of meaning-making in living—if we have enough practical wisdom to choose to use them.

If, against Rorty's best advice, we choose to reclaim social knowledge, careful memory, and what James called a vague sense of the divine acting within history as our best tools for forging the wider hopes and cosmopolitan and provincial loyalties that Josiah Royce mapped for the future and that all of our lives depend upon now, we would be wise to do so in a way that heeds Rorty's warnings about how these powerful concepts have been used as instruments of cruelty in the inquisitions and holy wars of the past. Instead, we must develop a democratic social epistemology that inclusively yet critically recombines and mutually corrects all the perspectival knowledges that flow from differing, often rival social locations, deepening these provisional knowledges with those existential truths-in-living on which each of us is betting our lives, and balancing its live intellectual "water quality" by adding the often reliable though always revisable generalizations of open, collaborative, future-oriented sciences and other cross-disciplinary inquiries. This is how we can create the kind of "common well of knowing" that James imagined—a pooled social intelligence that can enliven, correct, and guide widely shared, diversity-embracing social hopes. Drawing on Dewey's wise insights, we must inclusively reframe contemporary social epistemology in pragmatist terms that allow us to critically reclaim shared lessons from a contested geopolitical history and from the harsh clash of cultures and the global social-environmental erosions that mark our present time, in order to revitalize and to direct hope's progress toward more deeply democratic ends that collaborating peoples can sustain and progressively achieve in diverse global contexts.

Toward this larger purpose, it will be useful and perhaps necessary here, given Rorty's contemporary influence, to discuss in greater detail why he recommended against this choice. In suggesting his reasoning in *Achieving Our Country* and *Philosophy and Social Hope*, Rorty expressed some widely shared postmodernist sensibilities while reintroducing the intellectual resources of the classical American pragmatists and other great American thinkers to a wide international audience. Unfortunately, he did so in terms that significantly misrepresent their views and obscure some of their best insights, which would be of great help as guides to our reflection and action now. In order to reclaim pragmatism's meaning and methods from Rorty's neopragmatist appropriation, it will be necessary to show, first, that he systematically misreads both Dewey and Whitman, and second, that his neopragmatist alternative to a democratic social epistemology leads to a dead end that can be avoided by retracing our steps back to and then beyond the epistemological methods of the classical American pragmatists.

Remembering Dewey in this way will not be an example of the kind of change-denying anachronism that often attends philosophical retrievals from the works of earlier generations. Instead, it will be an example of what I call "pragmatist piety," which involves three phases:

- critically winnowing this earlier pragmatist's works to find aspects that represent areas of historical continuity and thus offer seeds of useful guidance for our own times;
- fanning out any "chaff" of Dewey's personal limitations, lapsed freshness, and now clearer wrong-headedness;
- adding complementary new theoretical concepts and methods that acknowledge and help us to handle the emergence of genuinely new, discontinuous events and strains within recent stretches of our ongoing streams of shared experience.

My choice of the phrase "pragmatist social epistemology" to describe the larger process of which such a textual retrieval is one part is an example of this kind of "pragmatist piety." My choice of this label for the larger project and process cues a still important emphasis on "the social" that characterized the works of classical American pragmatists such as Peirce, James, Royce, Dewey, Addams, Mead, and Locke, directing us toward aspects of their work that have continuing value for serious thinkers and world citizens of the twenty-first century. At the same time, it specifically rejects as wrong-headed one of Dewey's well-known conceptual advisories in "The Need for a Recovery in Philosophy," which many (including Rorty) have taken to mean that we should give up epistemology entirely. In contrast with this widely shared interpretation of Dewey's view, I believe that twenty-first-century pragmatist public philosophers must reclaim and reconstruct the broad philosophical field of epistemology, and especially deeply democratic social epistemology. Let me explain.

Beyond Ethnocentrism: Why We Need a Pragmatist Social Epistemology

In "The Need for a Recovery of Philosophy" (1917), Dewey famously criticized "the epistemology industry" as the preoccupation of mainstream modern philosophy, challenging its continuing tendency to chew the woody cud of originally misconceived, now traditional philosophical problems, such as the mind-body problem, while ignoring the contemporary efforts of both scientists and ordinary citizens to grapple with new, emergent problems that call for new ways of thinking. Regarding the proper work of philosophy as its original project of developing concepts and methods for the guidance of thinking, Dewey called for "a recovery of philosophy" that would return philosophers to valuable service as polymath "liaison officers" among diverse disciplines and contemporary projects of inquiry, interpreting participants to one another and helping them to work together more effectively in addressing real-world problems, "the problems of men [and women]." In order to fulfill this responsibility effectively, Dewey believed that philosophers must become collaborating partners in the various intradisciplinary and interdisciplinary conversations, instead of somehow riding on the air above and beyond them. A translator cannot interpret reliably between two languages without knowing both language worlds as an internal participant or at least as a frequent and welcomed sojourner.[7]

A community of such philosophical translators would have to work effectively together, with occasional side consultations among themselves, in order to serve as an effective liaison community within a world of differing intradisciplinary and interdisciplinary conversations, because even the most gifted polymath will never have "world enough and time" to know all the conversations well enough. Moreover, if the liaison role of public philosophers is to go beyond translation and interpretation to include effective, reconstructive criticisms of concepts, methods of thinking, goals of collaborative effort, and social composition and structure of groups participating in inquiry, as Dewey argued it should, then public philosophers will need a whole "tool set" of shared methods and acquired skills.

That is, in addition to shared methods of translation and interpretation, such "liaison officers" will need preferable methods of guiding collaborative inquiry, including clarifying methods of reconstructive criticism, inclusive methods of participant group composition, effective methods of continuing education, and reflective practices of ongoing evaluation. All of these will be necessary if the philosophical community is to do its job and if diverse communities of inquiry are to benefit from and to value that job. Moreover, these "specialist" inquirers—philosophers, scientists, and social-intellectual experts of other kinds—must continue to participate in the nonspecialist affairs, conversations, and collaborative inquiries of everyday life, and they must dedicate their more specialized efforts toward enrichment of these more encompassing inquiries. Thus, engagement and fluency within these diverse daily "worlds" also is part of the preparation, credentials, and ongoing responsibility of philosophers as Dewey conceived of them.

Dewey's analysis of the developed skills, credentials, and responsibilities that must become part of philosophy per se is his pragmatist prescription for epistemology, to be understood in relation to his pragmatist views about metaphysics and ethics. Unlike Dewey, James explicitly linked pragmatism to earlier philosophical positions about epistemology within the ongoing historical conversation by using the label "radical empiricism" for interlinked aspects of the converging or "family resemblant" epistemological views that he, Dewey, and other classical pragmatists were then developing, both in America and in other parts of the world. Dewey, like James, struggled repeatedly over the tricky business of naming new philosophical concepts within an already heavily laden philosophical lexicon. If one coins a new term to highlight new issues or new ways of approaching old problems, as Alfred North Whitehead chose to do, people may not understand the term or see how it sheds a different light on matters. On the other hand, if one attempts to use a long-familiar philosophical term in a new way, as James and Dewey did with the term "experience," careless or unsympathetic readers are likely to miss its new meaning or to systematically misread the texts in which it appears, as Bertrand Russell and G. E. Moore famously did with James's and Dewey's pragmatist metaphysical and epistemological proposals, and as I believe Richard Rorty did, too.

So this choice was continuously challenging Dewey, as it still challenges us: *what term* shall we use for pointing toward this particular domain or kind of philosophical work, to the concepts that can best guide it, and to its proper presuppositions, methods, and prerequisites? How shall we refer to the process of inquiry that seeks fallible truths about a changing world, within which we can never avoid influencing that matter about which we seek to know, even without certainty? Dewey generally eschewed the *term* "epistemology," leaving it to the philosophical mainstream whose views and efforts he criticized—as did Rorty. However, Dewey actually worked in the field of epistemology under various other names, whereas Rorty proposed to give up this whole project. I think both were wrong: Dewey in giving up the fight for the meaning of the term and the arena of philosophical work it designates, given that he recognized the need for the work; and Rorty in proposing to give up the work in favor of a dangerously unacceptable substitute, his critically un-checkable and self-consciously exclusive "ethnocentrism."

Rorty first outlined what he meant by "ethnocentrism" in an influential essay entitled "Solidarity or Objectivity?" (1985), which has been both wide-ly anthologized and widely criticized since that time. In that essay, which I quoted as the second epigram at the beginning of this chapter, Rorty mislead-ingly characterized pragmatism in the classical American stream of James and Dewey, arguing that pragmatism so understood sees no need whatsoever to continue to work on the traditional projects of metaphysics and epistemol-ogy, even in reconstructed forms. Moreover, he gave up on Dewey's pragma-tist projects of seriously reconstructing the concepts of truth, knowledge, and objectivity, recommending that we settle instead for a less ambitious ethno-centric search for beliefs that simply serve "us" well in some unspecified way, even though they offer us very little cross-difference critical leverage—includ-ing self-critical insight—and are warranted by nothing more than a narrow but potentially expandable range of agreement in opinions. This is what Rorty wrote:

> From a pragmatist point of view, to say that what is rational for us now to believe may not be *true*, is simply to say that somebody may come up with a better idea. It is to say that there is always room for improved belief, since new evidence, or new hypotheses, or a whole new vocabulary, may come along. For pragmatists, the desire for objectivity is not the desire to escape the limitations of one's community, but simply the desire for as much intersubjective agree-ment as possible, the desire to extend the reference of "us" as far as we can. Insofar as pragmatists make a distinction between knowledge and opinion, it is simply the distinction between topics on which such agreement is relatively easy to get and topics on which agreement is relatively hard to get.
>
> (Rorty, "Solidarity or Objectivity?" 5)

Rorty's choice of the term "ethnocentrism" for this ultraminimalist epis-temic standpoint was quite serious, suggesting that the possibilities of learning to see by other cultures' lights are so radically limited as to make the assump-tion of a privileged standpoint of one's own cultural tradition inescapable. And while the logic of his argument goes both ways, his emphasis was on privileging a Western liberal intellectual standpoint while rejecting the idea that we should make any effort to encompass very different traditions and worldviews. Rorty argued that "to say we must work by our own lights, that we must be ethnocentric, is merely to say that beliefs suggested by another culture must be tested by trying to weave them together with beliefs we already have" (8). He added that "the question is not how to define words like 'truth' or 'rationality' or 'knowledge' or 'philosophy,' but about what self-image our society should have of itself" (11). From this he concluded that "we must, in practice, privilege our own group . . . we Western liberal intellectuals should accept the fact that we have to start from where we are, and that this means that there are lots of views which we simply cannot take seriously," a view that he characterized as "this lonely provincialism, this admission that we are just the historical moment that we are" (12). In light of hope's great need now for critical intellectual instruments and substantial and deep cross-cultural solidarities in these times of global emergencies—an unlimited "war on terror," the rapid spread of nuclear weapons capabilities, genocides on almost every continent, world hunger, a worldwide AIDS epidemic, and a growing gap between the economic and existential capacities of developed and developing nations—adopting such a view seems akin to sinking into despair.

Why should contemporary philosophers and other citizen-thinkers adopt such a view? Rorty's answer in 1985 was this:

> The best argument we partisans of solidarity have against the realistic partisans of objectivity is Nietzsche's argument that the traditional Western metaphysico-epistemological way of firming up our habits simply isn't working anymore. It isn't doing its job. It has become as transparent a device as the postulation of deities who turn out, by a happy coincidence, to have chosen us as their people. So the pragmatist suggestion that we substitute a "merely" ethical foundation for our sense of community—or better, that we think of our sense of community as having no foundation except shared hope and the trust created by such sharing—is put forward on practical grounds.
>
> (15)

Thus, as a result of his rejecting any kind of potentially universal or even significantly cross-cultural project concerning reality and truth, Rorty's ethics also became ethnocentric—his social hope has no grounding other than being nationally shared or, in actuality, shared only by a small group of Western "intellectuals."

What shall we make of this description of pragmatism? If we take it merely as a description of Rorty's own views, which he subsequently more helpfully labeled "neopragmatism," it is undoubtedly accurate, even tautological, though we may wish to argue against its most important claims. If we take it as a description of pragmatism unmodified in the classical stream of James and Dewey, Rorty's description is simply wrong about at least seven key points:

(1) contra Rorty, James and Dewey both saw the need for a reconstructed metaphysics and a reconstructed epistemology (though Dewey was reluctant to use these heavily laden labels for his own pragmatist work in these philosophical work zones);

(2) James and Dewey both believed that truth is revealed by the consequences of believing and acting on a hypothesis, and that truth-seeking inquiries are of ultimate human importance because everything that matters to us depends upon their outcome, *not* because truth is simply whatever makes us happy or is more hopeful to believe, as Russell famously misrepresented their views, a mistaken reading that Rorty simply carries forward, although more sympathetically;

(3) though James and Dewey rejected the a priori existence of any universal human rationality that brings a uniform perceptual framework to bear on experience and that can somehow with certainty pierce to the heart of a deeper reality hidden by sensible phenomena, they nonetheless affirmed the importance of developing shared human potentials to achieve reliable, well-warranted knowing of true beliefs through cumulative and cooperative processes of collaborative inquiry, even though such true beliefs must be understood as fallible as we strive to correct and exceed them through ongoing processes of inquiry;

(4) what can and has undermined the credibility of well-warranted beliefs historically is new experiences in the sciences and in daily living that are grounded in and that benefit from collaborative reflection on the insights and the inadequacies of earlier beliefs as guides to consequences-bearing action because the world "pushes back," not just because someone has an idea that is "better" in terms of being simpler, more recent, or more popular;

(5) at their best, James and Dewey were *not* imperial ethnocentrists, generous in their willingness to include new citizens within the empire of Rorty's "we" whose shared beliefs guide the use of real power in the world; instead,

they were open-minded internationalists who tried to practice what Josiah Royce called "enlightened provincialism," cultivating their own American cultural garden as part of the flourishing of our world as a whole, while learning from other very different yet recognizably excellent "provincial" efforts, including those of the ancient civilizations of China and Japan, which they studied with great interest and which they respected as developing according to their own distinctive and semiautonomous metaphysical, epistemological, and ethical guidance systems;

(6) James and Dewey thought of knowledge as involving more than widely shared opinion or Rorty's "easy agreement"—instead, they took the sciences seriously and suggested new models and domains for scientific inquiry that would produce better-warranted new knowledge about matters of great importance for human living, concerning which we need to know "what's going on," what real choices are before us, and the likely consequences of placing our hopes in one course of action instead of another;

(7) James and Dewey took the expansion and reflective reconstruction of experience through collaborative inquiry and the inclusion of genuine differences so seriously because they thought that we need better grounding for ethics than custom and liberal orthodoxy, and better grounding for our hopes than merely the fact that they are shared, because justice matters, our future is uncertain, and so much is at stake in our lives.

Rorty himself responded to a few of the many critics of his key claims in "Solidarity and Objectivity," but seemingly was influenced in his own views by none of them.[8] This is because his philosophical method was postmodernist rather than pragmatist. Rorty did not believe that evidence and argument do or should persuade us about social-historical matters. He did not regard himself as a member of a continuing community of collaborative social inquiry, but rather as a lonely individual, a Nietzschean thinker who acknowledges a few heroic fellows within his Western liberal "we" who call themselves to poetic-political leadership in shaping the future in their own preferred image. Moreover, he did not believe that the matters at issue here concern truths about shared experiences already undergone, but instead are rather free-floating individual choices about what we will believe, what we will hope for, and who we will claim we are. There was an important "we" operating within Rorty's ethnocentrism, but its reference was unfixed, or rather fixed only by the author. It reflected his standpoint as the product of a particular cultural-historical stream who had been shaped by and who had reacted to a generically Western and specifically American story, as told and assumed by a particular privileged enclave of voices within which he proudly claimed his place. It acknowledged few internal critics within its shared *ethne* and treated those it named as marginal (e.g., those he called "the feminists"), except when an individual critic's power and influence equaled his own. It assumed that critical, cross-cultural discourse toward wider truths, shared values, and common purposes is neither possible nor important.

Strangely enough, Rorty claimed that this self-assertive, "ethnocentric" individualism was not his alone, but one that our classical pragmatist ancestor John Dewey shared or should have shared in his earlier tellings of "the American story." Rorty brought Dewey into the picture because he helped to widen Rorty's "we," offering it a certain kind of edgy yet respectable pedigree, and because some of Dewey's philosophical moves appear to agree with his own *if* they are truncated and reframed outside their original historical and textual locations to serve his own rhetorical purposes. In this way, Rorty created the appearance of broad, intracultural agreement, of historical continuity, of an inherited poetic-philosophical brilliance, and of testing by time for his own version of the American story. At the same time, he subtly insulated it from criticism and from a critical reframing of his own elusive language as a set of claims and proposals to which evidence and argument are relevant. Yet because no other comparably prominent philosopher was offering a comparably sweeping, eloquent, and hopeful counterstory during the frightening years that ended the twentieth century, Rorty's American story gained a wide audience that added to his prestige and to the influence of his nominally "neopragmatist" but actually postmodernist philosophical methods.

When we assess the insightfulness of Rorty's analysis with post-9/11 hindsight, we can see that he was right in calling philosophers and other citizen-thinkers to political reengagement and right in suggesting that Dewey still has something important to say to us about how to do this well. However, his more specific suggestions in *Achieving Our Country* about the kind of "liberal reformist" program of action we should undertake—as well as kinds of faiths, hopes, and loves that rightly could undergird and motivate such actions—would mislead our reflections and actions in these days of still emerging, multifaceted crisis for our country, our individual lives, and our wider world. Thus, in deciding whose American story to choose as the broad frame and guide for future-focused reflection now, we must decide whether to ignore Rorty's advice in *Achieving Our Country* or to learn what we can from it while seeking additional guidance for effective, hope-sustaining, collaborative inquiry and action to deepen democracy in global contexts. I believe that the latter is the wiser course, both because Rorty's influence has been wide and deep in the academy and with an international reading public and because he has important lessons to teach by his errors and insights. Therefore, in the next chapter, I will highlight Rorty's glancing evocations of his "ethnocentric" background views while critically challenging his central claims about history, knowledge, and social hope in *Achieving Our Country*: that seeking the truth about history cannot ground and guide a hope-sustaining pursuit of justice—and that John Dewey and Walt Whitman would have agreed with this judgment. We can begin this critical-hermeneutical process here by reclaiming the real Dewey's pragmatist intercultural epistemology as preferable to the views of the neopragmatist imposter Rorty presented to us in his place.

Reclaiming Dewey's Intercultural Pragmatist Epistemology

The real John Dewey was an internationalist who recognized both individual and cultural differences as potential sources of a richer, shared understanding and not just as obstacles to efficient choice and action.[9] As Scott Pratt points out, Dewey called for a hospitable open-mindedness to other cultures and new ideas that is similar to an intellectual virtue traditionally practiced among many Native American peoples—"an attitude of mind which actively welcomes suggestions and relevant information from all sides" (Dewey, *Democracy and Education*, 182). Such an attitude is a key element of effective processes of democratic inquiry and deliberation that seek better, shared answers both about what is going on in the world and about what we as humans can do together to improve our shared prospects for survival and mutual flourishing in the future.

> Through mutual respect, mutual toleration, give and take, the pooling of experiences . . . is ultimately the only method by which human beings can succeed in carrying on this experiment in which we are all engaged, whether we want to be or not, the greatest experiment of humanity—that of living together in ways in which the life of each of us is at once profitable in the deepest sense of the

word, profitable to himself and helpful in the building up of the individuality of others.

(Pratt, Native Pragmatism, 30–31, quoting Dewey,
"Democracy and Education in the World Today")

As this passage makes clear, Dewey's "we" is not Rorty's "we Western bourgeois liberal intellectuals" or even "we Americans"—it is the "we" that encompasses all of *humanity*.

Moreover, as Dewey's student, the American philosopher John Herman Randall Jr. has pointed out and supported with anecdotes from life as well as texts that Dewey took cultural differences seriously, being careful not to assume antecedently that the "common sense" or even the philosophical strategies for democratic transformation that fit one culture would play out equally well in another culture (Randall, "Dewey's Interpretation of the History of Philosophy"). Instead, Dewey argued, we must appeal to and honor an emergent democratic impulse within the world's history, not just America's, in framing processes of collaborative, cross-cultural inquiry that seek to understand how things are, how they have been, and how they could be better for all of us. Only by drawing on all of these differing bodies of experience can we shape feasible and desirable strategies for democratic transformation to foster the becoming of a worldwide "Great Community" (Dewey, *The Public and Its Problems*).

Thus, it is important to realize that Rorty's "Dewey" was an odd mixture of the real classical American pragmatist, who left traces in texts and in living memory, and a fictional character of Rorty's making who advances quite different, un-Deweyan arguments to serve Rorty's neopragmatist purposes—rather like Plato's Socrates in the Middle Dialogues. Rorty's Dewey has largely forgotten the community, actual and ideal, which was the focal center of the real Dewey's concern. Democracy is a dream for Rorty's Dewey: an image, a story, but no longer a guiding practical ideal that already has achieved partial actuality in history and in lived experience. The hopes of Rorty's Dewey are groundless, dependent on forgetting rather than knowing. Rorty's Dewey has given up on attempting to persuade others to adopt the pragmatist approach to fruitful, truth-yielding inquiry—in contrast, the real Dewey devoted at least three books and countless essays to explaining and arguing for his pragmatist method of inquiry, hoping to achieve its adoption within the various sciences and also within participatory democratic processes.[10] Likewise, the real Dewey argued in a multitude of books, essays, and speeches that political resolutions that are desirable and sustainable must acknowledge and adjust themselves with the help of the sciences to wider human and nonhuman forces that contribute inexorably to the shaping of that wider and deeper reality we coinhabit—a larger reality that "pushes back."

On the subject of truth, as on others the real Dewey considered, keeping one eye on his pragmatist reconstruction of metaphysics is the key to understanding both what he said and how Rorty misrepresented him. Like many earlier thinkers in the Western philosophical tradition whose work Dewey criticized, Rorty treated theory and practice as separable and as hierarchically related. Rorty merely inverted the traditional hierarchy to give greater prominence to the practical, claiming Hilary Putnam's companionship in stating that this was Dewey's view, and that it meant that we must always emphasize the agent's perspective. However, this was not the real Dewey's view. Instead, the real Dewey treated theory and practice—like the polar elements in other classical philosophical dualisms, such as mind-body, actuality-potentiality, permanence-change, and hope-anxiety—as inextricably interrelated, whether or not we intend and acknowledge them to be so in our philosophies and our ways of living. Likewise, the real Dewey argued that we are always both "agents" and "patients"—acting and undergoing simultaneously and sequentially, always becomings-within-Nature, both reflecting and collaboratively causing emergent outcomes that introduce new structures, new relationships, and genuinely new kinds of actor-patients.[11]

Moreover, in the real Dewey's view, humans are and need to be members of multiple, overlapping, many-leveled communities, which give our individual lives context, meaning, some measure of security, and various opportunities to develop some of our unique and eventually valued, individuality-defining potentials (Dewey, *Time and Individuality*). Over the course of human history, as Dewey envisioned it, the developed human potentials we have come to prize as defining our individualities have become increasingly complex, as the structures and needs of human communities have become increasingly complex. However those primordial events came to pass that led to humanity's emergence within Nature, we as a species are now and have been since our earliest human days an active kind of creature who needs to ask questions, seek answers, and reflect on our surroundings and on the events we undergo in our shared and individual lives. We semievolved humans need to do all these things in order to understand this awe-inspiring world we experience as exceeding our grasp—and also to gain at least some small measure of control in shaping the future's course in ways that matter to us in the undergoing, including but vastly exceeding a pleasure-pain economy (Dewey, *The Quest for Certainty*).[12]

Unlike Emerson and Rorty, who would attempt to shake off earlier layers of history and antecedent civilizations in order to give voice to a uniquely American experience, within which an unprecedented social-environmental context gives birth to unprecedented new beings with utterly new world visions, those who worked most closely with the real Dewey knew him as "the great traditionalist," reflecting on and sustaining continuities with earlier thinkers and treating the past as a fund of human experience and still potent longings that can offer at least some guidance in our new contexts (Randall, "Dewey's Interpretation of the History of Philosophy"). As human beings, the real Dewey suggested, we carry forward within ourselves an "immanent impulse" toward the conditions of our *mutual* human flourishing that we inherited from our biological and social progenitors—a longing inherited in our bodies, in our central nervous systems, in our deep emotions, and in our shared thought-world, and in the institutions, social practices, and ritual reenactments that sustain them.[13] Dewey called the future conditions that would fulfill this inherited, transgenerational longing "democracy," with each new generation expanding its meaning by adding insights about what must be avoided and what must be respected, what must be protected and how this can be done, what must be risked and what may be gained by such risks—and then passing the task of advancing this great continuing project to new generations in new circumstances, for which their progenitors' experience can be, at best, only a partial guide.

Instead of a utopian optimist of the kind Rorty called us to be, the real Dewey was a practical "meliorist," trying to improve hurtful, dangerous, and life-limiting aspects of our world in various ways. The real Dewey had experienced a great deal of tragedy in his own life, directly through wars and through the deaths of his first wife and two of his children, and indirectly through reports of others' experience that he incorporated into his reflections, including his reading of history and the daily news. These experiences of irrecoverable loss also taught him the importance of hope. Dewey's real and serious project of making the world better, if never free of tragedy, requires social hope, but it also requires us to seek the truths of the past and of the present, of the conditions of our being and of the possibilities we aspire to actualize.

To ignore its import is the sign of an undisciplined agent, but to isolate the past, dwelling upon it for its own sake and giving it the eulogistic name of knowledge, is to substitute the reminiscence of old age for effective intelligence. The movement of the agent-patient to meet the future is partial and passionate, yet detached and impartial study of the past is the only alternative to luck in assuring success to passion.

(Dewey, "The Need for a Recovery of Philosophy," 50)

Unlike Rorty and Rorty's "Dewey," the real Dewey did not make up his own goals single-handedly as a "strong poet's" act of imagination, though he claimed and reframed the democratic goals he had inherited. Nor did he listen only to his own heart in determining whether a course of action and the belief structure that directs and explains it are likely to advance those goals in a context of real dangers and serious obstacles. Instead, inquiring cooperatively with others, the real Dewey drew upon and added to the best evidence available, acting practically within a theoretical framework falliblistically adopted and put to the test, even as it was being relied upon to bring about consequences that mattered greatly to him and to others. In so doing, the real Dewey acted within his American cultural and historical context, yet on the basis of and for the sake of a wider world whose future welfare he rightly saw as inseparable from America's welfare and whose citizens he included in the "we" of his ideal Great Community.

The world's future welfare as Dewey imagined it included the satisfaction of the ancient human impulse to awe-filled wonder that stimulates our human need to understand how things are because we are fascinated by the world, semi-independently from our needs to know how to bend things to our will in creative play and to know how to enhance our mutual security through effective work and protective measures. Like Rorty, Dewey regarded humanity as part of the world, and our quest for knowing about it as interactively affecting our world, instead of giving us infallible insight about how it is or would be independent of us. Final justification of our truths from "on high" will never be forthcoming for the Deweyan knower, both because our knowing processes cannot exceed "this world" and because we are co-creators within its continuous process of becoming.

Nonetheless, the real Dewey took the quest for knowing seriously, as Rorty refused to do. Though the real Dewey advised us to give up "the quest for certainty," criticizing his intellectual progenitors' approaches to knowing

and their hopes for its certain and permanent security, he expressed a pragmatist kind of piety toward them, toward the past, and toward nature. He
called for a new model of inquiry and a new conception of truth, not in order
to end the quest for knowing as such but to redirect it more fruitfully, with
chastened hopes for collaboratively achieving a kind of knowing for which a
complete, final, and incorrigible certainty is not possible and never was the
right criterion.

If we renounce knowing entirely, the real John Dewey might have challenged Richard Rorty, we renounce thereby the possibility of fulfilling a deep
and ancient part of our humanity whose "wondering" and whose need for
practical guidance we cannot deny. At the same time, we give up thereby the
possibility of intelligent, experience-based guidance of our efforts to understand and participate successfully in the world-unfolding process in ways that
make it more secure and less precarious for us, more calming of our anxieties
and more supportive of our hopes. Without the processive development and
fulfillment of that part of our humanity that seeks understanding and some
measure of control of our world and ourselves within it, the other, inextricably interlinked parts of our humanity, including memory and imagination,
will be stunted or overblown, undirected and untested. Thus, in imagining
and acting according to Rorty's prescription to "achieve" our American nation alone (or our German nation, or our Chinese nation, or Botswana, or
Brazil, or whatever nation we claim as our own), we may forget the world of
which it is a part, as well as those other human and environmental processes
that already are active within the world's becoming, with which we must
reckon if we are to be successful in achieving both our ends in view and those
ancillary goals that we *will* come to regard as important at a later point in
time. Social agreement alone, even among committed members of a transfor-
mation-minded American coalition devoted to fulfilling the requirements for
domestic economic justice, is insufficient as a guide to feasible and desirable
social transformation processes, as students of ongoing struggles in Ireland,
Africa, the Balkans, and the Middle East have come to understand.

Fortunately, there is a pragmatist path to knowing that is metaphysically,
epistemologically, and morally preferable to calling upon Divine Authority to
validate our Super Truth and thereby refusing our human responsibility to inquire. This path is preferable to passively seeking validation for our beliefs by
appeal to a correspondence theory of truth that denies our inescapably interactive role within the world about which we inquire. And it is preferable to

Rorty's "neopragmatist" invocation of what James Baldwin in *The Fire Next Time* called "an invented past . . . [that] cracks and crumbles under the pressures of life like clay in a season of drought" (81).

This is the pragmatist path to shared social knowledge of the kind we need to ground and guide our hopes for deepening democracy in global contexts: We can draw upon and contribute to the growth of falliblistic, collaborative knowing by continuously improving our provisional "knowledges" within active processes of remembering, telling our stories, expressing our best hunches as hypothetical beliefs, testing these beliefs and our earlier "truths" by using and testing them in collaborative action with the guidance of our ideals, taking responsibility for the results, whether they tend to chasten or sustain our hopes, and then revising or expanding the range of our beliefs accordingly. The growth of such shared social knowing will require the work of both natural and social sciences pursuing a Deweyan pragmatist model of collaborative, truth-seeking inquiry. It will require citizen participation at many levels of government as both legally and customarily acknowledged ways of contributing widely dispersed "truths of daily living" that arise within individuals' and groups' differing experiences of specific natural and social locations. It will require empirical case studies that reflect the experience of nongovernmental organizations whose members strive to ameliorate social and environmental tragedies and build human capabilities. It will require national and transnational collaborations among scholars and citizen-experts who together can discover and express some action-regulating and hope-sustaining truths: that our world's dominant paradigms of human welfare, justice, freedom, legal entitlements, economic advancement, ecosystemic sustainability, and meaningful living are not inclusive enough in their conception, not directive enough in remediating past harms and unpaid debts, and not visionary enough to guide timely, effective, future-focused action. It will require artists of all kinds and all cultures to tell better, truer stories that remind us of who we are and where we come from, to demonstrate that our country's best potentials are not yet actualized and that humanity's unfinished world-making needs our creative imaginations, and to rekindle in our hearts that ancient human urge toward awe-filled understanding and hope-building, world-changing transformative action.

What kind of world-story should we choose to guide our understanding and our future-making in these perilous times: Rorty's postmodern, "neopragmatist" story, with its narrowly nationalist invented past, its rejection of historical truth, and its free-floating hopes—or Dewey's internationally minded pragmatist story, with its fallible but warranted truths, its deep reliance on past experiences of diverse cultures, and its collaborative inquiries and concerted actions to guide our future hopes? How should we conceptualize knowledge, history, and social hope now? Even supposing that I am right that Rorty misrepresented the real Dewey and that the account I have given here is closer to Dewey's actual texts and embodied living, why should this have mattered to Rorty or to Rorty's readers?

The difference should matter to all of us because Dewey's story is a larger and more comprehensive story, because Dewey's reasoning about the mutual implication of knowledge and social hope is more realistic and more inspiring than Rorty's revision, and because we all have a great deal at stake. What we need now is a globally inclusive, critically responsive, collaboration-welcoming, hope-building story of a world-in-the-becoming that can "take the heat" of a complex, painful past that is still powerfully present with us. At the same time, our world-story must successfully guide "common faith"–based efforts to revive and to fulfill widely shared social hopes, reframing and balancing what we once hoped for and hope for now by constructing and drawing on a recombinant well of active, falliblistic knowledges. Such a hope-sustaining well of historical and contemporary knowledges must pool contributions from widely dispersed and differing life springs, which are continuously expanded and corrected through processes of cross-cultural dialogue and collaborative inquiry. The resources of this shared, critically recombinant well of diversely originating social knowledges will allow us to meet various "truth tests" in action within diverse social locations, in differing kinds of collaborative inquiries, and at many levels in our lives as individuals, as citizens of our diverse and sometimes differing nation-states, and as members of an emerging, truth-loving, and justice-loving global community. Such a shared, critically recombinant well of social knowledges with the power and fluidity to guide our shared democratic hope's progress flows out of the histories of nations, communities, and individual lives that can never entirely disappear, even as human living flows together in a braided world-river through the present and into the future. In addressing this great challenge before us of constructing such a great, cross-cultural, critically recombinant well of social knowledges, John Dewey's words and example offer us wise guidance as global citizen-scholars of the twenty-first century.

Aiding Hope's Progress

After hearing my thoughts on this subject at the American Philosophical Association's Pacific Division Meetings in April 2005, Colin Koopman, a gifted
young Canadian philosopher who clearly has benefited from reading both
Rorty and Dewey, asked me how my approach is really so different from
Rorty's, given that both approaches are antifoundationalist and include non-
propositional narratives, cultural dimensions, and moral emotions. I replied
that Rorty's American story is too narrow for our problems now and what it
will take to solve them; we need a world-inclusive, intercultural story that
reflects the painful, still operative truths of our transactional history and that
acknowledges wider aspirations and different sources of knowing than those
of the Western liberal intellectual tradition Rorty regarded as all "we" need
and can hope to understand. Furthermore, I replied, Rorty's "neopragmatism" does not include "all the experience," as William James advised us to
do under the banner of his "radical empiricism," including those embodied
aspects of experience that many feminists emphasize, as well as those mysti-
cal-religious levels of experience that motivate many deep thinkers and committed moral actors in our world today. Finally, I argued, Rorty's narrative
approach goes too directly present-to-future, relying too heavily on dreaming
and denial and without enough critical-reflective circling back through the
difficult aspects of our shared past in order to understand what "now" comes
out of, to learn what we must do to pay still valid debts in order to claim our
shared inheritance, and on this basis, to forge and direct those democratic
solidarities amid our diversity that will allow us to struggle collaboratively for
a mutually desirable future.

A more seasoned philosopher from the American South responded that
Rorty could agree with much of what I have said here—that his goal was to
convince us philosophers to stop having endless, inconsequential arguments
within the academy about epistemology and truth, instead of attending to
the kinds of real-world problems I have evoked. I replied to him that we
also need to work for more effective solidarities among philosophers within
the academy, not only to undermine those theoretical obstacles to a deeper
democracy that our own discipline continues to create but also to contribute
more scholars with valuable knowledge and useful, well-honed skills to the
work of public philosophy: helping diverse citizen-thinkers to find their voices, fostering cross-difference conversations, and helping to raise up "publics"

who can effectively challenge the antidemocratic "powers that be." We cannot forge such academic solidarities, I argued, without investing some of our energy in wrestling with our colleagues about and amid our academic histories of differences—including our differences about metaphysics and epistemology—using that language because it is significant to our co-conversationalists in that context. At the same time, we must challenge our colleagues and ourselves to strive constantly to meet a wider test of the adequacy of our work as public philosophers: to seek truths and knowledges that make a difference in the future-forging work of public philosophy, expressing these in languages that can be understood and valued in the many other contexts in which we must work to aid hope's progress as Deweyan "liaison officers," Socratic gadflies, and active midwives of shared, cross-difference social intelligence.

When I shared some of these thoughts in late May 2005 with Chinese philosophers, educators, graduate students, and other citizen-thinkers at a conference sponsored by Fudan University in Shanghai on the contemporary significance of Dewey's thought, the topic of "hope's progress" went deep with many of the senior thinkers gathered around the conference table in the middle of the room and with younger scholars seated all around us. Each sentence was translated by a lovely and skillful young scholar, who conveyed with her body as well as her words the felt resonances of the ideas she fluently expressed both in Chinese and in English. After she and I finished speaking, a professor from another prestigious Chinese university greatly trusted me and others present when he said, "I am fifty-seven years old now. The average lifespan of a Chinese philosopher is now fifty-three years. I do not know why I am still alive, or how long I have to live—but it is hard for me to hope now." I imagined his life: born just before the formation of the People's Republic of China, coming of age just as the Cultural Revolution changed every Chinese citizen's felt destiny, perhaps being sent to a rural area to do the kind of labor-intensive agricultural work that was to teach him a more egalitarian outlook and to reeducate any lingering attachment to the Confucian tradition, yet somehow forcing himself to continue to live, to think, to aspire to the work of philosophy, and at some point encountering Dewey's ideas about democracy and education. Gathering all my resources as a philosopher and a fellow human being, I replied to him: "My age is closer to your own than you may think, though my experience has been very different. Nonetheless, I know this: the different contexts and stages of our lives call for different ways of expressing *ren*, that Confucian virtue of full humanity and highest human excellence. Your challenge now is to exhibit *ren* in this time and place, at this stage in your life. We will be thinking of you and working with you. This is what John Dewey offers to aid our hope's progress." I hope this helped him—I know that he, and I, and others felt the beginnings of a deep solidarity on that day.

Such a trust-based, hope-bearing solidarity can begin within shared pursuit of the truths we need to guide us in wrestling with the weights of our individual, national, and global histories, as we must in order to find a way forward, because the past is still with us, and it implicates our future. It is hard to undertake the risks of larger personal and social hopes like Dewey's and those of other pragmatist public philosophers—hopes of world-embracing local and national loyalties that can revive and sustain tragedy-chastened, knowledge-guided processes of recognizing and repairing past and continuing harms—hopes that can guide our shared efforts to achieve a global future in which each people's culture-specific dreams involve mutual commitments to every other people's well-being within a beloved human community. Though Rorty rejected such hopes when he rejected the "truths of history" Baldwin said we must face, we can reclaim such hopes little by little if we patiently and cooperatively employ a pragmatist social epistemology like the one I sketched in this chapter and now propose to apply to the process of wrestling with history, seeking truth and reconciliation across its deep divides. Together, we can create and continuously correct the kind of fallible but useful, perspectivally balanced, experience-warranted "well" of shared social knowledge we will need to guide hope-sustaining and hope-expanding collaborative projects of deepening democracy in diverse global contexts.

Chapter 4

Choosing Our History, Choosing Our Hopes
Truth and Reconciliation Between Our Past and Our Future

Democracy . . . has been and is carried on by all the moral forces, and by trade, finance, machinery, intercommunications, and, in fact, by all the developments of history, and can no more be stopped than the tides, or the earth in its orbit. Doubtless, also, it resides, crude and latent, well down in the hearts of the fair average of the American-born people, mainly in the agricultural regions. But it is not yet, there or anywhere, the fully received, the fervid, the absolute faith.

—Walt Whitman, *Democratic Vistas*

To ignore its import is the sign of an undisciplined agent; but to isolate the past, dwelling upon it for its own sake and giving it the eulogistic name of knowledge, is to substitute the reminiscence of old-age for effective intelligence. The movement of the agent-patient to meet the future is partial and passionate; yet detached and impartial study of the past is the only alternative to luck in assuring success to passion.

—John Dewey, "The Need for a Recovery of Philosophy"

In order to change a situation one has first to see it for what it is. . . . To accept one's past—one's history—is not the same thing as drowning in it; it is learning how to use it. An invented past can never be used; it cracks and crumbles under the pressures of life like clay in a season of drought.

—James Baldwin, *The Fire Next Time*

Stories about what a nation has been and should try to be are not attempts at accurate representation, but rather attempts to forge a moral identity. The argument between Left and Right about which episodes in our history we Americans should pride ourselves on will never be a contest between a true and a false account of our country's history and its identity. It is better described as an argument about which hopes to allow ourselves and which to forgo.

—Richard Rorty, *Achieving Our Country*

Are Knowledge of History and Hope Incompatible?

These uncertain, dangerous years at the second beginning of the twenty-first century are ones in which people everywhere call out for social hope, yet social hope is hard to find, hard to ground, and hard to sustain. Gifted young people become drug dealers, drive-by shooters, thugs, suicide bombers, ethnic cleansers, and religious warriors, destroying the hopes of other families and whole peoples because they can find no other more effective way to advance the realization of their own hopes for their families, their peoples, and this shared world. Other gifted young people join armies to fight them, to torture them, and to kill them—sometimes in violation of long-established international conventions and their own religious traditions—partly out of misguided patriotism and partly because military service offers their only route out of poverty and lack of adequate educational opportunities. As a people, we Americans stumble forward, hoping to resume the normal living of another time through sadness-tinged forgetting or through prosecuting a last great war to reclaim control of history. And then we stumble backward, stunned by the sense that neither of these solutions will work, that both require the sacrifice of our core values and basic aspects of our nation's democratic identity, and that neither will alter many other peoples' rejection of America's leadership in advancing global civilization and our self-proclaimed role as the sole arbiter of international justice—a rejection that Al-Qaeda's murder-suicide pact brought forcefully to our attention on September 11, 2001.

A profound and difficult lesson we must learn about this new era in American experience is the central importance of creating *a global network of social hope*. Our American hopes and the actions we take in pursuit of them are not separate or neutral on the world stage. They are potent, enhancing or clashing with those of other countries and peoples, who respond in ways that amplify or undermine their influence, helping to shape transactionally our specific, local contexts for framing or frustrating the best-loved projects of every individual's life. Where hopes and related actions collide, we experience fear, anger, depression, or despair, and soon thereafter we have terrorism and war, locality-specific economic breakdown, and environmental degradation, as well as familial inability to meet basic needs, increased domestic violence, increased suicides and murders, gang formation, drug use and drug dealing, and a stunting of individual lives. In contrast, where our hopes converge and our conflicts can be resolved, each people's aspirations to "achieve our country" can be advanced, and our cultures, families, and individual lives can flourish. Thus, "achieving our world," at least potentially, by democratically reconciling our aspirations, negotiating our conflicts, and initiating our active collaborations is the condition for humane and fulfilling living in the twenty-first century; shared hope is required, or none can last.

This may explain the recent reemergence of hope as a key category for philosophical analysis: hope's presence allows us to endure shock, heartbreak, and temporary defeat; hope's absence or malformation can destroy our lives and the complex edifices of our civilizations. In the wake of September 11, we need to reground our hopes within interactive global processes of person making and world making, in which no single, power-enforced "Super Truth" and no narrow set of "ethnocentric" beliefs but rather many revisable knowledges guide the formation of wider loyalties, balanced relational memories, and shared, cosmopolitan social hopes for more deeply democratic global and local futures. Ours is an era of omnipresent mass communication and widespread ultradevelopment of sophisticated skills for deploying boundary-destroying technologies of communication, international finance, transportation, and war. It is no longer possible to sustain once-viable lifeways of "subsistence hoping," in which a few geographically isolated or geopolitically fortunate people can carry on their lives relatively autonomously by remaining cut off from others or by ignoring systematic injustices and dangerous dissatisfactions in our wider world, attending only to their own families, work, and church, however they understand these. Now, we must be wide awake in our "American Dreaming" and in our attentiveness to others' equal need to dream.

My purpose in this chapter is to show how the "pragmatist social episte-mology" I sketched in the last chapter can help us to tell the kind of inclusive, truth-oriented, vision-guiding American story we need now and that other peoples in other global contexts also need to tell about their own countries. A few individuals will always survive and prosper in times of war, enslavement, pestilence, and famine, but all of us are diminished in our humanity by such experiences, and the cultural wounds they leave run deep and affect all of our future transactions. Just as all of our diverse American peoples with our rival memories of the past must be reconciled if we are to actualize our guiding democratic ideal's full meaning, all of these stories of now rival nations must be reconciled in various ways if we are to "achieve our world"—a more deeply democratic world—as a necessary condition for fulfilling all of our national, familial, and individual hopes.[1]

Richard Rorty understood the importance of this kind of cross-difference reconciliation, but he believed that there is no truth of history that can help us to achieve it, and, in any case, that the past is gone and the future must be our concern. On the important question of *how* to move forward together in actively striving to "achieve our country," Rorty deeply disagreed with James Baldwin, who argued that the past is far from gone and can never be for-given, and that it is only by facing its truths together that we will ever be able to reconcile across our nation's deep divides in order to work together for a better future. Though I disagree with Baldwin about the possibility of reconciling while refusing to forgive, I think he is right about the importance of establishing and mutually acknowledging certain truths of history. As the evidence in this chapter will show, Rorty misread key texts by Whitman and Dewey that he quoted to support his general claim that knowledge of history is neither possible nor necessary; moreover, he erred in his more specific claim that Baldwin made a "category mistake" when he argued that telling the truth about America's history must guide our future-oriented pursuit of justice and national unity. Baldwin's wisdom on this point has become even clearer since 9/11—although the continuing costs of America's chattel slavery, of seizures of Native American's lands, and of the social subordination of women, as well as of the continuing legacy of the Holocaust and of other tragic and un-necessary miscarriages of justice by formally democratic nations, should have provided extensive reasons for all of us to concur with Baldwin even before that awful day. Taken together, the evidence of these experiences shows that we need a collaborative, problem-focused method of social inquiry to guide our cross-culturally inclusive efforts to learn the truth of history and to rectify outstanding debts from our shared past. In turn, such a truth-and-justice process will clarify our communications about the present and help to guide key aspects of our cross-difference collaborations in future forging, including shaping and sharing our national and global story about America's transgenerational pursuit of deep democracy.

Choosing Our History, Choosing Our Hopes?

A few years before the beginning of this strange new era, which somehow grew out of our past yet seems to preclude all we once hoped for, Richard Rorty provocatively suggested that social hope and knowledge of history are incompatible, and between the two, we must choose hope. In fact, in the passage from *Achieving Our Country* I quoted above as the fourth epigraph for this chapter, Rorty suggested that raising questions of truth about a nation's history involves a kind of category mistake, because the point at issue in the relevant arena of cultural politics is not *truth* but *identity*, which is focused not on the past but on the future—on issues about *which hopes are permissible*. Rorty further argued that knowledge of the truth of our history, *if* it were possible and relevant, would contain within its deterministic, lawlike structure an inevitable path into the future that would block creative imagination, putting an end to hope as such: "Whereas Marx and Spencer claimed to know what was bound to happen, Whitman and Dewey *denied such knowledge* in order to make room for *pure, joyous hope*" (Rorty, *Achieving Our Country*, 23, emphasis mine).

Clearly, Rorty was suggesting in this passage that knowledge of a nondeterministic, pragmatist kind either is impossible or doesn't really count as knowledge, and that Whitman's and Dewey's only reasons for refusing to believe in historical determinism is that unfettered hope mattered so much to them existentially. Rorty then attributed to Dewey the proposal that the only or best warrant for any belief is that it helps us to meet a human need, *not* that it is confirmed by the tests of cross-difference experiences of inquiry and of living in a real world.

> Dewey abandoned the idea that one can say how things really are, as opposed to how they might best be described in order to meet some particular human need. In this respect he is in agreement with Nietzsche, and with such critics of

"the metaphysics of presence" as Derrida and Heidegger. For these philosophers, objectivity is a matter of intersubjective consensus among human beings, not of accurate representation of something nonhuman. Insofar as human beings do not share the same needs, they may disagree about what is objectively the case. But the resolution of such disagreement cannot be an appeal to the way reality, apart from any human need, really is. The resolution can only be political: one must use democratic institutions and procedures to conciliate these various needs, and thereby widen the range of consensus about how things are.

(34–35)

As I argued in the previous chapter, it is simply not true that Dewey entirely rejected any notion of objectivity other than intersubjective consensus. Instead, objectivity as Dewey conceived of it emphasizes collaborative inquiry and structured encounters with the wider reality in which humans transactionally participate, within which our needs as well as our ideals and our theories emerge and are *rejected* or *fulfilled*. Moreover, while Dewey argued that there must be a discussion-based aspect of dispute resolution within any well-conducted inquiry, this does not translate into a view that such resolution is "only political," whether we are talking about the latest findings of biomedical research or deciding whether today's newspaper told us the truth.

Rorty ended his story of *Achieving Our Country* with the claim that, given the incompatibility of knowledge and social hope, we should choose hope, as Whitman and Dewey did:

Whitman and Dewey tried to substitute hope for knowledge. They wanted to put shared utopian dreams—dreams of an ideally decent and civilized society—in the place of knowledge of God's Will, Moral Law, the Laws of History, or the Facts of Science. Their party, the party of hope, made twentieth-century America more than just an economic and military giant. Without the American Left, we might still have been strong and brave, but nobody would have suggested that we were good. As long as we have a functioning political Left, we still have a chance to achieve our country, to make it the country of Whitman's and Dewey's dreams.

(106–107)

In addition to radically misrepresenting the views of Whitman and Dewey, as well as the less ideological, more dynamic patterns of American political life,

Rorty made two important philosophical mistakes in addressing the intertwined issues of history, knowledge, and hope that run from the beginning to the end of *Achieving Our Country*. His first mistake was in yielding the still-crucial philosophical language of metaphysics and epistemology—including key terms such as "truth," "knowledge," "experience," and "history"—to those philosophical, religious, political, and legal conservatives who continue to argue for an antiquated and unachievable theory of truth that depends upon a correspondence between our ideas and a fixed, human-independent reality guaranteed by an objective, standpoint-free method of inquiry. Rorty's second mistake was advancing his narrowly grounded and insufficiently critical "ethnocentrism" as a substitute both for these older philosophical projects and for a Deweyan pragmatist social epistemology. The importance of these intertwined mistakes has become even clearer since 9/11, which has or should have taught us that in the future, widely separated peoples will need to converse, criticize, and collaborate across significant cultural and even civilizational differences—contra Samuel P. Huntington—to attain mutual security in mutual growth for our larger communities and for the diverse individuals who compose them in each rising generation.[2]

These two misguided philosophical suggestions, which Rorty had been advancing more abstractly for twenty-five years before writing *Achieving Our Country*, distort his advice to Americans about three important issues:

- how we should think of our history in the twenty-first century;
- how we can foster shared social hopes in spite of still-unresolved problems of our past;
- why his proposed "neopragmatist" method of fostering social hope would produce greater individual freedom and more effective modes of justice-focused collaboration than a different kind of method—a pragmatist philosophical method that requires us to test and guide our hopes for the future by drawing on the sometimes bitter well of historical truth—a method closer to the convergent insights of Whitman, Dewey, and Baldwin.

Rorty's application of his long-held "neopragmatist" views to the contemporary American situation began with his rejection of Baldwin's claim in *The Fire Next Time* that telling the unforgivable truth about America's history is a necessary prerequisite to the emergence of a cross-racial collaborative community who are ready, willing, and able to pursue justice together, thereby allowing the American people to hope again that the democratic promise of our country will be fulfilled some day.

Our nation was founded and is still based on a history of unforgivable crimes, Baldwin charged. Moreover, history is not as malleable as Rorty suggested. Though open-ended and always in need of interpretation, an adequate account of the past must be a true one, because it must withstand two kinds of "pressures of life" (Baldwin, *The Fire Next Time*, 81). First, real people still bear the real, painful, social-locationally specific, hope-destroying contemporary consequences of past laws, institutions, and individual choices-in-action. And second, we all must rely on reflection about our shared past to ground and guide shared hopes for our shared future, which is at least partly in our hands to make through broad social collaboration. Thus, telling the truth about our past and hearing it acknowledged by others—including by those now collaborating partners who have sometimes been our opponents—plays liberatory, regulatory, and sustaining roles in shaping effective, future-focused, cross-difference projects of hope-in-action. If *any* Americans are to have realistic, achievable hopes for the future, Baldwin rightly argued, instead of simply waiting to be consumed by "the fire next time," we *all* need truth-based, shared hopes for a common future, in which still outstanding debts from the past will be paid and Americans will work together as equals to fulfill our nation's democratic potential. Thus, telling our history's truths must ground the future-focused work of justice to which Baldwin called collaborating leaders from a still-divided American nation (105).

Though Rorty clearly was moved by Baldwin's powerful prose, he argued that Baldwin's *choice* to hope, to reach out, and to work in cross-racial solidarity to extend and deepen America's democracy—despite what Baldwin viewed as our country's unforgivable history of race-based chattel slavery and our ongoing, cross-generational racism—*cannot be justified* as reflecting a truer, more knowledge-based account of our country's history, present-day patterns, and future potentials than the rival choice of Baldwin's black Muslim contemporary, Elijah Muhammad, to *reject such hopes*, to condemn America, and to refuse to acknowledge any common moral responsibilities that others might associate with his unchosen American citizenship. Rorty asserted that neither was right, and neither was wrong, because *there is no truth of our history to guide us*, only a choice about our hopes for the future and how we will act now. For the same reasons, Rorty suggested, it makes no sense to ask whether Whitman and Dewey got America's continuing story right—and perhaps whether Rorty got Whitman and Dewey right—because *social hope concerns moral identity, national and personal, not knowledge and truth.*

How, then, are we to choose among different American stories and the different hopes that go with them, especially as a newly reawakened, deeply fearful, and hope-hungry people in a time of world crisis? Rorty offered no adequate answer to this question. In contrast, insights from Whitman, Dewey, and Baldwin that he misread or rejected offer helpful guidance concerning how we should proceed. Again, let me explain.

Rorty's Whitman: A World Without Sin and Knowledge?

Rorty's path to reviving shared social hope depends upon processes of forgetting and denial: forgetting the quest for truth on important matters, as well as previous generations' hope-grounding beliefs in an eternal scope of events and an extrahuman divinity acting within them, and denying the weight of any particular knowledge claims about the real world that might limit imagination and therefore hope, as well as all traditional claims of nonhuman authority. In attempting to persuade us that such forgetting and denial is both possible and well precedented, Rorty argued that Whitman's and Dewey's hopeful image of America retains the Christian scriptures' emphasis on fraternity and loving kindness while excising "supernatural parentage, immortality, providence, and—most important—sin" (Rorty, *Achieving Our Country*, 16). Such Luciferian pride, of which so many other peoples now accuse all Americans and of which the American "Right" typically accuses the American "Left," would no longer be a sin in the world of "Rorty the ironist," for two reasons: first, because there would be no more sins—the concept of "sin" would simply drop out of our language—and second, because we would deny any other source of our being, and any authority that we should respect in our creative becoming, other than our own imaginations and the active choices they guide.[3] Rorty's metaphysics of morals for Americans today would require only one thing of us: that we acknowledge in our freedom our fellow human "archangels" as equally potent and equally free from any external authority as we are ourselves.

In claiming that such a self-understanding has and should guide the American "party of hope," Rorty quoted—and systematically misread—passages from Whitman's *Leaves of Grass* with which he claimed Dewey would have agreed. Rorty suggested that these lines indicate the deeper democratic motive for pragmatism's rejection of the correspondence theory of truth, as well as any other conception of a preexisting, human-independent Super Truth that would limit humanity's imagination and unfettered freedom to agree among ourselves as the sole basis for what we will regard as binding upon us. Whitman wrote, and Rorty quotes: "I speak the password primeval . . . I give the sign of democracy; / By God! I will accept nothing which all cannot have their counterpart of on the same terms. / . . . Logic and sermons never convince, / The damp of night drives deeper into my soul. / Only what proves itself to every man and woman is so, / Only what nobody denies is so" (Rorty, *Achieving Our Country*, 26–27). Though Rorty did not offer a close reading of Whitman's lines, his praise of them, considered in light of his own explicit, long-term antireligious commitment and his own more detailed, ironist account of self-creation, suggests that he took these lines to express a moral egalitarianism grounded only in a personal stance of rejecting human inequality and any extraindividual basis for well-warranted belief other than universal agreement among our personal experiences. Perhaps, despite his stated "nominalist" metaphysical commitment, Rorty read Whitman's "password primeval" as referring to some kind of generalized, humanistic self-respect that human intuition or a shared "common sense" has always taught us—despite the imperious claims of philosophers, theologians, and religious mystics that there are other sources and standards of epistemic and moral validity that can and do exercise authority over the adequacy of our own determinations.[4] Rorty read Whitman's allusion to the authoritative witness of divinity—"By God!"—as a self-reference to the "strong poet" himself, while also claiming it as self-referring for him and for any other self-creating and world-shaping human being—even though many passages in Whitman's writings suggest that Whitman actually believed that human individuals participate in a divinity that includes but exceeds us.[5]

Reader beware: the real Whitman was not Rorty's Whitman. In addition to celebrating the creative potentials of his own body-spirit and those of his fellow individual men and women, the real Walt also lamented their collective role in causing Lincoln's death, as well as all the hopes that died with him, in such powerful and influential poems as "When Lilacs Last in the Dooryard Bloomed" and "O Captain! My Captain!" If we consider what Whitman himself probably meant by the lines Rorty quoted, while taking seriously his impulse to employ the human-connective, world-changing powers of communication—as did Dewey in *Experience in Nature*, calling them an achievement in comparison to which transubstantiation pales—we must conclude that Rorty misrepresented the real Walt Whitman in important ways.

Rorty's Dewey: A World Without Truth?

Rorty's misreading of Whitman's allusion to the "sign of democracy" in *Leaves of Grass* led into a brief sketch of the emergence of pragmatism's conception of truth, over the course of which he also misrepresented Dewey's views in order to serve his own rhetorical purposes.

> These passages in Whitman can be read as presaging the doctrine that made pragmatism both original and infamous: its refusal to believe in the existence of Truth, in the sense of something not made by human hands, something which has authority over human beings. The closest Hegel got to this pragmatist doctrine was his dictum that philosophy is its own time held in thought. Despite this historicism, Hegel could never bring himself to assert the primacy of the practical over the theoretical—what Hilary Putnam, defining the essence of pragmatism, has called the primacy of the agent point of view. Dewey, like Marx in the eleventh of his "Theses on Feuerbach," took the primacy of the practical all the way.
>
> (Rorty, *Achieving Our Country*, 27)

Rejecting any independent "Super Truth" (and also any Deweyan provisional truths of cross-cultural collaborative inquiry) as criterial for the descriptive accuracy and the moral adequacy of any American story, Rorty's neopragmatism treated American aspirations and needs as "we" understand these as the sole criterion for deciding which story about our nation's history warrants belief.[6]

In fact, Rorty misleadingly argued, Dewey's pragmatism was an answer to the question, "what can philosophy do for the United States?" rather than to the question, "how can the United States be philosophically justified?" As Rorty told American pragmatism's story, Dewey abandoned the question, "why should one prefer democracy to feudalism, and self-creation to obedience to authority?" in favor of the question, "given the preferences we Americans share, given the adventure on which we are embarked, what should we say about truth, knowledge, reason, virtue, human nature, and all the other traditional philosophical topics?" Importantly limiting the actual scope and grounding of the real Dewey's philosophical goals,[7] Rorty claimed: "America will, Dewey hoped, be the first nation-state to have the courage to renounce hope of justification from on high—from a source which is immovable and eternal. Such a country will treat both its philosophy and its poetry as modes of self-expression, rather than ask its philosophers to provide it with reassurance" (27–28).

In Rorty's view, philosophers have no basis other than personal opinion for criticizing America's self-preoccupation and no grounds to which we can appeal—other than agreement of our fellow citizens—in order to reassure (or perhaps to challenge) them in their belief that their country's institutions, international policies, and even perceived shortcomings are justifiable. Therefore, Rorty concluded, philosophers must recognize that we have no particular public role to play and thus can contribute nothing more or different in kind than what poets contribute to our country's guidance. We cannot serve as impartial arbiters of history nor can we provide impartial rules for arbitration among rival claimants. Neither poets nor philosophers can speak "Super Truth" to power, in Rorty's view. We can only express ourselves.

Moreover, we Americans like what we have achieved, Rorty asserted in Dewey's name, and our self-satisfaction is what makes an account of our history true or right.

> The culminating achievement of Dewey's philosophy was to treat evaluative terms such as "true" and "right" not as signifying a relation to some antecedently existing thing—such as God's Will, or Moral Law, or the Intrinsic Nature of Objective Reality—but as expressions of satisfaction at having found a solution to a problem: a problem which may someday seem obsolete, and a satisfaction which may someday seem misplaced. The effect of this treatment is to change our account of progress. Instead of seeing progress as a matter of getting closer to something specifiable in advance, we see it as a matter of solving more problems. Progress is, as Thomas Kuhn suggested, measured by the extent to which we have made ourselves better than we were in the past rather than by our increased proximity to a goal.
>
> (28)

Here Rorty distorted Kuhn's claim about the history of science while misleadingly characterizing Dewey as an ethical emotivist who reduced ethics to ethnocentric feelings and who has simply added descriptive criteria to the theory in order to better explain why we cheer what we like and boo what we dislike.[8] In spite of its multiple misreadings, however, this passage also contains a grain of insight concerning two important aspects of Dewey's conception of an action-guiding hypothesis for transforming a problem situation. First, we are motivated to act in order to change circumstances that have given us problems in the past. And second, the kind of ideal goals that guide our future-focused action are too open-ended, contextual, and processive to be achievable through antecedently specifiable, stagewise Platonic approximations.[9]

However, Rorty radically understated Dewey's pragmatist assessment of the importance of *provisional truths and guiding ideals* in our lives. For Dewey, scientists who rightly have given up belief in an independent and anteced-ent Super Truth still do and should seek provisional truths and better truths through ongoing processes of inquiry. Likewise, American citizens who *rightly* have given up belief in an American Manifest Destiny still do and should guide their actions by a shared democratic ideal. The term "rightly" as used in the previous sentence had significance for Dewey, expressing more than personal opinion or a widely shared social belief, even after one has given up both the correspondence theory of truth and belief in a divinely foreordained course of human history. For Dewey, the consequences that matter in testing the meaning and truth of an idea include much more than our personal satisfactions—and even these have social, cross-cultural, and time-tested dimensions that Rorty ig-nored. Ironically, Rorty's claims about Dewey's view echoed Bertrand Russell's famous, false, and damaging gloss on the meaning of pragmatism's conception of truth while simply inverting his verdict on its value.

For James, Dewey, and contemporary pragmatists, truth is more than what it is helpful for us to believe at some moment in time, more than what we choose to believe. Truths are achieved warrants for present inquiries that gained their current standing through past inquiries, in which our beliefs were tested against the world and others' reflective opinions, and they either stood up well or were revised accordingly. Though pragmatist truths are not Super Truths—not yet, anyway—they are valued, used to the farthest extent they can go, and then revised again when future experience shows us they must be. To say that they are our "instruments" is not to cheapen them but to compare the best-warranted of them to a priceless, seasoned Stradivarius vio-lin—to be used with care and with profound pleasure, because it was made to be used.[10]

Rorty's American Black Box:
A Substitute for a Pragmatist Social Epistemology?

With this favorable but misleading verdict in mind, Rorty asserted that Dewey's epistemic egalitarianism ultimately was motivated by and served the needs of his moral and political democracy, understood as a nominalist and ironist faith he shared with Whitman in the originary value and authority of individual human beings. Somehow, at the same time, this was a faith in our exceptional nation, America, which Rorty claimed came into being with both an ontological power and the tendency as an agent to create the conditions for diverse individual self-creations.

> Repudiating the correspondence theory of truth was Dewey's way of restating, in philosophical terms, Whitman's claim that America does not need to place itself within a frame of reference. Great Romantic poems, such as "Song of Myself" or the United States of America, are supposed to break through previous frames of reference, not be intelligible within them. To say that the United States themselves are essentially the greatest poem is to say that America will create the taste by which it will be judged. It is to envisage our nation-state as both self-creating poet and self-created poem.
>
> (Rorty, *Achieving Our Country*, 29)

This passage introduces a collective metaphysical entity, the American nation, into Rorty's analysis—a created entity, of course, as are all poems—but one that shares the power of its human makers to make new things, specifically the power of a poet to shape future human tastes. At the same time, this new entity is not separate from those who created it and those it shapes—it maintains and expands the richness and complexity of its life by spreading weblike among them, attaining thereby the status of a unique and unified being. It's great fun (and a little scary) to play with this idea—and yet, it straightforwardly contradicts Rorty's "nominalist" claim about Whitman's views: that there are no other moral agents than human individuals and that no artificial entity such as a nation has any claim on individuals' beliefs and loyalties. In that other passage I quoted earlier, Rorty had insisted that only such claims as the experience-shaped consciences of human individuals might prompt them to freely express from time to time, as they individually see fit, have any moral weight. A view that reconciles these two ideas would make a lot of sense—but it would be a pragmatist view, not Rorty's view.

Neither acknowledging this contradiction nor somehow "sublating" it within a Hegelian dialectic or a low-rise pragmatist metaphysics, Rorty the "ironist" here described the American nation as the active agent in a great project of self-creation, whose success will be assessed by the collective body of citizens to which it gives birth. Other nations' opinions will not and should not matter to Americans, Rorty asserted, unless these opinions agree with our own. Nonetheless, a harmonious global future is possible, Rorty predicted, because other nations will tend to agree with "us" to the extent that they democratically re-create themselves according to the American "ironist" model: becoming similarly self-generative nations that give birth to the same kind of self-creating, radically diverse Luciferian individuals who acknowledge no other creator, who reject group identities and inherited responsibilities as in any way binding upon them, yet who for some unexplained reason concur with one another in their views and values concerning all important civic matters.

> So much for my interpretation of Whitman's and Dewey's attempts thoroughly to secularize America—to see America as the paradigmatic democracy, and thus as the country which would pride itself as one in which governments and social institutions exist only for the purpose of making a new sort of individual possible, one who will take nothing as authoritative save free consensus between as diverse a variety of citizens as can possibly be produced.
>
> (30)

Paradoxically, in spite of his attribution of these views to Dewey, Rorty's American nation-state here replaced Dewey's "Great Community" as the indispensable future mode of human social organization.

Yet upon careful examination, Rorty's America is neither poet nor poem nor a web that works within and among us at some other metaphysical level—it is nothing more than a "black box" theoretical device that works by sleight of hand. It does not answer crucial questions about *how* deep disagreements within America and with other nations can be resolved in the best and most sustainable ways. It does not tell us *how* we can foster diverse individualities and a sense of shared responsibility simultaneously. It does not teach us *how* our differing, deeply valued cultural identities, practices, and institutions can be understood and respected, reconciled when they conflict in important ways, and effectively challenged in ways that lead to internal reconstruction when they do harm and resist change. As Ludwig Wittgenstein commented in another context, "The decisive move in the conjuring trick has already been made."[11] Rorty treated the end products of this national "black box" device—self-creating American individuals—as the arbiters of what is "objectively" the case by means of their democratic consensus. Our nation is not really a formative culture, but an empty shell, Rorty suggested: an open space or a drive-through for simultaneous but independent self-creations. Our fellow citizens' self-creative metaphysical freedom depends upon their shared refusal of any epistemological or moral limits on their choices other than their uncoerced mutual agreement not to interfere with one another's becoming and to work together to meet such needs as they severally agree are shared or can be traded off against one another. Their drive through the black box shapes no tastes, nor does their "deliberation" influence their thinking; they only negotiate and enjoy each other's company.

Of course, Rorty was partially insightful in emphasizing the importance, both for Dewey and for citizen-thinkers of our own times, of achieving a wide democratic consensus about "how things are," and also about what should be done if real people are to work together through democratic means toward more deeply democratic ends. However, Rorty offered poor advice—and certainly very different advice than Dewey offered—in suggesting that the agreement in question needs to be only that of the citizens of the American nation-state, and that such agreement requires neither rational and evidential warrants nor any deep openness to learning new truths that matter, either from other Americans or from the peoples of other nations.

We need evidence and argument to support, challenge, and continuously improve our beliefs, not just a tradition-based cultural consensus, not just pronouncement by experts, and not just opportunities to "speak our minds." Otherwise, we risk mob rule, authoritarian bureaucracy, or being drawn in by an illusion that our views and values matter in the outcome of a pseudodeliberation. Furthermore, other peoples also need the ongoing improvement of such truths, and they can contribute to this process, both because the commonalities amid differences in our cultural standpoints allow them to offer fresh, "outsider" experience-based insights. Moreover, our interests and our histories are intertwined in ways that are both quotidian and profound, which both entitles other peoples to be heard in the shaping of our nation and makes their "otherness" less significant than Rorty (and Huntington) suggest.

Instead of Rorty's "black box" theoretical device and self-expressive, dangerously parochial rhetorical gestures, what our country and the world need now is to employ a democratic social epistemology that can guide our processes of collaborative inquiry and personal reflection on urgent issues of history, social hope, and the future. In framing and employing such a democratic social epistemology, we would do well to thank Rorty for raising important issues and reminding us of the resources within the classical American pragmatists' texts and those of other great American citizen-thinkers like Whitman and Baldwin, but then we must go on to retrieve still-living truths from these texts for ourselves. We must seek to benefit not only from their hopeful, progressive spirit but also from their still-valuable insights about the past-laden, intercultural issues—metaphysical, methodological, moral, economic, educational, and practical political issues—that a democracy-deepening social epistemology that can guide sufficiently inclusive, future-focused projects of reflection and action in our real historical situations must help us to frame, inquire about, and actively address *together*.

Remembering Complex, Painful Truths of History as a Basis for Shared Social Hopes

Fostering diverse collaborations in truth-seeking inquiry and in global transformation—not to achieve American dominance nor solely to solve our country's domestic problems but rather to deepen democracy worldwide—will require us, as Baldwin advised, to remember much that Rorty advised us to forget. Though Rorty was right that we need to tell a new American story that can successfully re-call American citizen-thinkers to work together as respected, mutually transforming equals in a process of deepening and expanding our country's actualization of the democratic ideal, Baldwin offered an important negative criterion for adequacy in his warning that an "invented" story that denies our complex and painful history cannot offer the kinds of illuminating, motivating, and semidirective guidance that he and Dewey agreed we need from our past. Though our "official" American histories do not adequately acknowledge the multiple, rival stories that currently underpin differing perspectival "knowledges" among the various racial and ethnic member-communities that make up our culturally diverse American people, a new American story that can summon up an inclusively shared vision of who we are and who we together may hope to become must speak to, reflect, and interactively correct this unevadable and potentially valuable epistemological pluralism within our country. Moreover, it must acknowledge and engage the even wider epistemological pluralism that characterizes diverse global contexts that inextricably interweave through our American lives, now more than ever.

Rorty's worry about epistemological pluralism was that the effort to reconcile our rival histories as a diverse and contentious American people will lead us to focus too much on our troubled past, despair of any possibility of future national goodness, and unplug our motivations to advance a much-needed struggle for economic justice in our country. Somehow, he suggested, we must agree on a patriotic story that promotes unity, shared self-confidence, and a commitment to completing that final phase of achieving that "more perfect union" that Lincoln called for during the violent and uncertain days of our nation's civil war. The key to achieving economic justice in America, Rorty argued, is to regain our nation's "self-respect." We do not need to know the worst, most discouraging details of our nation's past, he asserts, to know both what justice requires in the future and how to achieve it.

Thus, with a wave of his hand, Rorty closed the curtain that hides the workings of his "black box" American nation-state with its diversely developing individual psyches: many things should "chasten and temper" our national pride, he announced, but "nothing a nation has done should make it impossible for a constitutional democracy to regain self-respect." Moreover, if we try to find out the truth about our nation's past and present moral failures, we abandon shared social hope for the vocabulary of sin (*Achieving Our Country*, 32). Rorty did not explain here or in *Philosophy and Social Hope* what he meant by a nation's "self-respect," or why the vocabulary of sin is necessarily incompatible with social hope.

Contrary to Rorty's unstated key premise here, however, extensive and reliable evidence about the past convinces most of us reasonable people now that citizens of constitutional democracies knowingly and willingly have been complicit in great evils in our shared human past by elevating to power those who have used the formally democratic mechanisms of their governments to wreak dreadful harms on millions of people in historical disasters that strain the imagination of later generations. This is why Germany, France, and Japan are so careful now about public claims about their national histories.

Remember the Holocaust. This is also why we as an American people must wake up from our historical amnesia, which allows us so easily to believe in an exceptional past, an exemplary present, and an unrivaled future. Remember two hundred and fifty years of American chattel slavery, and one hundred and fifty years of its lingering racist aftermath. Remember America's "Indian Wars" that legitimized genocide and seizure of lands from Native Americans, and the survivors' confinement to reservations and semisuccessful attempts at their forced reacculturation. We must stop fooling ourselves into believing and hoping that the structures of constitutional democracy unsupported by a deeper local and global democracy can save our future from equally evil acts and prolonged eras of unthinkable cruelty. Calling ourselves "a good nation" while washing our hands of the ongoing effects of these acts, events, and whole eras that continue to harm some and benefit others, merely because we are a democracy and democracy is a good thing—and besides, we have elected new leaders and passed new laws since our nation's earlier moral failures—does not change the still-present effects of our shared past. It offers an inadequate prescription for a well-founded national self-respect, an irresponsible approach to present living, and an unsustainable method of assuring that a different, more deeply democratic spirit guides our efforts to achieve our shared hopes and dreams for our common future.

Nonetheless, Rorty was right on a key point: misemploying the vocabulary of sin can worsen matters, not only by blocking the processes of shared social hope but also by trivializing our history's great evils in suggesting that an easy regret and a unilateral new resolve can change and protect us from those problems in human hearts and minds that brought these great evils into being. Instead, we must seek guidance and grounding for more widely shared social hopes from a more careful retelling of the complex and painful truths of history. Such a retelling requires acknowledging the unspeakably cruel actions of some human beings with whom we are historically linked and for which the vocabulary of sin seems woefully inadequate. Simultaneously, it requires acknowledging the courageously moral actions amid these horrors that were taken by others with whom we also are historically linked: actions of refusal and of self-sacrifice that can give rise to a fragile sense of a better possibility within us that can spur our own actions toward a future in which such horrors will never again occur. Rorty was surely right to call on Dewey's support in arguing that what makes us moral beings is that there are some things we at least think we would rather die than do—and for our lesser moral failings, Rorty was helpful in suggesting that *if* we do such things in spite of our sense that they are wrong, we must struggle to remain agents, resolving never to do them again (*Achieving Our Country*, 33). Rorty's advice may guide an appropriate, adequate, and effective response to many of our individual lies, broken promises, petty thefts, and minor acts of violence, verbal and even physical.

However, a prompt and simple new resolve seems wholly inadequate to greater crimes, individual or collective. These call for deep silence, for continuing reflection, for voicing our responsibility within processes of seeking truth and reconciliation with those we have greatly harmed. These also call for self-reconstruction, for making whatever reparations to victims may still be possible, and for working for social reforms to create individual and collective social defenses against future repetitions of such acts. Otherwise, the pledge "never again" is nothing more than a self-deceiving insult to the memory of the victims. "To forget would be a sin," Elie Wiesel wrote of the Holocaust. "To remember is essential; it is a worthy endeavor, a noble cause for which many of us have fought relentlessly" (Wiesel, "Only the Guilty Are Guilty, Not Their Sons"). Though Wiesel used the ambiguous, seemingly mental language of "sin" to characterize forgetting, what is involved in the alternative he urged—active remembering—is more than a pious mental act. It is a re-calling into being of an experience, shared with others, of as much as we can comprehend among us of what has been lost, combined with a demand for accountability, insofar as this is possible, and a forward-looking, energetic rededication to cultivating and protecting a shared sense of what is precious in our present lives, our rival pasts, and our shared future.[12]

Realistic social hope for our shared future requires such two-sided historical remembering. It requires personal acknowledgment of enormous harms that beggar the language of sin that elected leaders and ordinary citizens of constitutional democracies like our own have wrought in the still-living past. In combination with such truth-telling, it also requires energetic rededication to more widely actualizing the better possibilities that some of our prophetic brothers and sisters devoted their lives to manifesting, even in the midst of such horrors. Because Rorty was determined to avoid both truth telling and the religious language of sin, he failed both to clarify "sin's" limitations and to suggest a more adequate response to those great historic evils that desirable and sustainable social hopes for the future must acknowledge and reclaim in the course of framing effective motivations for engaged, transformative, more deeply democratic living in the present.

In proposing his own approach to future-focused living in a past-burdened world, Rorty endorsed Andrew Delbanco's explanation of how Dewey understood evil: as a "failure of imagination to reach beyond itself . . . to open oneself to a spirit that both chastises one for confidence in one's own righteousness and promises the enduring comfort of reciprocal love."[13] But Rorty disagreed with Delbanco that the inadequacy of such an analysis shows why humanity needs a fixed moral standard. However, Rorty's explanation of Delbanco's solution to the problem of great historical evils was itself woefully inadequate.

Rorty claimed that Dewey's intellectually courageous rejection of the language of "sin" in favor of a more hopeful conception of the human spirit was basic to the Progressive movement's confidence in education and social reform as the nineteenth century flowed into the twentieth. Thus, he claimed, their actual successes in advancing justice in America bear out the fruitfulness and thus the reasonableness of this linguistic, psychological, and political reorientation. For the real Dewey and his fellow Progressives, however, ungrounded hopefulness was not the answer to real human evils. Perhaps their intellectual courage was displayed most in how they confronted great difficulties and failures, often finding themselves divided and in need of major midcourse corrections in their efforts to understand and to transform America's multifaceted continuing problem situation as it expanded and mutated over time, in spite of their best collaborative efforts to advance a deeper democracy than the world has ever known.

Progressive public philosophers of the twenty-first century must remember that in spite of their shared social hopes, their shared pragmatist methods of inquiry, and their growing body of provisional truths, Dewey and his fellow original Progressives—James, Royce, Du Bois, Addams, Wells-Barnet, Mead, Locke, and others—were often deeply divided in their own minds and against one another about how to face the great evils of their times: war and peace, industrial violence against and by workers, lynching, exclusion of African Americans and women from higher education and the professions, and other Jim Crow–era manifestations of America's deeply ingrained attitudes toward race and gender. The original Progressives' challenge in dealing with their fresh history, like ours in dealing with the still-resonating horrors of our own time, was to take in experientially the inexpressibly evil actions of some human beings like us, in tension with the prophetically courageous moral actions of other human beings equally like us, as stimuli and resources for our search for language in action that profoundly and appropriately acknowledges our dual moral inheritance and that can help us to maintain lifelong, committed efforts to achieve more deeply democratic transformations in hearts, minds, and institutions.

For example, Jane Addams stood alone against the other Pragmatist-Progressives in her opposition to America's entry into World War I and all the "patriotic" repression of dissent that went with it, and she was pilloried by the press for it, feeling so much continuous pressure that it nearly broke her health. In spite of this, she worked with women leaders in other nations at war to found the still-living Women's International League for Freedom and Justice, which documented real conditions in war zones and promoted citizen efforts to bring about a negotiated solution to the carnage. Her friends Dewey and Mead communicated with her privately throughout the war and eventually realized that they had been taken in by the great idea of "a war to end all wars," which she had argued was practically self-contradictory. She eventually shared the Nobel Peace Prize with one of her wartime opponents who had called her "unpatriotic," and her insights about the peace process are still invaluable for us today.[14] We must learn her endurance and ability to forgive, as well as her Pragmatist-Progressive friends' ability to admit being wrong, to change, to reconcile, to carry on.

As we pursue our transformative inquiries, like the original Progressives, we must keep our eyes open to the disheartening possibility that our opponents may be working equally hard in pursuit of incompatible social hopes that, if realized, might devastate our own. Motivating and sustaining well-focused and effectively transformative social hope does not depend upon wearing world-narrowing blinders or minimizing the significance of history's moral horrors through solitary acts of "strong imagination," as Rorty read Dewey. Instead, it depends upon courage to reach out in a pragmatist "faith" without intellectual certainty toward what Delbanco calls "a spirit"—what Dewey himself, without dualistic metaphysics, called a "religious" spirit, drawing on the original Latin meaning of "tying together again"—a shared sense that has the power to move one's own heart and to bring together a transformative community whose goals and means of change arise through the powers and processes of interactive, truth-and-justice-loving, hope-grounding, future-making collaboration in transformative inquiries to deepen democracy locally, nationally, and globally.

In his desire to separate religion from public life, and thereby to free human persons for creative individual self-definition, Rorty settled too quickly for an impoverished language of social hope insufficiently complicated by the dreadful realities that certain other thinkers have sought to evoke, though perhaps inadequately, with the language of sin. At the same time, and because of this same fear of religious language in action, Rorty also failed to appreciate that there are other sources and processes for evoking and sustaining realistic social hopes within the life experience of an ideal-loving community—sources that are extrarational, though they need not be otherworldly. In a spirit of pragmatist piety, we must learn from Rorty's insights and mistakes while drawing on the best insights of the original Pragmatist-Progressives and other congenial "friends of the mind" such as Whitman, Baldwin, and Wiesel to guide us in bravely facing the new and frightening in our twenty-first-century situation, which demands a democratic social epistemology to revive and reground shared social hopes for that global "Great Community" we so desperately need now.

A Pragmatist Path to Social Hope: Critical Memories, Deep Truths, Democratic Loyalties

As Dewey sketched pragmatism's social epistemology, each local moral situation is unique in important ways. Thus, transforming it for the better requires collaborative inquiry to shape a fitting response that draws on the past's lessons in a balanced way while intelligently attempting to bring about what William James called "a genuine moral universe," if only in small, contributive ways.[15] Each of these focused objectives constitutes what Dewey called an "end in view" toward our larger, vaguely imagined ideal goal: a future in which our democratic ideals will be more fully actualized and every life's demand will be heard and valued.[16] Dewey's pragmatist method of inquiry, which he discussed in many works but focused on in some detail in his *Logic: The Theory of Inquiry* (1938), requires enough intellectual courage to stare evidence in the face and to change course when that evidence shows that one has been operating on an inadequate hypothesis. This is the real meaning of James's widely misunderstood but profound essay "The Will to Believe."[17] Otherwise, we cannot find better-warranted truths and more adequate grounds for a united response in more effective and sustainable transformative action, without which shared social hope eventually withers during difficult and dangerous times.

Though their times may seem far upstream from our own, the kind of democratic, intercultural social epistemology that can help us to find our way forward in the complex moral, political, and economic terrain of the twenty-first century was ably sketched in the first half of the twentieth century by a diverse cast of original pragmatist-progressive thinkers and their inheritors. Our challenge, to be undertaken in a spirit of pragmatist piety, is to critically winnow, affirmatively reclaim, and imaginatively expand this valuable inheritance, marking out our own pragmatist path to social hope guided by their reminders of the importance of critical memories, deep truths, and democratic loyalties. Tracing a path through their world-transforming life journeys marks out a good way to begin our own reconstructive efforts.

A good place to begin: Josiah Royce, who was William James's daily interlocutor as well as the great "ideal pragmatist" from whom John Dewey learned the language of "the Great Community," insightfully explained in the last years before America's entry into World War I that real communities are woven together by shared memories and hopes as much as by patterns of interreliance in daily living. Where rival memories divide, Royce pointed out, crisis situations may evoke shared new hopes that bring a new community into being rather suddenly—a "Beloved Community" if the hopes are great enough, and if mutual commitment in action exceeds the limited expectations that a past history of harms once made reasonable.[18] Building on these insights, Royce's and James's student, the great "critical pragmatist" Alain Locke, expanded this insight by suggesting the possibility and the importance of relationally reframing our rival histories of harms through face-to-face experiences of collaboration in hope-building, world-healing practical projects.[19] When such projects are effectively structured and sincerely entered into, Locke suggested, they can teach nonfundamentalists among both "victors" and "vanquished" of fresh historical struggles the practical meaning of a cosmopolitan "unity amidst diversity" as a shared guiding goal and "critical relativism" as its epistemological and interpretive principle. When it is properly understood, Locke's pragmatist "critical relativism" can be employed in reframing curriculums and educational processes to prepare every nation's students for a future of peaceful, relational living in a closely interconnected world in which a culture-transforming version of James's metaphysical and ethical pluralism has become a necessary intellectual tool for human survival and flourishing. Martin Luther King Jr., a self-described "personalist," was a student of Royce's students and knew both Locke's and James's work. He employed all of these insights in combination with Howard Thurman's critical reconstruction of Christianity and Gandhi's cosmopolitan religious and political transformative vision to frame the most effective nonviolent mass struggle for "the Beloved Community" the world has ever known—a river of shared social hoping that continues to carry forward invaluable deposits of memory and insight into our own times.[20]

We who need such expansive social hopes and such a world-changing movement now must link both of these to careful, double-edged historical memories if we are to gain and retain their lessons of conscience, committed effort against evil, democratic loyalty, and inclusive love. But we also must be prepared to reframe our knowledge relationally, accepting correctives from the differing perspectives of other members of a shared new community of hope and struggle in order to actively knit together a diverse, worldwide coalition in transformative inquiry that motivates us as a "Beloved Global Community." Such a national and worldwide community of hope and cooperative struggle for peace and justice already had begun to coalesce in the days immediately following September 11, before President Bush unleashed the dogs of war and threatened the destruction of all who are not "with us" on "our terms." Our challenge now is to revive this global community of hope and cooperative struggle into full and vibrant life.

Our "Beloved Global Community" of the twenty-first century must be more than an antiwar community. It must be a peace-forging community that uses effective, cooperative methods of social and scientific inquiry about causes of and possible solutions to our troubles, in concert with democratically open-minded interpretive processes that draw upon diverse, culture-linked "knowledges" of the present and potential meanings of history-with-us. It must foster those wider democratic loyalties among peoples that can emerge and mature within practical, concerted efforts to change mentalities, emotional economies, and globally interlinked social-material conditions that leave many members of our human family in so much want and despair that some willingly give their lives to build global tsunamis of history-changing violence.

Even if we have become firmly convinced, contra Rorty, that a careful, truth-seeking historical memory is necessary for moral and practical guidance in a dangerous but not possibility-closed world, we must face with him the reality of rival memories sometimes linked to narrow loyalties that seem to license terrible things: murder and war, famines and epidemics, religious intolerance, ethnic cleansing and cultural erasure, exclusion of women and ethnic minority groups from participation rights and educational opportunities, cruelty to other species, devastation of our shared habitat. If a pragmatist process of reworking history's probable future is to offer a better transformative path to widely shared, sustainable social hopes than Rorty's "neopragmatist" path, such a process must reasonably and realistically expand our deepest loyalties cross-culturally and transnationally, while guiding us in interactively judging together whether a particular story of shared group identity and past relationships with others is true or at least well warranted. Because Rorty believed it is impossible to state and rationally defend criteria for such a cross-difference critical-interpretive process, he rejected the possibility of historical truth and knowledge in favor of proposing that we tell stories that are motivating to "us" as a national culture and that illuminate "our" ideals in ways that make them more effective in guiding "our" actions. However, the human global community can and must do better than this now.

In our post–September 11 world, we must face history's painful truth that pursuing a Wilsonian conception of American-style democratization worldwide could lead and already has led to forced imposition of a set of uniform, "cookie-cutter" institutions in other global contexts that have very different histories and cultural traditions than our own. When American-style institutions are imposed on people outside their context of origin, instead of seeming natural, desirable, and progressive, as they do to most Americans, they often seem alien, oppressive, and Procrustean, forcing sudden and unsupported expansions or painful truncations of historically and culturally evolved lifeways to which they are uncongenial. Of course, there are no "pure" cultures in our world today that do not carry forward significant marks of past interchanges with other cultures, both for good and for ill, nor have there ever been such "pure" cultures. Nonetheless, there are deep differences among real, existing cultures concerning the ideals, practices, institutions, instruments, artifacts, and histories in terms of which they frame human lives, foster communal loyalties, and guide shared social hopes. These deep differences must be taken into account in critically open-minded, context-specific ways within our efforts to foster democratic global futures.

Within a field of cultural differences, a well-informed, open-minded, deeply democratic interpreter would understand some practices as what Alain Locke called "functional variants" that performatively express "common humane values," though in differing ways. Some study and reflection would suggest that many social, religious, governmental, and educational practices express this first kind of difference, as do the more obvious examples of differences in culinary, musical, and hospitality traditions.[21] As Locke suggested, we have good reasons not only to democratically tolerate these kinds of differences but even to celebrate them, because they are important to our sisters and brothers in other places. They are *their* traditions, and they connect them to particular communities of memory that stabilize and give meaning to *their* lives. At the same time, they can expand *our own* experience and stimulate *our own* reflection and growth.

However, as Locke pointed out, culturally differing practices of a second kind are "democratically intolerable" because they block some culture members' opportunities to meet their basic human needs, to participate fully in shaping the future direction of their society, or to experience flourishing lives that allow them to develop and enjoy their individual gift potentials. Concerning such practices, we as fellow world-citizens must find feasible and democratically desirable ways to influence and to support one another in seeking change within the affected cultures. In rare, truly serious emergencies, we must act directly, collaboratively, and effectively to prevent great harms—not only great harms of commission like wars and executions, but also great harms of omission, such as ineffective governmental response to famine and public policies that deny whole generations of girls and women opportunities to achieve literacy and active citizen participation.[22] In such cases, we must act both for these unknown sisters' and brothers' sake and for our own, because our world citizens' lives are no longer separable.

In our globally interconnected real world of the twenty-first century, curtailing such great harms of commission and omission while cooperatively creating new peace-fostering resources and opportunities to assist our sisters and brothers in other places to meet their basic needs and develop their human capabilities requires that member nations of the world community learn to actively and effectively make interculturally well-informed distinctions between functional variants of common humane values and democratically intolerable practices. This requires critically reconsidering their own cultural practices as well as those of others in these terms. Getting such distinctions right requires soberly reflecting on the truths of history, understood as a balanced, multisided, relational retelling of experienced events that hears other voices as well as the mainstreams of one's own tradition. It also requires fact-finding, truth-seeking, cooperative inquiries that involve the "best minds" among diverse peoples who have something in common at stake in creating the local and global conditions for a positive, cooperative peace that fosters democratically diverse instantiations of national, communal, familial, and individual flourishing.

Efficiency and simplicity weigh in as practical, action-guiding values within deeply democratic development strategies only in a secondary "lexical" relation to this pragmatist background requirement that our transformative efforts must foster complex, democratically interlinked heterogeneity in particular instantiations of the common goals we seek, rather than value-reductive, culture-destroying homogeneity.[23] It may be valuable at this time in history to encourage differing cultures and individuals to work first and primarily within and through their own country's government and socioeconomic institutions in striving to meet their basic needs and in seeking support and opportunities for the development of their complex human capabilities. At the same time, it may be most feasible and democratically desirable now for other nations, cultures, and individuals to assist their culturally differing sisters and brothers primarily through institutions indigenous to or highly compatible with their home places.[24] Of course, the reasonableness in particular contexts of this general, two-part democratic development strategy requires that relevant governmental and nongovernmental socioeconomic institutions display enough openness and transparency to serve those in need and to discourage corruption while allowing their activities to be understood and supported or challenged by interested parties inside and outside their countries who make the effort to know.

However, this two-part democratic development strategy of respectful cooperative assistance, with its operative requirements of inclusiveness, openness, and transparency, is compatible with wide-ranging democratic pluralism in institutional structures and processes. It allows for—even requires—a great deal of history-based, culture-linked contextual specificity in democratic institutional designs and processes, while also accepting significant "information costs," a concept from economic theory that reminds us that learning what we need to know comes at the expense of time and money that could have been employed in other ways. Working with culture-linked institutional diversity requires outsiders to invest a significant amount of study time to know what's going on in order to play helpful, integrative roles on behalf of the world community of nations as they work toward deepening global democracy in political, cultural, and economic relations. In fact, a carefully balanced, multisided, relational study of relevant examples from history will show us that intervening in others' local contexts, even with the most helpful intentions or to make our own lives more secure, is likely to do great harm to all concerned, unless we invest this kind of other-study time in preparing for those mutually illuminating negotiation processes. Through well-prepared, mutually framed, collaborative processes, as Jane Addams suggested, we can see how we can work together to improve things for all concerned.[25]

Such a pluralistic approach to world future-making is necessary—and it is the simplest and most efficient approach possible—if we are to achieve democracy's guiding goal: the liberation of diverse individuals who are always and everywhere culture members into ways of living that respect them in their particularity, that assist them in their needs and in the growth of their human capabilities, and that value their dispersed knowledges as priceless in the shaping of the mutually transformative practices and processes of a locally contextualized yet globally cosmopolitan "unity in diversity." A cosmopolitan respect for culture-linked differences that are democratically tolerable can be a source of strength in fostering worldwide support for the democratic ideal as an immanent transformative current within a shared present and a hoped-for future. If world citizens today are to take the right risks in encouraging and monitoring the progress of such cosmopolitan democratization processes worldwide while using America's historically evolved customs and institutions as only one set of still-unfinished models among many, we can and must retain the idea of truth, learning to understand its guiding roles in past-appraising and future-shaping processes in new ways: provisional, inquiry specific, and practical.[26]

Conclusion:
Only True, Shared Stories Can Restore Shared Social Hopes

In the twenty-first century, we have even better reason to believe that the original pragmatist, Charles Sanders Peirce, was right a hundred and fifty years ago about his metaphysical "tychism." This was Peirce's guiding metaphysical hypothesis that the developmental process of our cosmos is not finished, that genuinely new things emerge in the cosmos at all levels, from subatomic particles to galaxies, including in the structures and interactive processes of living things, and especially (with the help of new technologies and new ways of thinking about the lessons of experience) in human ways of living, loving, evaluating our lives, and imagining possible futures that we may be able to co-create. Peirce's "tychism" means that there is no fixed, unchanging "way things are" for us to know about nature, about democracy, or even about divinity. Furthermore, as Dewey pointed out, we cannot stand outside this process of world-becoming as uninvolved and disinterested observers in order to grasp some Super Truth about it. Not only do we care passionately about how things go in ways that unevadably affect our knowing and our doing, but we are "agent-patients" in the midst of events, interacting with other agents and processes while undergoing change ourselves, as events work themselves within and among us.

That sense of "the new" always stirring within the old that destabilizes any certainty about what is, or has been, or will be, is widely shared among our living human generations now, in America and in many other places worldwide. It is a source of existential nausea to some that drives them back to seeking fortification from older stories in which nothing important ever changes. At the same time, it is a source of liberation into hopes for wider possibilities in living for those who have found the world as circumscribed by the older stories suffocating and panic producing. If Whitman, Peirce, James, Royce, Dewey, Addams, Locke, Baldwin, King, Wiesel, and Rorty are still wise guides, this widely shared sense of "the new" stirring deep down that stimulates interest in both kinds of stories now is not merely interesting; it is important for the world's future, because people act on their stories.

Must the second kind of stories—the liberatory stories of a new era in world-becoming—be Godless, truth free, and history "lite," as Rorty argued, leaving behind all of these philosophical categories as already claimed and powerfully dangerous within the old stories, in order to make room for a "joyous social hope" of creative living unspoiled by the cries of those unfairly wounded by cosmically contingent and therefore changeable social histories? No. A careful reading of the original Pragmatist-Progressives and downstream "friends of the mind" as an aid to sober reflection on the searing experiences of so many people in these early years of the twenty-first century suggests that critical, dual-sided relational memories of history, an immanent sense of divinity, widely shared cosmopolitan loyalties, open-ended knowledges, provisional truths, and active engagements in cross-cultural collaborative projects of mutual aid and transformation are grounds and guides for a much-needed, globally shared social hope.

However, as Whitman and James clearly intimated, divinity must be understood to enter into and to dwell within the world in different ways than some of the older religious stories seem to suggest. As Dewey and Addams demonstrated, truth must lose its finality and coercive power while gaining in its transformative usefulness. As Royce suggested, our loyalties can and must become as ecumenical as they are deep. And as Locke, King, Baldwin, and Wiesel have shown by their lives as well as their works, history can and must remain present and unfinished for us, whispering different parts of the riddle to differing peoples, who must find ways to combine and correct their bits of experience and their differing interpretations so that a living, life-guiding, harmonious wisdom can sound forth.

To advance the kind of common story Rorty rightly called for in *Achieving Our Country* along the collaborative lines I have argued for here and in chapter 2, drawing on the kind of pragmatist social epistemology I have argued for here and in chapter 3, I have tried to show three things: first, that Whitman and Dewey did not in fact agree with Rorty's conclusions about history, knowledge, and hope; second, that Baldwin was right about the importance of historical truth for the pursuit of future-focused justice and the cross-difference unity and harmony to which justice is a prerequisite; and third, that a pragmatist social epistemology can meet our present need for effective, hope-sustaining guidance and reliable critical correctives within a worldwide, cross-cultural, collaborative process of future-influencing reflection and transformative action. Now it is time to draw on such a pragmatist social epistemology to retrieve and expand our stories of "achieving our country" and "achieving our world."

Chapter 5

Trying Deeper Democracy

Pragmatist Lessons from the American Experience

Part 1: A Dialectical History of American Democratic Theory and Practice

For after the rest is said—after the many time-honored and really true things for subordination, experience, rights of property, etc., have been listened to and acquiesced in—after the valuable and well-settled statement of our duties and relations in society is thoroughly conned over and exhausted—it remains to bring forward and modify everything else with the idea that Something a man is (last precious consolation of the drudging poor), standing apart from all else, divine in his own right, and a woman in hers, sole and untouchable by any canons of authority, or any rule derived from precedent, state-safety, the acts of legislatures, or even from what is called religion, modesty, or art. The radiation of this truth is the key of the most significant doing of our immediately preceding three centuries, and has been the political genesis and life of America.

—Walt Whitman, *Democratic Vistas*

At the end as at the beginning the democratic method is as fundamentally simple and as immensely difficult as is the energetic, unflagging, unceasing creation of an ever-present new road upon which we can walk together.

—John Dewey, *Freedom and Culture*

Sail on, sail on—O Mighty Ship of State!
To the shores of need, past the reefs of greed, through the
squalls of hate . . .
Democracy is coming—to the U.S.A.!

—Leonard Cohen, "Democracy"

Two Strands in American Democratic History: Representation and Direct Participation

It is time for me to offer a preliminary sketch of the kind of inclusive, truth-seeking American story and shared vision quest I think we need now to guide the pursuit of a deeper democracy in diverse global contexts. In this first part of this chapter, I will reply to the often-raised question, "if participatory democracy is such a good idea, why has it never been tried?" I aim to persuade my readers that this question rests on a mistaken premise. We have been trying a deeper, participatory democracy in America for as long as this place has a history. In fact, a second, Jeffersonian strand of our democratic theory and practice is interwoven with our constitutionally primary, representative strand in all aspects of our American life—not only in government, law, and politics, but also in our civil society and our practices of daily living. We have been learning from democratic participatory opportunities for hundreds of years, practicing unity without uniformity and solidarity in the midst of diversity, experiencing growth and strength because of our differences, and building a democratic culture in the process—though our efforts have been deeply flawed from the beginning by older customs, social institutions, and economic allocations that assume and maintain inequality. Moreover, our efforts have been actively opposed by those who think democracy is not a good idea, and they have been passively blocked by those who have not yet understood why and how we must work together to attain and sustain this new, more deeply democratic way of being together, even amid our difference-making legacy of harm and neglect, in order to begin, as James Baldwin wrote, "a new history of the world."

Fulfillment of the long-loved dream of a deeper democracy than the world has ever known will not come about in a moment or from following some "cookbook recipe," to use Dewey's phrase. It will emerge out of difficult dialectical struggles not only against democracy's active and passive opponents but also within ourselves, within our diverse social institutions, among the various culture groups and regions of our country, and against the inertia of weighty global tendencies and processes that only partially reflect anyone's intentions. However, without a deep-rooted, responsible, responsive, and more fully achieved "second strand of democracy" in our culture, civil society, and habits of daily living, we will find that our institutions of law, government, and politics are vulnerable to that fourfold democratic disease I wrote about in *Deep Democracy* and in the introduction to this book: institutional subvertibility, ideological hollowness, individual nihilism, and cultural anomie. As the world's experience in the weeks, months, and years after 9/11 has demonstrated, democratic politics without a democratic culture is neither feasible nor desirable. At the same time, a democratic culture is unsustainable without widely shared social hope, effective cross-difference collaboration to more deeply actualize that shared hope, and at least some institutional support from government, the economy, education, mass communication, and the most potent realms of local, national, and global storytelling, such as churches, sports, and the arts. Already obvious symptoms of the fourfold democratic disease in America's body politic before 9/11 suggest why our nation lost its democratic direction for a time after 9/11—and yet, the strength of our deeper, second strand of democratic culture, though imperfect, has allowed us to absorb this damage and to begin to rise up to reclaim our responsibility and our chance to work for the actualization of that dream of democracy Richard Rorty prophetically feared would be taken from us.[1]

Among many contemporary citizen-activists and influential democratic theorists such as Michael Sandel, Robert Dahl, and Benjamin Barber, who would regard a wider role for citizens in shaping global futures as desirable *if it were feasible*, there is widespread doubt about whether this condition can be met in an age of economic, political, and cultural globalization guided by the seemingly irresistible force of capitalist markets, culturally invasive Western materialism, a largely "formal" liberal political ideology that justifies expert decision making within powerful international institutions, and the habitual use of violent force as a means of conflict resolution.

However, since the late eighteenth century, direct citizen participation in government, as well as in nongovernmental organizations and social transformation movements, has constituted an important second strand of democratic theory and practice in various global contexts. Active citizen participation has been a well-documented, increasingly important aspect of democratic institutional life in America since the early nineteenth century, and it has gained substance and scope throughout the twentieth century. However, this second strand of democratic theory and practice has always been vigorously opposed, undermined, and hidden, both by antiparticipatory "democratic realists" and by antidemocratic cultural, legal, economic, and political forces in a dialectical power struggle that continues today. Some of these opponents, as well as some theorists who do not understand democracy's nature and purpose, tend to suggest that we must choose between the representative form of democracy stressed by many interpreters of the U.S. Constitution and an untried, utopian, impractical, and potentially dangerous participatory form—but this is a false dilemma. In its historical development and in its prospective transformative application as I and others envision it, the second, "republican" or participatory strand balances and complements the representative strand rather than replacing it.

At the beginning of the twenty-first century, cities have become the focus of the struggle over what kind and how much democracy we will strive to achieve, because they have become centers of a rapidly growing world population and nodes of various interlinked forms of global power. To show how this power struggle has shaped recent events, democratic institutions, and widely shared perceptions of the feasibility of active citizen participation in democratic self-governance, we must tell a story. To change our future, we must extend our story, perhaps in the ways I will suggest in part 2 of this chapter. Arguments and evidence are important, for reasons I gave in the last two chapters, but they never persuade without a story that links them to the world and to the individuals who will decide what to believe, what to hope for, and how to act.

The story I will tell in this chapter will be primarily an American story, because this is the one I know best. Nonetheless, travels and friendships formed in Ireland, the United Kingdom, Greece, Germany, Italy, France, Poland, Slovakia, the Czech Republic, Botswana, China, Korea, and Japan in recent years have taught me that related stories are being told, or waiting to be told, in those places and elsewhere.[2] My story will show that the second, "republican" strand of democratic theory and practice that emphasizes citizen participation in institutional structures of urban governance, as well as in nongovernmental democratic organizations, social movements, and expressive events, is alive and rising in its importance in America and elsewhere, though it is not yet as effective in deepening democracy as it can become.

Stories matter—especially those that get at something deep about our evolving human nature and the world's change processes—because they both inspire our hopes and set out cautionary markers as we imaginatively project a road forward for our lives as individuals and as members of a culture, a nation, and a global community. They affect what we will hope for and what we will do. Therefore, it is important that our guiding stories be *true*—provisionally warranted and critically advanced with help from a pragmatist social epistemology like that I described in earlier chapters—even though our truths may never be certain and final, and future events will always condition and test the meaning of the past. I believe that the story I will tell here is in this sense *a true story*, even though it is partial, provisional, and incomplete. My purpose in telling it is to reveal deeper possibilities within democracy's meanings that have already been named, advocated, and even experienced as important in earlier times, but that have been actively hidden by powerful opponents within our culture because they threaten other values and frighten some who still cling to older or rival ideals. However, I believe that when a more balanced history of American democracy is known and taken seriously in our imagination of American culture's future possibilities, it can inspire efforts that will have great transformative significance for us and for others, as their stories have great value for us.

Experimenting with Democracy: Our First Postrevolutionary Generations

Please let me begin my story by reminding my readers that America's most well-known "Founders," who prevailed against all odds in our world-changing revolution, were economically well-off men, many of them slaveholders, none of them feminists. When they affirmed that "all men are created equal," they meant free, property-owning *males* like themselves, not all of humanity and not all of "us," when it came down to who was actually entitled to have and to assert the rights that eventually would be guaranteed in their first formulation of our Constitution. None of these men could even begin to imagine a woman voter, representative, senator, or president. And when I say many of them were slaveholders, I do not mean to evoke the practices of ancient Greece, Rome, Africa, and parts of Native America, in which people who lost a war might be forced to serve the victors as household help for a time. I mean to say clearly that American slaves, and those of European nations during the same period, were treated under law and custom as "chattel"—not as human beings but as *things* like machines or cattle who have no greater worth than their worth in use and exchange in a market, things that can be whipped or beaten to make them compliant and raped to make more slaves. Most of our Founders knew this was morally wrong and metaphysically self-contradictory—this may be one reason why they counted slaves as partial humans in their way of determining how many political representatives each state would get in our House of Representatives. However, there were holdouts among them against abolishing slavery, so they maintained their solidarity by keeping it legal—even though some slaveholders like Thomas Jefferson wanted it abolished in order to create uniform economic costs of change and because he could not bring himself to end his participation in it alone. He also could not imagine how to fix this mess in which our new country was beginning—this is one reason why he supported an easy process for future amendments.

Though the voices of Alexander Hamilton, James Madison, and John Adams, who all emphasized the "first," representative strand of democratic theory, prevailed in the American revolutionary generation's design of a constitutional structure for the new republic, the "second strand," complementary emphasis of Thomas Jefferson and other members of the highly valued "republican" minority on the need for direct citizen participation in continuous processes of self-governance was not disregarded or forgotten in the generations that followed. It expressed the views and values of many Americans of the time, as well as the established practices of many of their communities, especially in small towns and frontier areas. American high-school students still learn that Jefferson called for a constitutional convention during each generation to make revising our constitution as easy as possible and to assure that the basic law of the land always reflected the will of those currently governed. However, this is only one application of Jefferson's general principle of active "subsidiarity" in institutional design, which would have acknowledged and nurtured citizens' capacity to participate in determining the entire range of local matters on a continuous basis of active, cooperative decision making in local "wards," with the facilitating guidance of an elected ward leader.[3] Reflecting his awareness of the democratic participatory practices of the Iroquois Confederacy[4] and his belief that direct responsibility for care for the land would shape the virtues that American citizens would need for active self-governance, Jefferson treated such ongoing participatory roles as definitive of democracy and as necessary safeguards for the basic human rights of life, liberty, and the pursuit of happiness that intelligent contemplation of Nature and of Nature's God reveals to all.

In "Presenting Thomas Jefferson," John Dewey reminded us that the rationale for Jefferson's proposal to institutionalize direct citizen participation in local decision making flowed from his belief that all other levels of democratic institutions derive their justification and must continuously determine their direction from the active will and capacity of citizens for cooperative self-governance. Their directive capacity included all local matters in its scope.

> While the first aim of the division into small local units was the establishment and care of popular elementary schools, their purpose extended, in the mind of Jefferson, far beyond that function. The aim was to make the wards "little republics, with a warden at the head of each, for all those concerns, which being under their eye, they would better manage than the larger republics of the county or State." They were to have the "care of the poor, roads, police, elections, nomination of jurors, administration of justice in small cases, elementary exercises of militia." In short, they were to exercise directly with respect to their own affairs all the functions of government, civil and military.
>
> (Dewey, "Presenting Thomas Jefferson," 215)

Jefferson viewed this self-governing capacity as rightly delegated to citizens' representatives at county, state, and national levels *only* in important matters that require translocal coordination. *Democratic representation* in such matters would require delegates to know and to reflect the will of all the citizens as determined within simultaneous meetings in their local units.

> In addition, when any important wider matter came up for decision, all wards would be called into meetings on the same day, so that the collective sense of the whole people would be produced. ". . . The elementary republics of the wards, the county republics, the State republics and the republic of the Union would form a gradation of authorities." Every man would then share in the government of affairs not merely on election day but every day.
>
> (215)

Though the institution-framing majority of America's leaders of the revolutionary generation did not agree with Jefferson's call for continuous direct citizen participation in processes of self-governance at all levels, they did adopt his revolutionary premise that democratic governance must reflect the will of the governed. They also agreed with his principle of subsidiarity: that law, public policy, and legal enforcement should be carried out at the most localized competent level, as specified initially in the Articles of Confederation and then restructured in the U.S. Constitution. Though a few of these founding leaders may have doubted the capacity to judge intelligently even about local issues of that minority of their fellow Americans who were then treated as citizen-voters, such a view was not widely shared and did not represent the customs of the day. As evidence of this, we have the amazed testimony a generation later of Alexis de Tocqueville (1835 and 1840), who commented on the active involvement of citizens of the various regions of the new republic in nongovernmental organizations of all kinds that aimed to do good directly and to influence the development of their society over the longer term, in addition to active citizen participation in local government decision making in the small towns of New England.

Speaking from the standpoint of New England's democratic experience during the years of Tocqueville's visit to America, Ralph Waldo Emerson offered his own postrevolutionary generation's justification for trusting to the developable capacity of citizens for intelligent self-governance, a rationale that Dewey in *The Public and Its Problems* later cited as his own: "We live in the lap of an enormous intelligence." Like Jefferson, Emerson regarded Nature as the source of this intelligence, as well as its best school. The world needs and looks for something new from "The American Scholar," Emerson argued, something born of our experience of directly interacting with Nature.[5]

However, in Emerson's generation, as in those before it, opponents of direct democracy joined with self-interested opponents of democracy in any recognizable form to legally justify slavery, the Mexican-American War, violent seizures of Native American lands, and continuing refusal of suffrage for women. These miscarriages of democratic justice by institutions and representatives who claimed to derive their authority from the consent of the governed moved Emerson's friend, Henry David Thoreau, to write "Civil Disobedience" (1849). They inflamed democracy-minded citizens to join together in mass movements, including the movement to abolish slavery, some of whose most effective advocates were former slaves, including Frederick Douglass and Sojourner Truth. By means of an aroused electorate, they aimed to influence their representatives to make new laws and public poli-cies—including constitutional amendments.

Abraham Lincoln's Republican Party arose in response to these convergent mass movements. While he sometimes felt obliged as a practical politician to resist their guidance on many points, his reframing of America's founding democratic vision at the blood-soaked Gettysburg battlefield during the most violent and uncertain days of our terrible Civil War—as "a government of the people, by the people, for the people"—reflected these "second-strand" movements' fundamental claim that citizens' direct involvement in shaping their shared future is wholly appropriate, even morally and politically im-perative, and that their governmental representatives at all levels must reflect their active will.

Nonetheless, Walt Whitman, the great poet and visionary of that Civil War generation, whose controversial poetry Emerson cautiously praised and Lincoln read closely, declared in the postwar years that Lincoln's compel-ling vision of a deep and extensive democracy was still very far from the practical reality of American life—that democracy's enormous transforma-tive potential had been foreseen but had not yet been fulfilled: "We have frequently printed the word Democracy, yet I cannot too often repeat that it is a word the real gift of which still sleeps, quite unawakened, notwithstand-ing the resonance and the many angry tempests out of which its syllables have come, from pen or tongue. It is a great word, whose history, I suppose, remains unwritten, because that history has yet to be enacted" (Whitman, *Democratic Vistas*, 348). With Jefferson, Emerson, Thoreau, and Lincoln, Whitman believed that institutional changes, cultural revitalization, and ef-fective nurturing of the latent capacities of ordinary citizens for intelligent, cooperative self-governance were prerequisites to the practical actualization of the deeper implications of the democratic faith that was already imma-nent in most Americans.

Whitman was insightful in his critique of the wide gap between this shared democratic ideal and the cruel price America and many of its willing citizens were even then exacting from others in order to expand the country's borders and to open up unequal economic opportunities. Our so-called Indian Wars against the original conservators and inhabitants of these lands had begun shortly after that great day in 1620 of intercultural peace and Native American hospitality in Plymouth, Massachusetts, that we still celebrate every year on Thanksgiving Day. This was the beginning of an inexorable, two-hundred-

and-fifty-year-long march of devastation, land seizure, genocide, and cultural erasures across the Americas. European Americans desirous of settling what Jefferson once called "empty lands" and corporations desirous of their natural resources persuaded the United States government to break treaty after treaty with the Native Americans, eventually removing them to remote reservations, seizing their lands, and making these lands available to others. On a few memorable days, the Native Americans won great battles, as on that day in 1876 when General George Armstrong Custer and his entire army were killed at the Battle of the Little Big Horn by a combined army of Lakotas and their allies. However, heartbreaking massacres of whole Native American communities, including old people and children, were far more frequent. The last of these occurred at Wounded Knee, South Dakota, on a cold winter day in 1890, when three hundred people, including infants, were shot down as they fled from U.S. Army troops.

This process of "opening up the West" was expedited by a public-private partnership to build railroads across this now-American continent, with the labor of poorly paid Chinese immigrants working from the west and poorly paid European immigrants working from the east, until they met near the Rocky Mountains and hammered in a final, golden spike, while their bosses looked on with pride and government officials gave patriotic speeches. This conjoined railroad became enormously profitable to the business magnates who owned it, and is was very useful to both the settlers who built small towns along its length and to the merchants who shipped the culture goods and tools of a multicultural American civilization on it from Saint Paul, my birthplace, to Seattle, the "Emerald City" on the Pacific Ocean. It also offered a moving platform for hunters to shoot down for sport the great herds of American bison who once were the "thunder beings" of the Great Plains and the cornerstone of Plains Indian lifestyles, reducing these herds from millions to the brink of extinction. During these same years, ironically, Nature's value as America's teacher and as a refuge for the weary urban spirit was reaffirmed, as William James's student, President Theodore Roosevelt, responded to calls from Sierra Club founder John Muir and other naturalists to end the wanton destruction of wildlife and wilderness by loggers, mining corporations, and thoughtless tourists. He designated California's Yosemite Valley and the surrounding highlands as the first of America's National Parks, which were to be dedicated to the preservation of wild, rare, and beautiful parts of the American landscape for the equal edification of all the American people and the enjoyment of future generations. Preserving nature is still a second-strand democratic cause.

Reconstructing America:
The Progressive Era and the City Beautiful Movement

The "second-strand" struggle to fulfill the prerequisites to a deeper realization of democracy in the face of continuous, active opposition was the shared focus of democracy-minded philosophers and urban activists of the next American generations. In the last years of the nineteenth century and the early years of the twentieth, America's cities grew rapidly and virtually without urban planning or democratic quality-of-life regulations, absorbing immigrants fleeing poverty and oppression in Europe and Asia and African Americans fleeing the rural South's sharecropping, lynching, and continuing antidemocratic social attitudes of the color-coded kind that had allowed the recently abolished legal practice of race-based chattel slavery to continue for more than two hundred years. As powerful business corporations rose to national dominance in the late nineteenth century with assistance from the U.S. Supreme Court's affirmation of the legal doctrine of limited liability, "muckrakers" such as Sinclair Lewis and Ida Tarbell called attention to widespread industrial practices of exploitation and neglect, demanding worker-safety regulations and legal limitations on monopolies. In opposition to Andrew Carnegie and other wealthy industrial magnates who advocated "benign neglect" and increasing social inequality as the path of civilization's advance, pragmatist "progressives" such as John Dewey, George Herbert Mead, and Jane Addams called for more inclusive and more effective education, criticized corporate violence against workers, and organized practical social interventions such as Chicago's Hull-House, a "settlement house" in which Addams and other resident women, with Dewey's and Mead's active support, worked with and learned from new immigrants in a cooperative struggle to transform their situation, and later, to work for peace.

In the wake of the U.S. Supreme Court's disastrous, antidemocratic majority verdict in *Plessy v. Ferguson* (1896), which established the racialized legal standard of "separate but equal" as the highest law of the land, validating the patterns of racist "Jim Crow" laws that had been adopted by Southern state legislatures since 1870, Ida B. Wells Barnet cried out in speeches and editorials for an end to the practice of lynching, which was used as a form of cultural terrorism to enforce the real "separate and unequal," antidemocratic customs of many white-dominated communities in various parts of our country. During this same period, with support from an interracial committee of prominent citizens including Dewey and Addams, W. E. B. DuBois organized the National Association for the Advancement of Colored People to promote positive race consciousness and self-help among African Americans. DuBois advocated a broad, three-part strategic agenda to transform America into a racially inclusive democracy, which he summarized in *The Souls of Black Folk* (1903): "Work, Culture, Liberty," all requiring education as their indispensable means.

During these same years, the City Beautiful Movement for comprehensive city planning sprang into life under the inspiration of the 1893 Columbian Exposition in Chicago, with the leadership of influential landscape architects such as Daniel Burnham, Warren Manning, Charles Mulford Robinson, and Frederick Law Olmsted, who served many American cities as their first urban planning consultants. Burnham's 1901 master plan for the City of Chicago still serves as its framing planning document.[6] The citizen-led Governmental Reform Movement achieved such widespread influence by the early years of the twentieth century that a 1912 summary report documented planning efforts in twenty-eight cities, including New York City, Los Angeles, Waterloo, Bangor, Reading, and Oklahoma City. Despite the concentration of American energy and resources on World War I, the disillusionment and domestic upheavals that followed, and the powerful opposition of laissez-faire market proponents, the city planning movement's energy continued. In fact, it was so influential that then-U.S. Commerce Secretary Herbert Hoover's Advisory Committee on City Planning and Zoning issued a Standard Zoning Enabling Act of 1926 and a Standard City Planning Enabling Act of 1928 as model laws for use by the states, most of which adopted them in some form. An important aspect of these model laws was the call for appointed planning commissions of citizens.

The Struggle Widens and Deepens: The Interwar Years and Their Aftermath

In the years between the world wars, controversies over the importance for democracy of direct participation by ordinary American citizens in actively influencing the conditions that framed their lives expanded to the economy and the workplace with the rise to power and respectability of the union movement, which led to the passage of key pieces of labor legislation at national, state, and local levels. During the 1930s, the widespread economic devastation of the Great Depression made economic rights part of the basic meaning of democracy, including the right to work and the responsibility of government to provide work as employer of last resort, for which purpose the Works Progress Administration and related programs were created. These were the years when John Dewey wrote his greatest books, as well as a continuous stream of essays in magazines and newspapers, interconnecting the events and issues of the day with broad philosophical discussions of the growth and values of scientific inquiry, techniques for democratizing education, and the urgent need for a more personal, participatory experience of individuality-enhancing, cooperation-fostering, democratic citizen participation. In many of these books and essays, Dewey identified the emergence of genuine individuality through taking an active role in the process of democratic cultural transformation as the ultimate meaning and means of actualizing the democratic ideal, which requires active citizen participation in determining the guiding values and goals of all the institutions of adult living.

> Democracy signifies, on one side, that every individual is to share in the duties and rights belonging to control of social affairs, and, on the other side, that social arrangements are to eliminate those external arrangements of status, birth, wealth, sex, etc., which restrict the opportunity of each individual for full development of himself. On the individual side, it takes as the criterion of social organization and of law and government release of the potentialities of individuals. On the social side, it demands cooperation in place of coercion, voluntary sharing in a process of mutual give and take, instead of authority imposed from above.
>
> (Dewey and Tufts, *Ethics: Revised Edition*, 348–349)

These were the years when Alain Locke, "the Dean of the Harlem Renaissance," encouraged the expression of African American voices and transformative visions through the arts, promoted African American identification with struggles for liberation from colonial domination in other parts of the world, and theorized that economic motives underlie attempts by powerful nations to manipulate other cultures and the self-concepts of their members. To oppose these powerful economic and cultural forces, Locke called for an interdisciplinary "anthropology in the broadest sense" to discover and to teach common humane values. On that basis, Locke argued, even former antagonists could foster stepwise projects of cross-difference cooperation to deepen peace-making democracy and to extend its practical influence. These were also the years when direct citizen participation in the economic sector and, broadly, in government planning and decision-making processes was vigorously and influentially opposed by elitist critics and "democratic realists," including Walter Lippman, Gaetano Mosca, Joseph Schumpeter, and F. A. Hayek, who eventually argued that democracy must be abandoned in order to promote liberty.[7]

Nonetheless, the widely shared sense that all American citizens deserve an economic stake in democracy and that this requires active government planning was institutionalized during the post–World War II years of the 1940s and 1950s by our Federal Highway Program. The new network of fast roads opened up America to long-haul trucking and tourism (which linked our diverse regions) and to suburban automobile commuting (which made it possible for city dwellers to spill out into rural lands and to claim their own little place in nature, which was now radically changing). Post–World War II egalitarianism was fostered even more strongly by the G. I. Bill, which funded college education and home-mortgage guarantees for veterans, and by the Housing Act of 1954, which included a subsidy for local planning, the 701 program, to encourage development of local comprehensive or master plans. These education and housing programs had profound impacts in increasing working-class and middle-class citizens' capacity and expectations to participate actively in self-governance at local and national levels, because they now had the means of understanding and forming judgments about complex issues, as well as hope-grounding stakes in the future of their communities and their country. Speaking to these new stakeholders about the need to protect the land in the midst of profound social and technological changes, Aldo Leopold's *A Sand County Almanac* (1949) reenergized the American conservation movement, offering a new vision of human responsibility that he summed up in his "land ethic" as a moral imperative to draw upon emerging ecological knowledge in protecting the health, integrity, and beauty of the biotic community.

During this same period, however, powerful opponents used Congress, the courts, and the Federal Bureau of Investigation to delegitimize activists who sought new institutions and new opportunities for direct citizen participation in continuous social planning within both government institutions and nongovernmental organizations, especially those activists whose agenda for such citizen-voter influence included changes in laws that affected economic powers and civil rights. Although Senator Joseph McCarthy and the House Un-American Activities Committee specifically targeted members of the Communist Party for persecution, their wider intent and actual effect were to create a chilly climate for all proponents of the "second," Jeffersonian strand of democratic theory and practice, implicitly threatening all of them with the same loss of employment and even imprisonment that were being meted out to academics, writers, and film artists who could not prove they were not Communists, as a fascinated and horrified television, radio, and print media audience nationwide followed daily developments.

Nonetheless, in spite of this threat, Saul Alinsky and his fellow citizen-activists for urban democracy taught neighborhood organizations in many American cities how to press their claims in the courts, in the streets, in the media, and in direct negotiation for decent housing, fair labor practices, and equitable influence in city governance.

Under this same high level of scrutiny and threats to life, liberty, and livelihood, Martin Luther King Jr. and his fellow citizen-activists in the civil rights movement used the mass media to reason eloquently—and to display courage and dignity in the face of intransigent cruelty—in order to make race-based inequalities in federal, state, and local laws, and disparate treatment in the application and enforcement of the laws, a matter of national social concern. These active, nonviolent demonstrations of ordinary citizens' desire, developed capacity, and moral commitment to participate intelligently in shaping important national as well as local public policies eventually made the race-based inequalities they protested matters for legal and political concern by the courts, by Congress, and by the president of the United States. At the same time, these ordinary citizens taught their fellow Americans and others worldwide that such methods for advocating a deeper democracy are legitimate and can be effective.[8] Among those who learned these lessons well were newly resurgent Native Americans and Nelson Mandela's eventually victorious African National Congress in South Africa.

Winning and Defeating the "War on Poverty"

President Lyndon Johnson's "War on Poverty" of the mid-1960s was a direct result of the civil rights movement's activist-citizens' efforts, which persuaded a critical mass of their fellow citizens and key political leaders that the American nation as a whole had a responsibility to transform the conditions of race-linked poverty and inequality that our country's basic laws had played a role in creating. As Berry, Portney, and Thomson explain in *The Rebirth of American Democracy* (22–23), the key piece of federal legislation authorizing the War on Poverty's economic equity-focused transformative interventions, the Economic Opportunity Act of 1964, represented a major departure from the representative conception of the requirements of American democracy that framed previous governmental responses to the civil rights movement. It shifted emphasis from expanding participation in voting to sharing government decision making with citizen-participants in local community action programs (CAPs), "tapping the energies and imagination of those on the local level" in order to find "local solutions . . . tailored to fit local problems." However, both this broad goal and the War on Poverty's central transformative strategy—the CAPs were to be "developed, conducted, and administered with *maximum feasible participation* of residents of the areas and members of the groups served"—were actively opposed by powerful intellectual, political, and economic forces throughout their duration.

Among the most active and effective intellectual critics of the CAPs was sociologist Daniel Patrick Moynihan, later an influential senator from New York, then a member of the Johnson administration task force that developed the CAP program proposal to Congress and an antagonist of Sargent Shriver, who became director of the Office of Economic Opportunity and was popularly known as the "poverty czar." Moynihan's *Maximum Feasible Misunderstanding* (1969) "skewered the program by portraying CAPs as local free-for-alls, abetted by a vague law and conniving liberal social engineers" under Shriver's leadership (Barry et al., *The Rebirth of Urban Democracy*, 23). More importantly, Moynihan attacked the inclusive conception of participatory democracy underlying the program, arguing that it is unrealistic to expect the poor to participate effectively in promoting their own welfare within any "advanced society," and that the goal of expanding democracy through "maximum feasible participation" in "participatory democracy" is both ambiguous and dangerous: "It may be that the poor are never 'ready' to assume power in any advanced society: the exercise of power in an effective manner is an ability acquired through apprenticeship and seasoning. . . . We may discover to our sorrow that 'participatory democracy' can mean the end of both participation and democracy" (Moynihan, *Maximum Feasible Misunderstanding*, 136–137;

quoted in Berry et al., *The Rebirth of Urban Democracy*, 29). However, contrary to Moynihan's second criticism, any ambiguity in Congress's original language about "maximum feasible participation" had been removed by explicit legislative clarification and reaffirmation a year later (1965), four years before his book was published.

In 1966, Congress went even further in specifying that Community Action Program directors must include those poor citizens whose situation the War on Poverty aimed to transform. The Quie amendment to the Equal Opportunity Act (named for its chief author, Representative Albert Quie, Republican of Minnesota) required "at least one-third of the membership of local antipoverty boards to be composed of poor people. . . . This amendment was intended to *increase* citizen participation in the wake of reports that the White House wanted to pull back because some mayors were complaining about the independence of the community action agencies" (Berry et al., *The Rebirth of Urban Democracy*, 28). Though any American schoolchild could recite Lincoln's dictum that democracy requires government *of*, *by*, and *for* the people, "good government" activists from the middle class had become the perhaps unwitting partners of antidemocratic wielders of cultural, economic, and political power in their willingness to rush in to help expand programs of governance *for* poor people that were not governance *by* poor people. Sixty years earlier, having learned from their partners in struggle, Jane Addams and the women of Hull-House had criticized such well-meant but patronizing acts of *noblesse oblige*. Nor were they appreciated in the 1960s by cynical, often disappointed poor citizens, especially by those who had developed aspirations and effective capacities for democratic self-governance through their work with Saul Alinsky's organizers and within the civil rights movement.

The Quie amendment called for the Community Action Programs (CAPs) to make space for poor citizens on their boards; some members of the middle class would have to step down so that poor people could stand up for themselves. Given this clear directive, this is what happened:

In San Francisco in 1965, not a single member of the CAP board or executive committee came from the CAP's target neighborhoods. By 1966, members from the target areas had majorities on both. This was a common pattern as pressure from community activists and from the federal government (soon manifested in the Quie amendment) led to significant representation from poor neighborhoods. By 1967 Sargent Shriver could proudly tell Representative Quie that 10,000 poor people served on CAP agency boards and another 30,000 on neighborhood advisory councils.

(Berry et al., *The Rebirth of Urban Democracy*, 31)

Congress further reaffirmed this commitment to the importance of citizen participation in city planning processes by the poor in its 1966 enabling legislation for the Model Cities Program, which called for "widespread citizen participation" in model cities planning.[9] "In short, citizen participation was not something that departed from congressional intent. Congress wanted meaningful and recurrent participation of the poor; it did not have to be dragged along by bureaucrats wishing to ignite a social revolution" (Berry et al., *The Rebirth of Urban Democracy*, 29).

Nonetheless, powerful and experienced political opponents of this increasingly effective kind of direct citizen participation by the poor in local self-governance brought their influence to bear against the Community Action Programs, because they could not control them. Instead of treating representatives of the poor as a leaven and a lure to expand forms of transformative citizen participation by those the CAPs were designed to empower, many big-city mayors regarded meeting the statutory requirement specifying a minimum level of participation by the poor as sufficient or even as tending to give too much voice to the wrong poor people—those who undermined their power base and made new demands. This opposition was effective. The Office of Economic Opportunity adopted representation at the level required by statute as an adequate indication of participation by the poor. Turnout in target neighborhood elections for members of CAP boards was very low (1 to 5 per cent), perhaps because the presentation of issues and candidates was not compelling and because poor citizens had little confidence that the CAPs would make a difference when previous antipoverty efforts by the government had been unsuccessful (Berry et al., *The Rebirth of Urban Democracy*, 31).

This powerful opposition from elected big-city politicians, in addition to the influential intellectual critique from Moynihan and others, effectively unplugged the U.S. Congress's support for direct citizen participation by the poor in shaping government initiatives to transform the conditions of their poverty. However, it left untouched or even tended to add credibility to much older claims about the value of citizen participation by the middle class in government planning processes. In fact, Congress reaffirmed its importance in a series of more than 150 new federal mandates for citizen participation in planning processes, even though the CAPs came to be regarded as failures and the once-broad support for participation by the poor had eroded in the corridors of power.

> Implicitly members of Congress and agency officials believed that the failure of community action programs resulted from the poor's cynicism, lack of education, and weak political skills. The expectation was that *middle class people* would know how to use the programs, and bureaucrats and citizen participants would work together harmoniously. Thus, when legislation was passed creating health system planning agencies, revenue sharing, and product safety standards, citizen participation requirements were incorporated into the statutes. Public involvement programs were made part of such diverse laws as the Coastal Zone Management Act of 1972, the Airport and Airways Development Act of 1970, and the Energy Reorganization Act of 1974.
>
> (Berry et al., *The Rebirth of Urban Democracy*, 35, emphasis added)

Citizen representatives became members of planning and regulatory boards in many of the new federal agencies concerned with intergovernmental relations, the environment, and the public's health, safety, and welfare. In addition, many American cities developed still-active neighborhood associations that are run by and open to citizens and that have a formal role in local government concerning planning, zoning, city services, and proposed developments.

Peacemakers and Anarchists: The Anti–Vietnam War Movement and Its Offspring

During this same period, both support for and opposition to active citizen participation in shaping America's public policy intensified in the wider culture because of strong feelings evoked by the Vietnam War. As Martin Luther King Jr. brought his influence to bear in this struggle, the antiwar movement (referred to by King and some others as the peace movement) replaced the civil rights movement as the focal center of moral urgency for a large number of middle-class partisans of direct democracy. These included growing numbers in my rising "baby boom" generation who were coming of age just in time to be drafted or to watch helplessly as the evening news on television brought vivid images of the killings and the body bags into their homes and dormitories. Prominent among the student groups that organized and directed mass demonstrations against the war and efforts to transform campus cultures nationwide was Students for a Democratic Society (SDS). Regrettably, the visionary 1962 Port Huron Statement of the SDS's Deweyan participatory democratic principles lacked any feasible transformative structures and processes in its broad call for "the establishment of a democracy of individual participation, governed by two central aims: that the individual share in those social decisions determining the quality and direction of his life; that society be organized to encourage independence in men and provide the media for their common participation" (Westbrook, *John Dewey and American Democracy*, 549).[10]

Given this lack of attention to well-thought-out democratic transformative means, as well as the enormous existential stresses in SDS members' lives and the untimely death of one of its most experienced intellectual leaders in a plane crash only a month after the adoption of the Port Huron Statement, we should not be surprised in retrospect that the original SDS vision of participatory democracy gradually eroded in practice into anarchism and poetic self-assertion, strategically expressed by breaking store windows on mass-march routes and provoking violent confrontations with police. For many citizen-activists who interpreted antiwar marches and rallies through the hopeful lens of a democratic struggle for cultural change toward the ways of peace, these horrifying experiences of watching and experiencing police violence being inflicted on fellow citizens evoked both anger and intellectual confusion, due to the knowledge that these violent, television-attracting clashes had been orchestrated in part by supposed "peace activists."

Nonetheless, in addition to its effectiveness in ending the Vietnam War, citizen participation in the peace movement gave powerful support to many Americans' growing participatory democratic expectations, while at the same time developing in them the practical citizen capacities to organize related democratic movements. As Sara Evans has persuasively shown, the American Women's Movement owes its revitalization around 1970 to the combination of women's capacity building and their frustration at the sexist limitations on opportunities for participation in collaborative leadership they experienced in the civil rights movement and "the New Left," including the peace movement.[11] Similarly, the American environmental and consumer rights movements reemerged in the late 1960s and early 1970s out of a culture-wide experience of heightened personal responsibility for the conditions and impacts of shared social life spurred on by the convergent impacts of these other mass movements, and inflamed in part by their elected government representatives' undue responsiveness on these issues to antidemocratic forces and corporate interests. The passage of the controversial 1972 Federal Water Pollution Control Act amendments showed the effectiveness of citizens' heightened environmental concern and commitment to active participation in shaping the future; its section 208 authorized an Environmental Protection Agency subsidy for regional planning for sewage treatment, which led in turn to development of the environmental databases that were prerequisites to such planning.

The Trilateral Commission Strikes Back

The great interactive impact of these powerful mass movements on American culture and the resultant federal authorizations for direct citizen participation in an increasingly wide range of areas of social planning struck its intellectual, economic, and political opponents as dangerously out of control and as tending to undermine representative democratic governance as they conceived of it. Therefore, with funding from the Rockefeller Foundation, the Trilateral Commission was called into being, bringing together that generation's "democratic realists" from all the "experienced democracies" for conversations across disciplines and areas of professional responsibilities. The chief document emerging out of their collaborative research, *The Crisis of Democracy: Report on the Governability of Democracies to the Trilateral Commission* (1975), whose section on the United States was written by Samuel Huntington, argued that the "surge of participatory democracy" of the 1960s and early 1970s had "weakened American government because it had been unable to satisfy the conflicting claims made upon it," thereby making people "cynical and disrespectful of government" (Berry et al., *The Rebirth of Urban Democracy*, 8, 198). The solution Huntington proposed was less direct democracy. This so-called Huntington Report became the theoretical warrant for some of Ronald Reagan's earliest acts as U.S. president, when he set members of his administration the task of systematically deauthorizing existing federal practices and requirements for citizen participation at other levels of government that depended upon federal executive directives and discretionary funding.

The Reagan counterattack against direct citizen participation in government framed such opportunities as incompatible with the American commitment to individual liberty as well as a dangerous form of interference with the operation of free markets, which were treated as partially constitutive of democracy and as providing an important shield against communism. This thinking was echoed by Margaret Thatcher in the United Kingdom, who used her power as prime minister to privatize state-owned firms and utilities, to deconstruct Britain's practices of direct citizen participation in government, and to culturally marginalize groups who supported and exercised power through them, including labor unions and advocates for the poor. The profound international, cross-cultural impact of these ruling views of the political leaders of two of the world's most powerful "experienced democracies," in combination with the greater exposure they provided for the views of libertarian economists such as Milton Friedman, resonated globally throughout the remainder of the twentieth century. Among those influenced were the newly independent states of Central and Eastern Europe, which were then struggling to formulate the meaning of a democratic alternative to communism.[12] These countries still struggle to democratize their laws and public institutions in the context of global economic, political, and cultural forces and agencies that practically limit their alternatives, as well as the scope of their hopes for national autonomy.

Though rival political parties friendlier to limited forms of democratic citizen participation gained control of the executive branches of government in both Washington and London in the early 1990s, Bill Clinton's and Tony Blair's economic views showed little change from those of their predecessors. At the same time, the global influence of their economic views expanded exponentially due to the end of the cold war, their countries' dominance within international economic organizations such as the International Monetary Fund, the World Bank, and the World Trade Organization, and the radically expedited pace of computer-assisted financial movements worldwide. The world-changing significance of these events, institutions, and economic globalization processes has paradoxically changed citizens' expectations and the practical value of their developed capacities, leading both to expanded support for formally democratic institutions and to increasing frustration with the ineffectiveness and unresponsiveness of such institutions to citizens' views and more deeply democratic values.

In the 1990s, some countries' currencies lost so much value in a matter of days that elected governments fell, and the International Monetary Fund attached the culturally humiliating price of coerced institutional changes to its financial bailouts. The numbers of the desperately poor began to grow rapidly in ecologically and socially unsustainable hypercities in many parts of the world, prompting Ismail Serageldin, the World Bank's vice president for sustainable development, to warn, "the poor will consume the planet unless we build bridges that give them means and hope" (Serageldin, "The Environment and Development"). During these same years, global climate changes occurred that ecologists attributed primarily to chemical emissions from industrial processes and automobile exhausts. The Kyoto Accords were drafted and signed by the majority of the world's countries, mutually committing themselves to changing their modes of production and consumption to rapidly diminish their contributions to this critical problem. This effort was rebuffed, however, by a coalition of elected leaders of developing states, who believed such regulations would limit their opportunities to rapidly increase their countries' wealth, converging in their opposition with powerful transnational corporations and "conservative" members of the U.S. Congress. At the same time, middle-class American citizens, like citizens in every other country, lost confidence in their government's ability and willingness to protect their economic and social security.

During his first days in office, President Clinton's successor, George W. Bush, enthusiastically embraced the interests of transnational corporations and systematically eliminated federal requirements for environmental and worker protection. That process continued and expanded after September 11 into attacks on hard-won American civil liberties and prosecution of a global war on terrorism "by any means necessary," guided by a neoconservative vision of American global military and economic dominance in conditions of stability assured by enforced "democracy" on an American institutional model. Because of this brief period's world-changing, hope-shaking events, as well as short memories, systematic attempts by opponents to undermine belief in the feasibility and desirability of active citizen participation in government, and a fifty-year democracy gap in Central and Eastern Europe and many parts of Africa, South America, and the Middle East, the "democratic realist" view became "normal" to many people and therefore seemed true. This explains why, despite the long history of the second, participatory strand of democratic theory and practice, many thoughtful, democracy-minded intellectuals now ask, "what makes you think citizen participation is such a good idea, if it's never been tried?" Nonetheless, just as the "democratic realists" have told only part of the truth, they have not had the final word.

Part 2: Participatory Democracy:
Movements, Campaigns, and Democratic Living

Political democracy, as it exists and practically works in America, with all its threatening evils, supplies a training school for making first-class men. . . . A brave delight, fit for freedom's athletes, fills these arenas, and fully satisfies, out of the action in them, irrespective of success. Whatever we do not attain, we at any rate attain the experiences of the fight, the hardening of the strong campaign, and throb with currents of attempt at least.

—Walt Whitman, *Democratic Vistas*

The end of democracy is a radical end, for it is an end that has not been adequately realized in any country at any time.

—John Dewey, "Democracy Is Radical"

The cultural Left has contributed to the formation of [a] politically useless unconscious . . . by adopting ideals which nobody is yet able to imagine being actualized. Among these ideals are participatory democracy and the end of capitalism.

—Richard Rorty, *Achieving Our Country*

Participatory Democracy:
A Useless Ideal for the Twenty-first Century?

These are paradoxical times for the ideal of participatory democracy in America, the land that gave the world Jefferson as its intellectual midwife, Whitman as its poetic spur, and Dewey as the visionary seer of its future global scope and culture-transforming depth.[13] In the months and weeks just before September 11, 2001, the majority of the American people, whom Alexis de Tocqueville had described a century and a half earlier as always meeting and organizing for democratic social betterment in all its myriad forms, had slumped into apathy, perhaps even mild despair, about civic participation's efficacy, combined with a too busy preoccupation with their own narrow interests. Half of America's citizens did not even exercise their right and duty to vote in the 2000 presidential elections, finding neither presidential candidate inspiring and believing that their individual votes made little difference, until the dramatic events of the Florida electoral recount put Miami and Tallahassee on the worldwide list of place names. Many citizens' sudden spurt of interest in the power of the vote during those days was quashed again, however, when the U.S. Supreme Court decided the outcome of *Bush v. Gore* by a single-vote majority and the electoral college subsequently declared Bush the winner, despite the fact that Gore had won a majority of the popular vote. The American economy slowed during this same period, and most American citizens slumped back into their previous apathy and preoccupation, which was now tinged with anxiety about their own economic survival, so that there was very little outcry against the new Bush administration's immediate attacks on the greatest achievements of America's participatory democratic movements of the previous century: civil rights and liberties, environmental protection legislation, occupational health and safety regulations, and affirmative programs to equalize opportunities for women and members of racial and ethnic groups who have been burdened with legal limitations and social exclusions of various kinds throughout our nation's history.

Then came September 11, and with it came an immediate revival from apathy and alienation into civic fellow-feeling, as members of a wounded American nation grieving together and determined not to allow hardhearted terrorists to destroy the democratic ideal we saw at that moment as precious, hard won, and fragile. Almost immediately thereafter, however, President Bush declared a war of reprisal on Afghanistan, further limited Americans' civil liberties, and began to speak of an "axis of evil" in the world that must be defeated by American might in a war against terrorism and its supporters in which "those who are not with us are against us."

I told the next part of our American story in more detail in chapter 1, so let me highlight here only those parts of it that relate to the second part of our question in this chapter: how can we go forward in these times with our world-historic project of trying a deeper democracy? As my readers will remember, Americans who spoke out against expanding President Bush's "war on terror" into a second war of invasion, this time in Iraq, were branded unpatriotic, and members of Congress who expressed reservations were effectively targeted for defeat in the midterm elections of 2002. Nevertheless, a new participatory democratic movement began to emerge throughout America, using the Internet and full-page newspaper advertisements to communicate with a wide public, despite the exclusion of their message from most of the traditional news media. During the early months of 2003, in coordination with similar movements worldwide, millions of these actively participating, democracy-minded citizens staged massive demonstrations in opposition to the proposed invasion of Iraq—the largest and most rapidly constituted antiwar movement in the history of the world. President Bush and Prime Minister Tony Blair of the United Kingdom ignored these mass demonstrations and invaded Iraq. Nonetheless, the experience of participating in this massive, international, though short-lived antiwar effort marked a new generation and revived members of older generations who had allowed their participatory democratic commitments to sleep for a time.

The question these activists and their fellow citizens must ask themselves now, in light of their post–September 11 awareness of democracy's fragility as well as their subsequent experiences of watching world leaders of the "experienced democracies" unravel the work of earlier democratic movements and then ignore their own citizens' time-consuming though exhilarating antiwar efforts is this: how should we imagine and pursue "second-strand" democratic citizen participation, now and in the future? Should we declare the participatory democratic ideal that so motivated Jefferson, Whitman, Dewey, and generations of American activists "a dead dog," whatever its beauty and usefulness when it was still alive and alert to its times? Is participatory democracy now nothing more than a "nostalgia magnet" that keeps us from facing the reality we now live in: a supremely dangerous, globalized world in which democracy can mean no more than governance by those chosen by the wealthy few and their like-minded "experts," whose carte blanche we Americans are constitutionally entitled only to reendorse through our electoral college at regularly scheduled intervals? Dare we frame our lives to include at least occasional participation in limited campaigns to remedy specific harms or miscarriages in the way such formally democratic governance proceeds? Or dare we go even further: shall we risk our hopes, our time and other resources, and our sense of meaning in living on a commitment to lifelong participation in local, national, and international movements to more fully actualize this deeper dimension of the democratic ideal that some of us glimpsed again, in spite of the frustrations and real dangers of advocating its global instantiation in these violent and unstable times?

The last of these alternatives suggests the risky adventure to which this book invites the reader: actively embracing participatory democracy as a necessary complement to representative democracy—as the crucial, weaker "second strand" of our long-loved democratic ideal we need to strengthen now in order to heal our country's "democratic disease"—and as a great goal that can give meaning and energy to our way of democratic living as individuals and as citizens.[14] My story in the first part of this chapter reminds us that in our future efforts to deepen democracy in America, we can claim and learn from a proud though painful history, though our objectives and strategies to advance this goal—our ends-in-view, to use Dewey's term—must be framed in light of the twenty-first century's new obstacles and new opportunities, in order to give good guidance to transformative efforts in diverse global contexts.

Anticipation of these obstacles, as well as a combination of misguided suspicion about the supposedly Marxist origins of the participatory democratic ideal, anxiety about its vagueness, and distrust of the competence of ordinary citizens to fulfill the parts it calls them to play led Richard Rorty to conclude in *Achieving Our Country* that "participatory democracy" is a bad idea and should be replaced by the goal of making periodic contributions to "good causes" that aim to fulfill America's long-term goal of equal economic opportunity for all. However, careful analysis of Rorty's thinking on this subject against the background of our American history shows that the effectiveness of the kinds of "campaigns" he endorsed actually depends upon the broader, ongoing, movement-building commitments of a critical mass of energetic, insightful, risk-taking real people who do the hard work of organizing, who harvest the lessons of both success and failure, and who successfully inspire and teach their successors how to carry on the participatory democratic struggle in other times and places.

This conclusion suggests that, instead of being "a dead dog" whose burial cannot be finished too soon, as powerful "neoconservatives" have joined the "reformist liberal" Rorty in asserting, participatory democracy is exactly what the world needs now. Therefore, we had better get to work on more fully developing a general theory of participatory democracy for the twenty-first century, including both context-sensitive guidelines for effectiveness in diverse global locations and a motivating rationale for our fellow citizens to make it part of their approach to living.

Rorty's Hero-Based Claim:
Campaigns, Not Movements, as Frameworks for Living

The seeming contradiction of Rorty's brusque dismissal of "participatory democracy" while evoking the vision of Dewey and Whitman in the context of recalling late twentieth-century American thinkers to active, collaborative participation in great campaigns of democratic reform sends a confusing signal to the careful reader, one that requires interpretation and critical assessment. This confusing signal and the key to interpreting it are both included in Rorty's dedication of *Achieving Our Country* to two great heroes of his youth, Irving Howe and A. Philip Randolph Jr., who modeled very different approaches to living within the context of transgenerational struggles to deepen America's democracy. Rorty's quick dismissal of "participatory democracy" seems to spring from two autobiographically linked causes. First, he dismissed it as a slogan of "the New Left," whose necessary and effective participation in the anti–Vietnam War movement he acknowledged in *Achieving Our Country*, only to quickly forget it. As a slogan, "participatory democracy" suggests no specific reforms and thus does no work, in Rorty's view; instead, he claimed, it masks an antidemocratic Marxist agenda that history has proven to be disastrous. Second, he dismissed the desire to work for "participatory democracy" as an expression of what Kierkegaard called a "passion of the infinite" and the need for "the assurance of purity" that typically characterizes movements (Rorty, *Achieving Our Country*, 114). He favored limited campaigns over movements because, he suggested, movements are ineffective in achieving concrete reforms, they are performatively self-contradictory over the long term because they become the kind of rigid establishments they originally sought to replace, and they are too dangerous to their partisans' hopes and values as individuals because they demand uniformity. As Judith Butler wrote in *Gender Trouble*, "insistence in advance on coalitional 'unity' as a goal assumes that solidarity, whatever the price, is a prerequisite for political action" (20). In Rorty's view, the democratic ideal calls us to fuller individuality; it cannot be achieved by sacrificing our individual projects and voices at the altar of the needs of "the Movement."

Though Rorty rejected movements in general and Marxism in particular, his secondary hero, A. Philip Randolph Jr., was self-identified with and shaped within two of America's great, transgenerational democratic movements. He was "a race man" and "a union man," the founder of the Black

Sleeping Car Porters Union, known to its members and friends as "the Chief," and he was the editor of *The Messenger* and an original American thinker who found much to agree with in Marxism.[15] Though Rorty's comments on this subject were brief and dismissive, he seemed to think that American Marxists, like the "cultural Left" he criticized in greater detail, fostered national self-disgust while being so preoccupied with abstract theoretical issues and intracurricular struggles that they failed to engage with the real, practical issues of the day. Moreover, he saw their dreams of "the end of capitalism" and of "participatory democracy" as vague, unachievable, and otherworldly as the dreams of heaven of Christian fundamentalists, which he believed similarly block the way to "achieving our country." Thus, though Rorty praised Martin Luther King Jr. and Walter Reuther, leaders of the civil rights movement and the labor movement respectively, as well as Randolph, who was a leader of both, he rejected movements as such, at least in part because he associated them with Marxism.

Ironically, however, movement partisans' allegedly inevitable attachment to a "quest for purity" was one of the reasons why Rorty rejected movements in favor of "campaigns." In this he claimed guidance from the lived example of the primary hero to whom he dedicated *Achieving Our Country*, Irving Howe, who parted ways in 1954 with *Partisan Review*, the movement-oriented journal of the intellectual "reformist Left" because it had lost its radical edge, founding *Dissent* as an alternative, independent journal of individual Left opinion. Howe's prose once inspired Rorty to seek to combine "critical consciousness" and "political conscience" in his way of living, as he thought Howe succeeded in doing (Rorty, *Achieving Our Country*, 112). However, by 1982, when Howe published *A Margin of Hope: An Intellectual Autobiography*, he and Rorty had both come to regard this aspiration as unrealizable, apparently in part because they both had decided that good minds do not operate well within an organized, unified structure. They are and must remain independent, Howe and Rorty both suggested, and thus cannot pledge their loyalty to a movement, although they can properly contribute their energetic gifts to more limited campaigns or "good causes." Membership in a movement, Rorty claimed, requires partisans to interpret events as "parts of something much bigger, and as having little meaning in themselves" (Rorty, *Achieving Our Country*, 114). Somehow, literature, art, history, and philosophy are combined together through a movement's imaginative alchemy in order to create "a larger context in which politics is no longer just politics, but rather the matrix out of which will emerge something like Paul's 'new being in Christ' or Mao's 'new socialist man.'" This kind of movement politics, Rorty said, "assumes that things will be changed utterly, that a terrible new beauty will be born" (115).

The impossibility of such a complete social transformation and the pain of disillusionment when one discovers that impossibility is apparently the reason why Howe stuck to campaigning and Rorty did likewise: avoiding movements, delinking his critical consciousness from his political conscience, and giving up the aspiration of perfectly synthesizing work with life (115). Rorty said admiringly of Howe: "He wrote as he pleased and about what he pleased, without asking which larger goals he served or how his work tied in with the spirit of the age" (116). Though Howe himself confessed he was troubled by his inability to "reconcile my desire to be a writer with remembered fantasies about public action," Rorty dismissed such a concern, stating that Howe was "the envy of his contemporaries, precisely because he was able to find the time to be both an accomplished man of letters and the unpaid editor of his country's most useful political magazine" (116).

America's Historical Experience: Effective Campaigns Require Broader Movements

It is hard to compare an approach to living like Howe's, which was influenced by the warnings of political novels, with one like Randolph's, which was learned in active self-identification within movements, yet they offer very different life models, and if we use these to measure the value of movements, they suggest very different conclusions. Rorty's approach suggested that we could say everything important about Randolph's life and about the way such a life has meaning and impact within the project of "achieving our country" by telling a narrative of "a very large number of small campaigns" (Rorty, *Achieving Our Country*, 121)—but such a story does not bear up well under scrutiny. Reflecting on real historical interconnections among some of the great American social movements, the kinds of lives they have framed, and the campaigns whose eventual success they have made possible shows that, without the movements Rorty dismissed, the effectiveness of the campaigns he endorsed and even our evaluation of them as "good causes" would be impossible.

Randolph became the kind of man he was because the great movements that framed his life, including the influential individuals he encountered and the decisive events in which he participated, required and called forth the development of the great potentials we retrospectively regard as characteristic of him. As Dewey suggested in his essay "Time and Individuality" (1940), any human being encompasses myriad potentials, only some of which will actually be developed in the course of living a particular life in a particular social and historical context. We are not born as finished individuals, nor do our families, our early friends, and our childhood circumstances complete the individualization process, though all of them are important in shaping who we become. Formal education (or lack thereof) also is important, though not finally decisive—remember Abraham Lincoln. Certainly choice and chance are important factors in our ongoing individualization throughout our lives, as Rorty rightly reminded us. Nonetheless, the educative associations and opportunities of our adult lives are profoundly formative, especially our daily work, because it takes up so much of our time and energies and because our culture strongly influences us to treat it as self-definitive, but so are our families and friendships outside the workplace, as well as the often related "avocational" interests and commitments to which we devote our "free time." Gardeners, birdwatchers, fishers, and wilderness lovers become special breeds; couch potatoes and Internet trawlers are other kinds of people; singers, painters, and mystery writers are shaped by the media they shape; and citizen-activists become what their causes need and stimulate them to become in the course of their collaborative efforts to transform institutions and social practices from without and from within.

A. Philip Randolph Jr. became the man he was because the parents who named him and the community that cared for him as a child taught and embodied idealistic values as well as needs related to "race" and to economic opportunity within the still-unfinished America they claimed as their country. In response to that caring, those values, and those needs, he chose to become "a race man" and "a union man." Chance combined with his own hard-wrought talents and the hard work of many others who also identified themselves with these great movements to create the extraordinary opportunities and circumstances that helped to form the adult individual who, as Rorty acknowledged, "symbolize[s] my country at its best." Without the movements that formed him, *that* Randolph would never have lived—nor *that* Martin Luther King, nor *that* Walter Reuther.

None of these highly effective movement leaders willed "a single thing," as Rorty suggested one inevitably must if one commits one's loyalty to a movement. Instead, each was a complex individual responsive to multiple loyalties, guided by a broader democratic vision, and appreciative of others' efforts and commitments to achieve different aspects of "our country." Participating in their particular movements during their moments in shaping history was a calling to them that came with a high price, yet with great rewards: a sense of larger meaning in their lives than if they had focused only on a predefined career and a narrowly conceived family, opportunities that otherwise would not have existed for their own development and that of others like them who would come after them, a sense of doing right in the face of great wrongs that could not be denied, and sustaining and exhilarating friendships with other committed, creative, actively developing, change-making individuals.

Those American movements, and other equally great participatory democratic movements before them, were more than "a very large number of small campaigns" in their goals, in their social and organizational structures, in their duration across the lives of many generations, in their capacities to sustain hope and loyalty through times of adversity, in their potentiality-developing powers, in their moral significance, and in their transformative effectiveness. For example, like the movement to abolish slavery, the American women's rights movement that emerged out of it spanned many generations, guided by American precedents and by broader democratic ideals. These were powerfully expressed by Elizabeth Cady Stanton, Lucretia Mott, Frederick Douglass, and others in their Seneca Falls Declaration of 1848, which focused movement participants' energies into a series of great campaigns to achieve both immediate and larger objectives, many of which were not accomplished until many years after these leaders' deaths. These larger ends-in-view on the road to women's equality within a deeper American democracy include women's suffrage, access to higher educational institutions and the professions, legal guarantees of equal pay and equal employment opportunities, and legal control of their own finances and of their own reproductive capacities. Some of the objectives that the American women's movement has sought at various times have subsequently come to seem ill advised or no longer necessary. For example, special protective labor legislation decreeing shorter hours for women, lighter loads to be lifted, and a chair on which to sit during breaks came to seem unnecessary, because the broader labor movement eventually achieved legal and customary protection of safer and more humane working conditions for most workers in most fields, and women gradually have become accepted as coworkers in most kinds of employment, though women still are paid less collectively in America and still are less likely to be chosen for top leadership positions in many fields. Other goals and examples of the early American feminists were ignored with embarrassment for a time but were later regarded by many of their movement inheritors as prophetic: Elizabeth Cady Stanton's *The Woman's Bible* (1895) and the feminist, interracial wedding party of Angelina Grimke and Theodore Weld,[16] for example.

All of these goals, strategies, campaigns, and symbols were adopted and justified to others not only in terms of the mysterious workings of individual conscience but also in terms of broadly shared moral values and guiding ideals for whose meaning partisans of the women's movement contested with both their intellectual-cultural tradition and the dominant members of their contemporary society. Part of their effectiveness was due to persuading others by reasoned argument. Part was due to their ability to demonstrate by their living example that another kind of life was possible. And part was due to the practical capability that their committed relationships with one another and their stable alliances with members of other movements gave them to maximize their inferior political, legal, economic, and cultural powers in ways that allowed them over time to influence laws and social institutions, as well as the outlooks and preferences of others.

Similar stories can be told of the Progressive movement, the labor movement, the civil rights movement, and the peace movement: effective movements require well-focused campaigns, and effective campaigns that can be recognized as "good causes" require the practical and interpretive context that larger ideals and longer-term transformative movements provide. Many contributors to the effectiveness of "good causes" may not choose to dedicate themselves to the movements that organize and direct such campaigns. They may, like Henry David Thoreau, have other life business to be about. However, it is important to realize that Thoreau's life, like Randolph's and Howe's, would not have been what it was without the gifts and the willingness of others to organize and to sustain movements in support of the democratic ideal and in opposition to the great evils of his day: the movement to abolish slavery, the movement in opposition to the Mexican-American War, the movement for universal public education, the budding movement to cherish and protect the land. To each of these, Thoreau occasionally contributed his own great gifts, and through such contributions, his conscience could obtain absolution for his choice to lead a predominantly solitary life.

Transformative Movements and Democratic Living in a Dangerous, Uncertain World

Movements end, and sometimes they achieve some of their great goals while failing to achieve others, but if their partisans' ultimate commitment is to an ideal like the democratic ideal, the longing that gives rise to these movements, the relationships they shape, and the special skills they develop usually continue to seek new transformative outlets. Former partisans who fail to find new opportunities to foster change collaboratively with many others often long nostalgically for "the Movement." Those who move on to new activist commitments form new friendships and develop new aspects of their individualities while building on and continuing to revise their active "how-to" knowledge and their senses of "what" and "why" they gain through civic activism. The attraction of such engagement for them (and for me) is not "purity" or "infinitude" but a meaningful life and one's own better becoming through participating in a shared, transgenerationally effective agency in shaping a world that reflects our ideals.

Such a life is "alive" for democratic partisans. It need not entail greater dangers to one's psychic integrity than other kinds of lives, especially the life of skeptical apathy so many fortunate young Americans seemed to find themselves living until recently. It does require mature response to disappointment and disillusionment, because more hope is felt and risked. Nonetheless, a democratic movement's guiding ideals and an experienced, multigenerational community pursuing them together can offer resources to shape and to sustain a response of continuing hope, enlightened dedication, undamaged personal worth, and undiminished regard for partners in struggle who live up to shared values.

Such a life could become existentially more sustainable and practically more effective with insights from an experience-based general theory of democracy-deepening processes that would illuminate the various practical, ethical, and psychological issues we contemplate when we consider the activist's life as a "genuine option."[17] These include:

- how to sustain ourselves in protracted democratic struggle while surviving devastating setbacks, hard life choices, personal harms, and daily costs to ourselves, our families, our friends, and our heroes, long enough to make deep personal, institutional, and cultural changes;

- how to understand the relationship between these deeper, ideal-guided, long-contested, hard-won changes and the related prospects of the particular campaigns we envision;
- how to recognize the difference between what coalitions can achieve in the short term and what it takes King's committed "beloved communities" to achieve in the longer term;
- how to create or to find the ways in which, as Dewey understood, committed democratic engagement can open up possibilities for developing desirable individual potentials, instead of stifling them in routine or in the conformity Rorty feared;
- how to reflectively welcome the ways that such wider engagements change the meaning of our own mortality, as Whitman understood;
- how to understand the deeply democratic ideal as a guide to our movements, our limited campaigns, and our individual consciences, as Jane Addams's life has modeled for many.

This book, like my earlier *Deep Democracy* and the other books that will complete this trilogy, aims to contribute some elements for such a general theory of democracy-deepening processes. The larger theory, however, like the public philosophy it aims to assist and reflect, must evolve through the collaborative efforts of many thinkers and activists in diverse global contexts.

Earlier stages in our American story of "achieving our country" suggest that this great good will not emerge solely from small campaigns with limited horizons and episodic contributions of "spare energy" from the "free time" of anonymous, unrelated individuals pursuing essentially private lives. It is by its very nature the kind of grand project that frames lives and requires the conjoint efforts of multiple democratic movements that can learn from, build on, and revise the shared understandings that emerge from past efforts. Likewise, as I will suggest in chapter 6, "achieving our world," the even more ambitious project that now must frame more realistic, effective, and morally justifiable American aspirations toward "achieving our country," requires learning from recent democratic movements in many other places:

- from Solidarity in Poland and related liberation movements in Central Europe;
- from the African National Congress and democratic transformation efforts in South Africa;

- from struggles against dictators and for indigenous peoples' rights in Latin America;
- from the student-led Otpor ("Resistance") movement in Yugoslavia that overthrew the dictator Slobodan Milosevic in October 2000 and made an obstacle-strewn opening there for democratic self-governance;
- from continuing human rights struggles in Burma, Tibet, and China;
- from local and global environmental struggles in every nation;
- from ethnic struggles in Europe, Africa, and Asia;
- from struggles for democracy within and through churches in all parts of the world.

Instead of being a useless slogan of Marxist revolutionaries, as Rorty feared, "participatory democracy" is a distinctively American way of expressing the "second strand" of our shared democratic ideal and of evoking some of the most effective methods that have developed over time within diverse, localized movements for "achieving our country" and "achieving our world." It is a phrase that reflects the heritage of Jefferson, Stanton, Mott, Douglass, Truth, Lincoln, Whitman, Dewey, Addams, Randolph, King, Reuther, and many other visionary heroes who committed their lives to making such "second-strand" democracy a living reality. It is a framing value that guides the culturally differing, situation-specific approaches to living of many committed members of contemporary democratic movements worldwide—a value that focuses their emerging transformative future-visions, stimulates the development of much-needed individual potentials, and motivates effective cross-difference communication. These contemporary democratic movements, more than any other factor, support a shared social hope that "achieving our world"—a more deeply democratic world—is possible. Thus, we who can contribute to developing a general theory of participatory democracy had better get on with the job.

Chapter 6

The Continuously Planning City
Imperatives and Examples for Deepening Democracy

Every people have their own particular habits, ways of thinking, manners, etc., which have grown up with them from their
infancy, are become a part of their nature, and to which the
regulations which are to make them happy must be accommodated. . . . The excellence of every government is its adaptation
to the state of those to be governed by it.

> —Thomas Jefferson,
> in Dewey, "Introducing Thomas Jefferson"

In the minds of many persons the very idea of social planning and of violation of the integrity of the individual are
becoming intimately bound together. But an immense difference divides the plan*ned* society from a *continuously* plan-
n*ing* society. The former requires fixed blue-prints imposed
from above and therefore involving reliance upon physical
and psychological force to secure conformity to them. The
latter means the release of intelligence through the widest
form of cooperative give-and-take. The attempt to *plan* social organization and association without the freest possible
play of intelligence contradicts the very idea in *social* plan-
n*ing*. For the latter is an operative method of activity, not a
predetermined set of final "truths." . . . Until that method of
social action is adopted we shall remain in a period of drift
and unrest whose final outcome is likely to be force and
counter force, with temporary victory to the side possessed
of the most machine guns.

> —John Dewey, "The Economic Basis of the New Society"

It would be a mistake (and most un-Deweyan) to recommend an uncritical or wholesale recovery of Dewey's philosophy. But it merits another closer look. If we are to enact the history that Whitman envisioned, we could do worse than turn to Dewey for a full measure of the wisdom we will need to work our way out of the wilderness of the present.

—Robert Westbrook, *John Dewey and American Democracy*

Urban Schools of Deeper, "Second-Strand" Democracy

It may aid and comfort us as we analyze our complex, anxiety-provoking, global problem situation in these early years of the twenty-first century to remember that proponents of a "second," deeper strand of democratic theory and practice have been arguing and demonstrating with some success since the days of the American Revolution that it is a feasible and desirable complement to the "first," representative strand of democracy, which today's neoconservative "democratic realists" regard as "democracy enough" but long experience shows to be neither stable nor consistently democratic in the absence of ongoing, active citizen participation. In the view of a wide range of contemporary democratic theorists, the "second" or "republican" strand of democracy, to use Michael Sandel's term, for which these earlier generations of citizen-activists struggled, must be revived and expanded if we are to achieve what Benjamin Barber calls "strong" democracy—strong enough to predominate in shaping local and global futures while struggling simultaneously against both "Jihad" and "McWorld."[1] Unless we can more effectively interweave the influence of this "second strand" of democratic theory, institutions, and cultural practices within the operations of the now dominant representative strand, it may be impossible for "experienced" democracies to fulfill their potentials in the twenty-first century, as Robert Dahl in *On Democracy* has worried—or even to withstand the cultural stresses of globalization processes, as Richard Rorty in *Philosophy and Social Hope* feared. Fortunately, there is good evidence to suggest that cities can be important sites for strengthening this second strand of democratic theory and practice by expanding existing, hard-won opportunities for active, ongoing, real citizen participation:

- within government, including well-established processes of urban planning;
- within nongovernmental organizations that influence government, the civic sphere, and democratic culture, as well as humanitarian relief and environmental protection;
- within gatherings of scholars and other citizen-thinkers to inquire together, tell stories, reconcile conflicts, and seek guiding visions for our shared futures;
- within mass protests and reconstructive movements focused on peace, economic and social justice, democratic cultural inclusiveness, and environmental sustainability.[2]

In the twenty-first century, cities have become our world's centers of population and power, as well as centers of opportunities for citizen participation in shaping preferable global futures. In various American cities even before September 11, formally authorized and even mandated real participation by diverse citizens in ongoing processes of planning for interlinked aspects of local and regional futures had proved itself useful in overcoming barriers to effective cross-difference collaboration and mutual democratic empowerment. During those same years, nongovernmental organizations, community-based coalitions, and democratic change movements of both national and international scope had begun to stabilize their interconnections and to share their lessons from experience. Since September 11, this process has continued, supplemented by active citizen participation in issue-focused communicative events. For example, the felt importance of more deeply democratic opportunities for citizens to exert "real" influence in planning lower Manhattan's redevelopment prompted urban planning professionals to spend countless volunteer hours organizing all-day mass meetings at which thousands of citizens helped to identify civic functions and to influence the designs for buildings and a memorial to replace New York City's terrorist-destroyed World Trade Center—meetings that would never have been held had they not been so strongly demanded, making choices different from those that would have been made by elected representatives and business leaders if citizens had not expressed their thoughtful, information-contributing views.[3]

Moreover, the speed and scale with which widespread opposition to the Iraq War was brought to global attention at urban locations worldwide should evoke its own "shock and awe." While it did not prevent an American-led invasion, this massive show of strength may have succeeded in postponing it for several months. In addition, these protests galvanized major international powers to speak out against the use of war as a normal tool for twenty-first-century global transformation. Last but not least, participating in these antiwar protests was of great existential significance in waking millions of Americans from their post–September 11 grief and depression into activistic questing for an honorable and effective approach to democratic living in times of terrorism, civic repression, and an ascendant "neoconservative" global agenda for regaining American security and prosperity by means of overwhelming military force.

Many theorists from various disciplines have been documenting and detailing such recent urban experiences and the felt imperatives toward a deeper democracy they express, converging to support my social hypothesis in this chapter: direct citizen participation in shaping "the continuously planning *city*" may be the key to achieving Dewey's "continuously planning *society*" on local, national, and transnational levels. My existential hypothesis, which I will explain in greater detail in the final chapter of this book, is that active citizen participation can deepen the "personal democracy" John Dewey rightly argued we need, sustaining shared social hopes while guiding the development in each of us of the kinds of individual capabilities and collaborative lifeways that deepening democracy in global contexts will require. The four kinds of urban "schools" for effective, "second-strand" democratic participation I will discuss in this chapter can raise up organized, experienced, interconnected, democracy-minded "publics" to counter the forces of globalization and resentment that now threaten democracy's viability everywhere. With time, hard work, and the long-term personal commitments of millions of world citizens who have awakened, educated themselves, and interconnected through such urban "schools" of a deeper democracy, we can creatively transform these economic, political, and cultural forces into powerful engines for shaping preferable global futures.

Building on Dewey's theoretical legacy and his living example of political engagement, the following discussion will show that many contemporary democratic theorists working within a wide range of disciplines have contributed converging insights about the imperative importance of citizen participation in addressing twenty-first-century social problems in ways that fulfill the meaning of the democratic ideal. At the same time, there is good evidence, some of which I will outline here, that opportunities for "second-strand" democratic citizen participation have become increasingly available, both in America and elsewhere in the world, especially in our cities. My purpose in this chapter is to show *why* and *how* twenty-first-century world citizens can claim and expand existing opportunities for real and ongoing democratic participation within our double struggle—against powerful antidemocratic forces and for meaning in living in the wake of tragedy—by working together to achieve hope-sustaining influence in shaping our shared future.

Contemporary "Second-Strand" Imperatives for Democratic Citizen Participation

As the previous chapter showed in some detail, conservatives have opposed direct citizen participation on theoretical, legal, and political grounds since the founding of the American Republic, arguing that the "first," representative strand of democracy is sufficient and all that nations can accommodate in the real world. In the twenty-first century, these opponents have included the "democratic realists" of the Bush White House and their colleagues at the International Monetary Fund, who together have responded to and wielded daunting concentrations of political, economic, and military power. In spite of this, or perhaps in part because of this, the "second," participatory strand of democratic theory and practice is experiencing a revival of intellectual, popular, legislative, and institutional support, even in the World Bank, which in recent years made local citizen participation in shaping particular project-based loan proposals a condition for funding.[4]

This revival of intellectual support for democratic citizen participation is evident in many academic disciplines, including philosophy, sociology, political science, history, religious studies, public administration, and urban planning. It is reflected in activistic "civic republican," "democratic socialist," "civic renewal," and "communitarian" works by diverse thinkers.[5] It is manifest in a resurgence of interest in advancing the work of the classical American pragmatists—Charles Sanders Peirce, William James, Josiah Royce, John Dewey, Jane Addams, W. E. B. DuBois, George Herbert Mead, and Alain Locke—which has been expressed in books and essays by contemporary theorists from many disciplines.[6] It shows in critical theory's "pragmatist turn" toward an emphasis on an inclusive, democratic "discourse ethics" as a necessary element in well-grounded social critique and a basic model for effective processes of social transformation.[7] The importance of women's democratic participation in transforming their cultures, empowering their own voices, and influencing the resolution of the great problems of the twenty-first century has been stressed in recent works by feminist thinkers from a wide range of theoretical orientations.[8] A postinstitutional emphasis on "second-strand" democratic theory and practice characterizes the work of many influential contemporary political scientists, including Benjamin Barber's analysis of the conditions for "strong" democracy, Robert Dahl's diagnosis of the need for "deepening" experienced democracies, Archon Fong's emphasis on "empowering" citizen participation, and a growing body of work on "deliberative democracy" building on the convergent liberal theories of Jürgen Habermas and John Rawls.[9]

Many urban planning theorists also have come to believe that ordinary American citizens can and must play an active, participatory role in future-shaping if we are to transform urgent problems that face our cities and metropolitan regions today: urban sprawl, central-city decay and its associated poverty and crime, traffic gridlock, endangered air and water quality, disappearing open space, lack of attention to land-use aesthetics, national and global challenges to regional economic sustainability, and adverse interactions among all these factors that harm citizens' experienced quality of life. This imperative toward citizen participation has motivated the proponents of a "New Urbanism" to argue that the goal of urban and regional planning processes must be *to build communities*, not just to reenergize urban economies or to build more demand-driven but civilly disconnected tracts of suburban housing.[10] To this end, they have advocated various "neotraditional" aesthetic and functional changes in built urban environments that reflect citizen input and that encourage people to interact with their neighbors in ways that foster the sense of having shared stakes in their local community's future. Thus, the design hallmarks of this "New Urbanism" include tree-lined streets, sidewalks, picket fences, front porches, and "human-scale" downtowns that combine "mixed" land uses, such as stores, offices, art galleries, and restaurants, with housing above them. They call for locating such mixed downtowns as well as traditional housing blocks and factories in close proximity to community centers, parks, and open space. And they call for interconnecting all these areas of a community with bicycle and pedestrian paths and with readily accessible, environmentally friendly, attractively designed mass transit, in order to offer practical alternatives to the socially isolating and environmentally costly private automobile. For similar reasons, in hundreds of projects across the United States, proponents of "Sustainable Development" and "Smart Growth Initiatives" have advocated citizen participation in urban planning processes, "trying to take a long-term systems approach to community problems by addressing environmental, economic, and social issues in an integrated manner" (Lachman, *Linking Sustainable Community Activities to Pollution Prevention*).

Among these diverse, contemporary "second-strand" democratic theorists working in various disciplines, the rationales for reviving and expanding opportunities for citizen participation are largely complementary, yet their differences are so often emphasized that significant areas of convergence are obscured. Most communitarians and pragmatists agree in viewing citizen participation as a necessary and effective way to fulfill a widespread longing for experiences of community and for future-shaping influence among modern and postmodern urban peoples. They also agree in treating active democratic participation both as a means of developing the civic virtues and the mutual commitments necessary for democratic governance among socially interdependent individuals and also as a set of cross-difference transactional processes for mutual adjustment in outlooks, capacities, and relationships among unequal and historically antagonistic social groups through which diverse publics with shared aims and institution-transforming power can emerge. In turn, many communitarians and pragmatists broadly agree with those critical theorists who analyze democratic citizen participation in terms of prerequisites for and actual processes of mutually respectful yet critical and reconstructive communication through which new knowledge and ethical solutions to social and cultural problems can be discovered and shared. Members of all of these groupings agree with feminist theorists from various theoretical orientations who argue that democratic citizen participation must involve processes for admitting women and other marginalized groups into social processes of future-shaping, so that their gifts can develop in transactional employment and so that their experience-based wisdom about the needs of the poor, the disempowered, future generations, and the Earth can influence the goals and the values that guide democratic social collaboration. Finally, members of all of these groupings broadly concur with Barber's prophetic sense that democratic citizen participation is the only social response that has the potential to redirect the global forces of both "Jihad" and "McWorld" by channeling resistance to global capitalism's new forms of economic and cultural colonialism into collaborative struggles to create local and international conditions that foster diverse forms of human liberation. A theoretical coalition is warranted, and it is emerging. Its solidarity is not the kind of unity based on required sameness against which Judith Butler warned. Rather, it is based on shared deeply democratic values, shared practical concerns, and family resemblances among their theories that help them to appreciate each others' work, to learn from it, and to look to the communicative and transformative effectiveness of their differing approaches as the key criterion for improving and further developing their theories.

At the same time, the ethical, existential, and practical political imperatives that this emerging coalition of "second-strand" democratic theorists have variously expressed and validated as problem-focused guides to transformative action already are embodied to a great extent in the thought in action of increasingly visible, issue-focused coalitions of diverse, democracy-minded nongovernmental organizations, including churches, labor unions, environmental organizations, and student networks. Such participatory democratic organizations and coalitions employ a wide range of means to spread their convergent messages: face-to-face meetings, letter writing, telephone calls, e-mail lists, Web sites, newspaper advertisements, lobbying, lawsuits, and carefully orchestrated, coalition-based mass protest events. Their various calls for active citizen participation in local, national, and transnational efforts to deepen democracy converge on five critical claims:

(1) the future-shaping processes of the emerging global socioeconomic order are profoundly undemocratic, disempowering, and suppressive of a deep human impulse to seek influence in shaping the conditions of our own lives, in spite of the fact that this new global order's financial and regulatory institutions are created, supported, and directed by the world's most powerful, "experienced" democracies;

(2) the effects of this kind of globalization are profoundly damaging to the integrity, stability, and beauty of the Earth's biotic community;[11]

(3) its effects on the value depth and diversity of human cultures in their history-bearing, meaning-carrying, autonomy-shaping roles are devastating;

(4) it ignores and in some cases worsens the unequal condition of women worldwide;

(5) its injustice in widening local and international gaps between rich and poor, and in fostering conditions of working and living that violate basic human rights, is staggering.

Like participatory democratic theorists, these democracy-minded nongovernmental organizations and the issue-focused coalitions they have formed, including the individual citizen-activists who participate in their mass events, call for more responsive representation from elected officials. They also call for and exemplify the need and the hope for something more: direct participatory democratic roles for citizens in helping to shape global futures. Their convergent positive premise is that many citizens of the "experienced" constitutional democracies, as well as some citizens of less democratic societies, already have developed the expectations and readily can develop the requisite capacities for more active, effective participatory roles in democratic future-shaping institutions of various kinds at all geopolitical levels. Applying and expanding the insights of Jefferson, Dewey, and contemporary "second-strand" democratic theorists, these citizen-activists argue that direct and ongoing participation by "ordinary" citizens in future-oriented public decision making must complement the roles of elected representatives, if democracies are to fulfill their promise of meeting humanity's basic needs while also advancing three great social hopes: liberating diverse, humane individual potentials; supporting progressive transformations within semiautonomous cultures; and drawing upon widely dispersed, experience-based wisdom in partnership with the sciences to shape sustainable, responsible human communities within our global biotic community. Their opponents, and even some of their concerned friends, regard this convergent positive premise as unrealistic, arguing that in an era of transnational economic, political, cultural, and military power, it is either too soon or too late to guide global democratization by empowering and coordinating diverse human expectations and capacities through the processes and projects of participatory democracy.

If we are to resolve this controversy, which we must do for both practical and existential reasons, we must find the answer to three closely interrelated empirical questions: What opportunities for *real* citizen participation in shaping local and global futures—in contrast with *pseudoparticipatory* diversions of time and energy—currently exist in America and elsewhere?[12] What is their probable impact on developing citizens' democratic expectations and capacities? What is the actual ability of citizens to use such participatory democratic opportunities to influence the outcome of emergent issues that concern them? Answering these questions in ways that show the feasibility and the desirability of active citizen participation to deepen democracy in diverse global contexts will be the project of this and the following chapter. Let me begin here by focusing on our American experience, in earlier years and in recent times.

Deepening and Expanding America's Cultures of Democratic Participation

Alexis de Tocqueville noted with amazement in reflecting on his travels in America during the early 1830s that the new culture then emerging here from the transplanted root stocks of diverse older cultures took opportunities for active, ongoing, democratic citizen participation very seriously. A passion for democracy was reflected not only in widespread, persisting interest in national and state affairs but also in active, ongoing participation in social and political institutions and issues at local and regional levels. Through "formal" (elected or appointed) roles on city councils and school boards, and also through informal (volunteer) roles in meeting community needs in various reliable ways, these ancestor Americans throughout all of our new nation's regions expected to participate continuously and effectively in shaping a shared future, and actually did so with enthusiasm.[13]

This is our heritage as an American people—a distinctive heritage we can draw upon today that is very different from those of many peoples in other parts of the world, but also a heritage at odds with many of our contemporary cultural habits, especially as these are aided and abetted by influential ideological claims, uninviting institutional forms, and a major shift in the balance of practical powers that has emerged in the years after Tocqueville's visit. Since the early 1960s, Americans' shared heritage of direct democracy often has been an influential rhetorical resource for justifying the creation of a wide range of formal and informal opportunities for citizen participation in government and in other future-shaping processes and institutions. During the same period, however, dangerous habits of daily living have become increasingly widespread—constant busy-ness, fashionable cynicism, reliance on experts, willful ignorance of our nation's history and of current events, materialism, personal greed, and, especially since September 11, feelings of "ontological insecurity," generalized anxiety, and personal impotence. These shared bad habits have interacted in a caustic combination with the antiparticipatory rhetoric of "democratic realists," the seeming inaccessibility of bureaucratic governmental and cultural structures, and the twenty-first century's daunting concentrations of economic, legal, communicative, and political power to discourage many people from using both traditional and recently created opportunities for democratic citizen participation in America—if they even know these exist.[14]

Thus, our challenge in the twenty-first century is to renew and expand America's cultural habits of democratic participation at all levels—national, state, regional, and local—in ways that realistically take into account these various obstacles and work effectively to overcome them. We must guide these efforts with a two-sided goal: (1) to correct and balance otherwise unreliable aspects of representative democracy and (2) to provide existentially vital opportunities for individual growth, valuable experiences of community membership, and a shared, well-founded sense of collective efficacy. Our recent history shows that the process of deepening and expanding America's cultures of democratic participation works not by once-for-always legal fiat or by unidirectional influence (whether top down or grassroots up), but through ongoing, mutually influential transactions among all our levels of government and community living. Sometimes these work in close coordination with one another, and sometimes their proponents face off in pitted struggle, but both our complex democratic form of government and our complex democratic culture evolve through creative tensions among diverse opponents and diverse proponents of citizen participation activated by equally imperative but differing visions.[15]

Moreover, our recent history also shows that effective citizen participation of the kinds that have deep and lasting effects on our wider regional and national cultures does not occur because of individual choices and actions alone, though it does require *competent, energetic, democracy-minded individuals* who expect to exercise influence. It also requires *valued communities of struggle* that can stimulate and support such individual citizen-activists, working through *established participatory organizations* with their own shared visions and operative structures, and *formal or informal institutional ties with government*, or at least with other democratic participation-minded organizations working within *reliable, well-coordinated coalitions* that allow such organizations together to exert effective influence, whether of an occasional or of an ongoing nature. The process seems to work as follows: Valued communities of competent, energetic, participation-minded individuals found or revitalize democratic-change organizations and coalitions, and similar individuals who hold representative roles within democratic government and other cultural institutions reach out to or at least respond to them in order to form a network of cooperative ties. The participatory democratic organizations and coalitions these collaborating individuals create or revitalize reciprocally influence their own further individuation and growth in leadership capacities, while functioning as "schools of democracy" for the education of new citizen-activists and also as stabilizers of patterns of cooperative ties and coordinated influences that allow these coalitions to last long enough to have real and enduring effects within the wider culture.[16]

Through the efforts of such visionary citizen-activists, democracy-minded organizations, issue-oriented coalitions, and reliable collaborations with elected and appointed representatives, many formal and informal opportunities for direct citizen participation in American government at all levels have come into existence since the late 1960s. America's great mass movements of that era—the civil rights movement, the antiwar movement, the women's movement, and the environmental movement—energized and educated an enormous cadre of experienced citizen-activists who learned the hard way that the occasional, informal influence of unaffiliated citizen-activists tends to lack staying power in government and other future-shaping institutions, even though it profoundly affects the activists' individual lives and has some effect on their larger culture.[17] Many of those who have sustained their activist commitments over time have learned to value the influence-stabilizing, hope-sustaining function of continuing nongovernmental organizations and their movement-shaping coalitions, and also of "formal," elected or appointed insider roles in influencing government policies.[18]

Thus, in the late 1960s and early 1970s, in response to the federal government's decisions to disband programs that formalized ongoing roles for citizens in shaping and administering local government policies, such as the War on Poverty's Community Action Program, some of the wisest and most experienced of these citizen-activists began organizing to introduce issue-focused legislation at all levels—national, state, regional, and local—that would create active, ongoing roles for citizen participants in developing public policies in areas of focal concern. For example, working with friends in the U.S. Congress whom they had helped to elect, environmental activists successfully influenced the framing of the Clean Air Act and the Clean Water Act in the early 1970s to include a requirement of active, ongoing citizen participation in developing locality-specific regulations and in monitoring compliance. At the same time, working in partnership with state legislators, citizen-activists motivated by concern about fragile ecosystems in Hawaii, Vermont, and Florida succeeded in shaping this concern into a politically operative cultural value for the majority of their states' voters, leading to the adoption of the first statewide Growth Management Acts.[19] Environmental activists and their legislative partners in other states in the Northeast, the Midwest, and on the Pacific Coast rapidly followed these examples.

Thus, even during the 1980s, when President Ronald Reagan used his considerable executive authority and influence to defund and undercut the influence of citizen participation at the national level, cultures of participation persisted, resisted, and even grew at the state, regional, and local levels in many parts of America. Additional states adopted Growth Management Acts (GMAs) during the Reagan era, and many of those adopted during the 1970s were revised to mandate citizen participation more strongly in order to enhance their political viability, especially to remedy the significant difficulties some cities and regions had experienced in implementing their comprehensive plans due to a widespread sense that these were politically illegitimate because citizen stakeholders were not included throughout the planning process. All of the sedimentary layers of established planning law and practices within the various levels of government and within the topical areas of public policy (such as transportation, housing, economic development, and open space) were gathered together in revised Growth Management Acts. These required citizen participation in determining where urban growth would occur, who would approve it and on what basis, what kinds of infrastructure and social amenities must accompany it, and who would pay for them.

These widespread, state-level efforts were encouraged and given federal clout when the U.S. Congress passed the 1991 Intermodal Surface Transportation Efficiency Act (ISTEA), which required citizen participation in planning processes if states and localities were to receive federal funding for transportation system improvements. In one of American history's ironic reversals, ISTEA was chiefly authored by that devastating opponent of the War on Poverty's Citizen Action Programs, Senator Daniel Patrick Moynihan, at the urging of state and local governments, as well as that of the American Planning Association and various citizen groups concerned with enhancing alternative, nonautomobile transportation modes. While ISTEA focused on transportation, it interlinked many other strands of public policy in its requirement that states and localities must provide for citizen participation in developing comprehensive plans that considered related land uses, air and water quality impacts, and other quality-of-life issues. These requirements were carried forward in the 1999 reauthorizing legislation known as the Transportation Equity Act for the Twenty-First Century (often referred to as TEA-21).

Over the past thirty years, such state and federal mandates for real citizen participation have effectively stimulated the growth of expectations and capacities among a core group of citizen participants to whom these opportunities seemed important and attractive, helping to foster the emergence of participatory cultures in some American states and urban regions that contrast markedly with the political cultures of other states and regions in which more limited citizen roles or even "pseudoparticipation" remains the norm. For example, in Portland, Oregon, the process of comprehensive planning for growth management has gone smoothly, and a growth boundary within which urban resources will be focused was adopted early on. Based on Portland's successful model, over fifty major urban centers in America have adopted growth boundaries as part of their comprehensive plans.[20] Portland succeeded in this effort because a participatory urban culture fostered by strong neighborhood associations found a powerful partner at the state level, the Speaker of the Oregon House of Representatives, who represented a rural area and was himself a ranch owner and a social conservative. Together, they worked effectively to build consensus across the political spectrum about the importance of planning for growth management and of citizen participation in the ongoing planning process.

In contrast, the city of Seattle, Washington, fewer than two hundred miles to the north, found very different results in its efforts to involve citizens and other stakeholders in its neighborhood-based approach to GMA-mandated comprehensive planning in the mid-1990s. Only one of the city's neighborhoods, the traditionally Scandinavian Crown Hill–Ballard neighborhood, succeeded in completing its preliminary vision statement by consensus and within the allotted time frame. Under our collective banner as GreenWoods Associates, David Woods and I served as professional planning consultants to the Crown Hill–Ballard neighborhood for the visioning stage of Seattle's comprehensive planning process, and thus we are particularly familiar with this example. Working with a diverse group of citizens, some of whom had long histories in movement efforts and as neighborhood citizen-activists, we helped to bring together diverse stakeholders to educate one another and to consider problems, needs, and alternative possibilities for interlinked housing, transportation and land use, recreation and open space, economic development, arts and culture, and social-services elements of the neighborhood vision, as per federal, state, and city requirements. Like Portland's neighborhood associations, the Ballard Neighborhood Association had already developed a high level of cooperative social capital and individual citizen leadership capacities through earlier projects and coalition efforts even before the comprehensive planning process began. On the basis of their experience with one another as a community of activists working within and through established organizations, Ballard-based members of the steering committee were able to work effectively with residents of adjoining Crown Hill to involve over seven hundred neighbors in the visioning process, work through their disagreements, and adopt a comprehensive vision by consensus. In contrast, all of the other Seattle neighborhoods, many of which had minimally functional neighborhood associations and unreconciled factional differences, failed to complete the visioning process as originally designed. This happened in part because, even though the state had approved a Growth Management Act, some deep, partisan divisions in the Washington State legislature about the desirability of citizen participation-based comprehensive planning processes sent a signal to Seattle-based opponents that a failure in citizen participation there would be desirable and might contribute to ending the state requirement.

There are now many formal, periodic opportunities for real citizen participation in comprehensive planning processes within American cities and their surrounding metropolitan regions through which citizens can make an important difference in shaping their local and regional futures, especially when the state and local cultural preconditions are supportive. There are also many permanent participatory roles for citizens within local governments on planning and zoning boards that approve more limited development plans and variances and on civic boards concerned with the arts, historic preservation, parks and recreation, and regional transportation. In addition, citizens can take up traditional formal opportunities to serve as elected representatives on city councils, school boards, water district boards, metropolitan planning organizations, and so on.

All of these formal opportunities for real citizen participation can help urban dwellers to grow in their knowledge, skills, and democratic capacities, to expand their networks of social capital, and thus to sustain and give realistic focuses to their hopes for future-forging influence. Equally important, and closely connected, are real though informal opportunities for citizen participation in the kinds of nongovernmental, voluntary organizations that have, since the days of Tocqueville's visit, influenced the future as well as the daily operation of American society: churches, labor unions, student groups, community service and civic improvement associations, and various issue-focused organizations that devote their energies to protecting nature and promoting social justice. Most visible of all in recent years, especially in times of crisis, cities have been sites for more limited but nonetheless real opportunities to participate in social movements and in value-expressive events that have been organized and supported by coalitions of democracy-minded nongovernmental organizations and sometimes by government officials. These continue to be starting places for raising citizens' expectations, for building their democratic capacities, and for giving them a voice in local, national, and global futures.

The questions we must ask next are: Who is taking up such opportunities for citizen participation in American cities today, how representative of our nation's diversity are their voices, and what kinds of influence are they actually having? How can we create new forms of "second-strand" democratic participation and expand its influence on the "first," representative strand? As Robert Westbrook rightly argued in *John Dewey and American Democracy*, we need much more empirical research and many more "best-practices" analyses to answer these crucial questions. However, some highly suggestive studies have already begun to show that *real* participatory opportunities for shaping urban and regional futures now exist and that these have great potential significance. Such studies are important both practically and existentially. They offer us crucial evidence about the conditions of feasibility for more widespread institutionalization of direct citizen participation in governance, in America and elsewhere. At the same time, they contribute a criterion for individual life decisions about whether we should invest our time and our hopes in committed, long-term efforts to expand and actively employ such potential avenues to more deeply democratic living within what Dewey called "democratic planning societies" of the future.[21]

Some Urban Experiments: Institutionalizing Direct Citizen Participation in Government

In one of the largest and most insightful American "best-practices" studies, *The Rebirth of Urban Democracy*, Jeffrey M. Berry, Kent E. Portney, and Ken Thomson presented empirical evidence with important prescriptive implications to show that contextually well-designed, neighborhood-based citizen participation in American city governance can "achieve the theoretical goals of democracy," including "the conditions necessary to develop, support, and sustain citywide systems of public participation" (v). One of the important features of their research model is their refusal to draw a strict boundary between representation and direct citizen participation, which they treat as complementary and interactive elements of democracy, in contrast with many opponents and proponents of more active participatory roles: "Participatory democracy is offered by theorists as an alternative to representative democracy; in the real world, institutions for strong democracy must be integrated into a system that also includes institutions of representative democracy" (293). Another important feature is their decision to focus on citizen participation at the level of the neighborhood as the common denominator among urban localities of all sizes, because neighborhoods offer opportunities for the kinds of face-to-face experiences that others have treated as necessary for the kinds of collaborative interactions that can transform individuals and influence issues (10). Much of the earlier urban politics literature had dismissed neighborhood associations and other citizen groups as "ineffective." However, these three authors were motivated to undertake their study by two well-established conclusions in other social science disciplines' empirical literature: (1) a sense of shared group identity leads people away from narrowly self-interested behavior toward concern for shared group benefits that may trump the desire to have one's own preference chosen, and (2) cooperative behavior is strongly influenced by frequent contact and opportunities for discussion (10–11, 289). On the basis of these well-established "truths," they framed their research hypothesis that citizen participation at the neighborhood level could be transformatively effective *in the right conditions*.

Drawing on this body of interdisciplinary empirical evidence while realistically limiting their own claims, the authors argued that neighborhood-based participatory government within a decentralized city structure represents "a sensible compromise" between the requirements of participatory democracy and "the realistic needs of efficiency and scale for some services" (12). The authors selected five American cities for detailed study—Birmingham (Alabama), Dayton (Ohio), Portland (Oregon), Saint Paul (Minnesota), and San Antonio (Texas)—because they have made this sensible compromise, creating differing but context-appropriate participatory democratic neighborhood systems that manifest at least limited forms of the benefits its proponents expected and none of the dangers its opponents feared.[22]

In contrast to the critics' predictions, these strong participation systems have not functioned at the expense of governability. They do not produce policy gridlock or increased political conflict. The systems do not seem to introduce racial or economic biases into the policymaking process. There is no evidence that the city-supported neighborhood associations at the core of the systems in four of the five cities are less effective in translating citizen demands into governmental action than are independent citizen groups. Instead of chaos, there is a degree of empowerment. Participation in these systems tends to increase confidence in government and sense of community. Within a certain range of issues—particularly land use and planning issues—neighborhoods generate city policy. High levels of face-to-face participation are linked to increased responsiveness by City Hall.

(14)

Berry, Portney, and Thomson's research was organized around three empirical questions, as well as a fourth prescriptive one: (1) whether rank-and-file citizen participation is practically possible; (2) whether local government responds significantly and equitably in policy matters to the neighborhood associations in these cities, and whether their influence is narrowly parochial rather than contributive to larger community interests; (3) whether participation in these neighborhood associations increases citizens' capacity to take part in cooperative decision making amid major social differences, builds a sense of community, and increases confidence in government or leads to increased conflict; and (4) whether these exemplars suggest "practical steps that can be taken to increase political participation in urban America" (16–17).

The authors concluded that the answer to all four of these questions is a qualified affirmative: "When one forgoes a utopian vision of [ideal participatory democratic] political systems, the five cities are remarkably vibrant examples of structures of strong democracy. . . . The neighborhood associations fail in some respects but are very effective in others. Overall, though, they are positive forces that enrich and improve city politics" (283–284).

Amplifying their qualified affirmative as it relates to *participation*, the authors note that though other citizens in the five exemplary cities clearly respect the neighborhood associations, the data *do not* show that their neighborhood structures increase the number of political participants relative to those in ten comparison cities: "The structures of strong democracy do not bring people out of the woodwork" (284). Nonetheless, they conclude, the neighborhood systems in four of the five cities clearly *do* facilitate direct involvement in government for large numbers of urban people: 16.6 percent of these cities' populations participate in the neighborhood associations, which is a substantial proportion of those who participate in politics in any way. Though the authors could not explain why a wider than expected cross-section of citizens choose to participate at the neighborhood level in these five cities, they note that *local political cultures* seem to play an important role in involving citizens from all socioeconomic backgrounds.

> This finding deserves some elaboration, for the data demonstrate that the relationship between participatory structure and actual participation is a complicated one. Although the focus has been on the five core cities, the entire data set was built on interviews done in fifteen cities. The overall levels of participation in these fifteen cities do not conform to the standard model in which socioeconomic status [SES] is a reliable predictor of participation. The range of participation in these fifteen cities is substantial, and citywide measures of SES do not explain the rankings, independent of their socioeconomic standing and their structures for participation that takes place. *Each city seems to have its own political culture that nurtures participation.* Just how tradition, norms, and expectations mix with structural opportunities to facilitate or inhibit participation is not well understood by political scientists.
>
> (284–285, emphasis added)

Thus, contrary to common criticisms in the political science literature, the authors' findings do *not* show that neighborhood associations tend to worsen America's political class bias. Active participants in the neighborhood associations in the five cities include low-income citizens, though their numbers are smaller than those of middle- and high-income citizens (285). Moreover, the data show that other citizens of low-income neighborhoods in the five cities respect their neighbors who *do* participate actively in their neighborhood associations and regard them as accurately representing their neighborhood's views (293).

The three authors insightfully argue that it is unrealistic to expect that there will be no representative element within direct citizen participation, especially given the practical obstacles that face many poor people who work at more than one poorly paid job and have limited transportation choices, little free time, and little or no help with child care. In addition, "the daily burdens of low-income people are powerful forces that may work to make them feel inadequate, apathetic, or alienated; such attitudes are not easily ameliorated by easier opportunities to become involved in politics" (285). Moreover, many people of all socioeconomic backgrounds may choose not to participate actively in local self-governance, either because they are intimidated about speaking in political meetings or because they prefer to spend their very limited "free time" on other activities. Given these real-life constraints on time and hope, as well as the various competing alternatives for their investment, the level of direct citizen participation in neighborhood associations the authors found in the five exemplary cities must be regarded as highly significant, especially in light of their finding that many nonparticipant citizens regard actively participating neighbors as reliable representatives.

Commenting on the *responsiveness* of these five central city governments to their neighborhood associations, the authors note that the neighborhood associations have more influence over matters of direct concern to them than they do over citywide issues, perhaps in part because they are not federated in any effective manner. Nonetheless, the authors add, city administrators tend to work hard to get along with neighborhood associations, perhaps because the perception of conflict can be damaging to their careers. Businesses, too, while exercising considerable influence in city governance in these five cities, have accommodated themselves to neighborhood control over zoning. Thus, "the result of neighborhoods' empowerment is not increased conflict but a smoothly functioning policymaking system in which there is *decreased* conflict" (289). On all the measures of responsiveness, the neighborhood associations scored highly as effective advocates, even for low-income communities: "low-income neighborhoods have fared well under the citizen participation systems in the core study cities. The citywide systems go a long way toward getting equal access to government for all neighborhoods" (293).

Commenting on the impact of the neighborhood associations on *citizen empowerment*, Berry, Portney, and Thomson note that "participation per se is a stronger force than participation in the neighborhood associations, but the neighborhood associations contribute to the development of some empowering attitudes as well," especially the sense of community, which shows a strong, positive association with level of participation (290). In addition, their participation clearly enhances citizens' sense of "*external efficacy*" (the belief that the political system will respond to citizens), though not their sense of "*internal efficacy*" (the belief that they personally can influence the political process). However, increasing knowledge about local government and neighborhood associations is positively related to increasing levels of effective citizen activity: "Community participants learn how to get things accomplished. . . . The concentration of political activism on the neighborhood level works to empower the whole neighborhood and not just the activists who go to the meetings" (293). Directly addressing the ongoing theoretical dispute about the desirability of direct citizen participation in democratic government, the authors found *no support* for the central claims of the Trilateral Commission's Huntington Report: that citizen participation is destabilizing to society, leads to the alienation of participants, tends to make them more intolerant, and threatens democracy itself. "We find no support whatsoever for these charges. The survey results disproved each of the anti-participation hypotheses examined" (291).

Berry, Portney, and Thomson conclude that, if we adopt a realistic conception of the nature of direct citizen participation in local government, one that includes a representative aspect, these five American cities offer good examples of effective structures of formal citizen participation, contextually tailored to each city's geographical location, demographic composition, political traditions, and local culture (292). In claiming that their five exemplars offer lessons for others, the authors do not mean to suggest that the citizen participation structures and practices in these five cities have achieved a final stage in their own development. They point out that many citizens of these cities have criticisms of the present structures, that many others choose not to participate, that participation is uneven across socioeconomic levels, and that many citizens are not aware of their opportunities to participate while still tending to be skeptical about their ability to influence government. Thus, "even the five cities are still far from achieving the ideals of strong democracy" (14).

Nonetheless, Berry, Portney, and Thomson argue that these five American cities suggest three important conditions that citizen participation programs must meet: (1) "exclusive powers [e.g., concerning zoning] must be turned over to the citizen participation structures . . . they must have authority to allocate some significant goods and services in their communities . . . [and] what neighborhood associations do must be integrated into the existing administrative structure of the city," (2) "accompanying such structural changes must be an administrative plan that creates sanctions and rewards for city hall administrators who must interact with the neighborhood groups," and

(3) "citizen participation systems must be citywide in nature" so that *each* community has "a single, officially recognized neighborhood association that represents an area with well-defined boundaries," instead of explicitly structuring such efforts as "programs to help low-income or minority neighborhoods," which tend to provoke backlash while failing to create the conditions for positive cross-difference cooperation. Absent these three important conditions, the authors warn, "cities should not attempt to create citizen participation programs" (295–296).

Among cities that have attempted to institute more limited forms of citizen participation or even pseudoparticipation in government, failures have been frequent and their cost has been high, tending to alienate people and to undermine respect for incumbent administrations: "More often than not, citizen participation has earned little more than empty rhetoric or lame efforts, such as the open office hours New York Mayor David Dinkins held for one day. Twenty-two hundred people showed up to tell him how to improve city government, and fifty-four were permitted brief audiences with the mayor" (294).

Creating Linkages: Government Partnerships with Nongovernmental Organizations

San Antonio is different from the four other American cities that Berry, Portney, and Thomson analyzed as models of effective citizen participation because it does *not* provide for official, citywide structures of neighborhood involvement in urban governance. Nonetheless, it is exemplary because an effective citizens' association representing poor, predominantly Hispanic neighborhoods—Communities Organized for Public Service (COPS)—has succeeded over the past twenty-five years in becoming a respected player in shaping local and regional politics, thereby overcoming to some extent a long-term and continuing bias in favor of more affluent, better-educated Anglo neighborhoods.[23] COPS is the oldest, largest, and most influential member organization of the Industrial Areas Foundation (IAF), an umbrella organization reflecting a more cooperation-focused transformation of Saul Alinsky's conflict-harvesting community organizing practices in the 1940s, 1950s, and 1960s.[24] Growing out of the Industrial Areas Foundation Training Center that Alinsky and associates founded in 1969, IAF shapes its general principles and its situation-specific strategies by creatively illuminating a tension between "the world as it is" and "the world as it should be" (Boyte, *Common Wealth*, 82). San Antonio's COPS is organized along "parish" lines and, like other IAF member organizations, works to build relationships between its "community-sustaining" member organizations—typically churches, labor unions, worker cooperatives, and universities—and those decision makers in government, business, and benevolent foundations who are in a position to help them fulfill their felt democratic imperatives to create more equal economic, educational, and civic opportunities. Like those of other IAF organizations, the strategies COPS developed include information, negotiation, and public "actions" that bring large numbers of the members of their community-sustaining organizations together in creative, nonviolent ways that attract media attention for the purpose of stimulating public interest and support that can, in turn, be used to influence potentially helpful decision makers. As sociologist William Julius Wilson has argued, the success of COPS in influencing public policy, not only in San Antonio but also in the Texas legislature through its partnership with ten other local IAF organizations statewide, offers a powerful example of what community-based organizations grounded in shared values that can bridge their differences in race and class can contribute toward solving shared problems and creating "affirmative opportunities."[25] It is important to note that neither Wilson nor Mark Warren nor Harry Boyte has found that differences among culturally and linguistically diverse COPS members carry with them a "values gap" that makes them unable to understand one another and to work for shared goals, as Samuel Huntington and others have led us to expect. How they reference and employ their values may differ initially, which explains the importance of IAF's evolved conversation-framing process in helping COPS members get to know each other well enough to set shared goals, to strategize with regard to differing strengths and obstacles, and to work effectively together to achieve the goals they set.

The Industrial Areas Foundation now includes more than forty member organizations in urban American locations, including Seattle's King County Organizing Project (KCOP), of which David Woods and I were active participant-leaders in the mid-1990s. We represented two of the local community-sustaining organizations, Seattle University and Saint Therese Catholic Church, both of which later sent citizen-activists to the 1999 demonstrations against the World Trade Association during its meetings there. Beginning in the mid-1990s, KCOP sought to emulate the successful COPS strategies through a cooperation-based CHANGE campaign ("Communities Helping to Achieve a New Generation of Equity"). This effort brought together KCOP member organizations, which also included labor unions and worker cooperatives working in coalition with government leaders, neighborhood centers, major area employers, and educational institutions, to collaborate on job creation, prospective worker identification, and effective worker preparation through education, child-care provision, expectation setting, and job-related practical skill building.[26] Thus, KCOP was an example of effective university-community partnership—a form of transformative democratic collaboration that links citizens with the resources of universities and other nongovernmental organizations, thereby enhancing their public policy–shaping effectiveness while helping to "democratize the universities," enhance the impact of nongovernmental organizations, and create "schools of democracy" for citizen participants.[27]

As Berry, Portney, and Thomson's neighborhood associations study and these examples of IAF collaborations show, both intragovernmental and nongovernmental opportunities for real citizen participation in shaping local, regional, state, and national futures already exist in America and already have begun to prove their effectiveness. Moreover, some of these locations of opportunity are already interlinked. For example, national federations of regional government organizations for most of America's major urban areas offer underutilized opportunities to share information and to foster cooperation among state-mandated regional planning organizations. Among the other responsibilities these regional government organizations have gained since the early 1970s, they typically house the Metropolitan Planning Organizations (MPOs), which have citizen-participation requirements that states must establish in order to qualify for transportation funds from our federal government. The value of further cross-location linkages that would allow democratic citizen participants to share transformative experiences and to multiply their influence is clear. If neighborhood associations and other community-based democratic transformation organizations became federated within cities, regions, states, and across the country, as are the IAF member organizations, citizen groups could learn more easily from one another's experiences and could collaborate on matters of common concern. This same model of federating citizen participation organizations could be expanded to the international level, helping to stabilize democracy-minded citizens' aspirational and organizational ties while expanding already existing processes of cross-context communication and collaboration.

Other Sites for Direct Citizen Participation: Courts, Campuses, Movements, Colloquies

The courts provide another kind of location for individual citizens, nongovernmental organizations, coalitions, and movements (as well as corporate interests) to directly influence local, state, national, and global futures. In a litigious society in which "anybody can stop anything," in Daniel Kemmis's phrase, the courts provide a last-chance opportunity for citizens to participate in future shaping. Yet they also show the limits of the standard institutions of representative democracy, when these are divorced from a culture of ongoing, real participation by diverse stakeholders who have developed the virtues, cooperative practices, and mutual stakes of deep democracy.[28] For example, during the Clinton administration and later during the Bush administration, the U.S. Fish and Wildlife Service complained that it received so many citizen requests to classify various plants and animals on the endangered species list, which would trigger special legal processes and requirements for their protection, that it could not respond to all of them. In addition, the Fish and Wildlife Service was legally required to respond to lawsuits from environmentalists and countersuits from logging and mining corporations as well as local interests that seem hopelessly irresolvable. In a disingenuous and legally questionable attempt to unblock or to end this process of citizen participation through adversarial litigation, the Bush administration included a provision in its 2001 budget proposal that would relieve the U.S. Fish and Wildlife Service from its obligation to receive such petitions and to respond to new lawsuits for one year—a provision that could be indefinitely renewed if it were once adopted and allowed by the U.S. Supreme Court to stand.[29] Clearly, legal avenues to challenge public uses of power and to demand the institution of new public regulations on private action must be available to citizens in a democracy. However, if these are the only avenues that seem likely to allow individuals' and groups' voices to be heard in future shaping, the attempt to use them in this way is likely to become self-defeating. At the same time, it can foster misuse of executive power, distort the legislative process, and fail to solve the underlying cultural problem. For example, during the Bush presidency, American conservatives successfully changed their site of long-time cultural struggle against abortion, same-sex marriage, affirmative action, and environmental protection to the selection process for justices of the U.S. Supreme Court, who hold lifetime appointments. In the first year of the Roberts court, majority decisions repealed key elements of earlier landmark precedents in *Brown v. Board of Education of Topeka* (1954 and 1955), undoing the sacrificial work of countless civil rights activists who demonstrated at great personal risk that "equal protection of the laws" requires telling the truth about our history, as well as substantive efforts toward reconciliation across the lines of harm, including cooperative creation of new opportunities for education, employment, and inclusion in the future-making process for descendants of those whom our nation greatly wronged who would otherwise continue to bear history's heavy burdens. This decision shows that the necessary interpretive role of the courts must be checked and balanced, not only by the other institutions of the representative strand of democracy but also by the second strand of citizen participation, and with the democratic education and empowerment of citizens to play such roles.

Frustration, in America and elsewhere, with the ideological hollowness, subvertibility, and unresponsiveness of our "first-strand" representative institutions to the more deeply democratic concerns and values of many ordinary citizens has led to the revival of student-led organizations and movements on many of our college and university campuses, making them schools and sites for "second-strand" citizen participation. In the United States, student organizations are using e-mail, Web sites, workshops, and mass rallies to build coalitions that link the local with the global in their demands. These include ending the continuing role of "The School of the Americas" at Fort Benning, Georgia, in training Latin American police and military leaders to use high-tech weapons and high-force techniques to control citizen opposition; ending sweatshop labor conditions that their university bookstores support when they buy clothing from firms that employ them; ending "prisons for profit" that their universities support when they choose campus cafeteria food purveyors who benefit from prison labor and service contracts; and just compensation for janitorial and food service workers on campus. An important challenge that these revitalized, democracy-minded student groups now face is to find ways to involve a wider student constituency while working in close partnership with those they seek to support. Both kinds of connections are important, not only to improve their chances of achieving their immediate goals but also to educate themselves and their fellows in the knowledge, skills, and capacities of active citizenship through participating together in the democratic transformation process. As an e-mail essay that was widely circulated among progressive student organizations at many American colleges and universities queried, "How can we reach and involve more people so we don't become widely separated in our thinking and our change efforts from the rest of our community, like progressive groups in the past?"

The potential transformative influence of student groups and movements working in coalition with other nongovernmental organizations and their elected representatives was demonstrated at the level of history-changing significance in Yugoslavia in early October 2000, where Otpor ("Resistance") surprised the world when their nonpartisan efforts to build a student protest movement focused on the shared value of freedom of speech evoked such a widespread response from participation-hungry ordinary citizens that it became the basis for an eventually successful but breathtakingly risky democratic revolution. Otpor's core constituency was students and other young people who felt weighed down by the Milosevic regime's limits on self-expression, cross-cultural communicative experience through the arts and the mass media, job opportunities, and democratic self-governance (Erlanger, "From a Summons to a Slap"). However, because Otpor focused on change rather than partisan advantage and offered resistance-based hope as a heady alternative to the despair that had become a deeply embedded element of Serbian culture, it was able to function as a gathering place for a coalition that also included opposition political parties, labor unions, democracy-minded elected officials from towns and villages all over the country, and many other citizens whose lives had been touched by the violence that maintaining such repression required.

Founded in Belgrade in October 1998 by a handful of student survivors of unsuccessful protests in 1996, Otpor chose a clenched fist (black on white or white on black) as its symbol for T-shirts, posters, and graffiti. As Roger Cohen ("Who Really Brought Down Milosevic?") analyzed their transformative approach, which eventually was effective, wrote:

> Otpor's founding principles were straightforward, refined by the failure of earlier agitation: remove Milosevic because otherwise nothing will change; spread resistance to the provinces; galvanize a cowed population by providing examples of individual bravery; be hip, funny where possible, in order to create a contemporary message; avoid a hierarchy because the regime will co-opt any leader.

"The idea was, cut off one Otpor head, and another fifteen heads would instantly appear."

Disciplined nonviolent resistance to President Milosevic's authority, even when enduring police beatings, was a crucial part of their strategy, as was seeking to win over the police and the military, who were called on to enforce orders to repress dissent violently. Encouragement and training in these strategies came from American sources, as did funding for T-shirts and spray paint, but the courage to face very real violence, and the communicative effectiveness to convince others to do likewise, was all their own.

Mass protest events like those organized by Yugoslavia's Otpor, by the justice-focused movement interlinking students at many U.S. colleges and universities, and by the worldwide movement in opposition to the preemptive war on Iraq can be very effective social instruments for expressing a clear, single-note critique. They also offer citizens a starting place for developing expectations and skills for more extensive democratic participation. However, they are not very useful as sites for developing a positive, alternative vision that draws upon citizens' more deeply democratic experiences and values.

For this kind of citizen participation in reconstructive social visioning, story-telling gatherings and issue-specific public colloquies that bring scholars and other citizen-thinkers together can be highly effective. This is the kind of series of gatherings to tell our "American Dreams" I called for at the end of chapter 2. These are the kinds of gatherings that already have become a part of urban planning in America, especially in long-range and comprehensive planning. This is the nature of the "town hall meetings" that were sponsored by Manhattan's Civic Alliance through its post-9/11 "Listening to the City" program, which involved thousands of citizens in planning for redevelopment of New York City's lower Manhattan neighborhoods, especially at the site where the World Trade Center once soared. Because of their issue-focused character and their high tech–assisted, on-site aggregations of participants' local knowledge and judgments about the desirability of alternative future plans, such public conversations have offered opportunities for participants to develop democratic skills and capacities for wider and even more effective public future-shaping involvements. At the same time, each event has been existentially important for participants, offering them opportunities to share their stories within constructive channels for their grief and anger and providing some small sense of shared control within a nightmare world that suddenly and horribly emerged as out of control.[30] In fact, the "Listening to the City" gatherings that were called together to find a reconstructive response to the events of that terrible day may represent a pioneering effort to combine the mass presence of a protest event with the face-to-face experience and opportunity to be heard individually of a town hall meeting.

The "Civic Alliance" of four major community organizations that sponsored the "Listening to the City" mass meetings and many other related events came together shortly after 9/11 to begin to plan a response that would give citizens democratic opportunities to be heard. Beginning in February 2002, just five months after the September 11 attacks, the Civic Alliance, with a large presence of architects and urban planners who volunteered to serve as small group facilitators, began to organize and publicize these mass events for civic participation in determining what values and visual images should guide the replacement of the World Trade Center and the design of a memorial to all those who were lost with them. Hundreds of participants turned out for the first of these meetings, and thousands more for those that followed.

From the beginning, however, these ordinary citizens from all walks of life and a wide range of ethnic, racial, religious, and generational backgrounds were locked in a struggle with their elected officials over their right to participate in such a public process. The governor of New York State, the mayor of the City of New York, appointed representatives of the Port Authority of New York and New Jersey, the Lower Manhattan Redevelopment Corporation, and various other national, state, and local officials asserted their legal entitlement to make all decisions concerning the site. Many of these elected and appointed officials expressed their determination to make these decisions on the basis of "expert" advice while paying attention primarily to what they regarded as the undisturbed property rights of the World Trade Center's primary leaseholder. Of course, they were also aware that their personal political hopes and ideological commitments would be on national display in the rebuilding process. These elected and appointed officials chose a firm of architects to develop six "concept designs" to guide their deliberations, which went on simultaneously with, but independent of, the public process.

Nonetheless, on July 20, 2002, responding to extensive public outcry as well as pressure from the planning and architecture community and the *New York Times*, these officials acceded to the proposal to hold a "Listening to the City" event at which public comments on their six "concept designs" would be elicited. Nearly five hundred professional facilitators, including representatives from all fifty American states and many other countries, arrived a day early for training, and on July 20, they welcomed five thousand citizen participants to carefully organized roundtable conversations whose results were electronically collected, rapidly analyzed with computer assistance, and displayed on large screens at intervals throughout the day. Some participants at the tables had lost family members on September 11. Others included survivors and eyewitnesses, people from the surrounding neighborhoods, and people from other parts of the city and the region who felt directly affected and concerned about the matters under discussion. All felt that they had been heard that day—and in their collective voice, they rejected all six "concept designs" and the "official" process by which these designs came into being so unanimously that the designs were withdrawn and the process transformed into one in which public comment became a legitimate, necessary, and influential element. This process eventually led to broad agreement on an inspiring new design for the World Trade Center site, with somewhat different functional components than those that the elected and appointed officials originally had regarded as basic and nonnegotiable. Regrettably, the soaring beauty of this concept design was weighed down by the leaseholding developer's own architect, aided by the New York City Police Department's advisor, who insisted on extensive use of reinforced concrete around the building's entrance to give it bunkerlike security from future attacks. Most of the spaces planned for the arts and for museums were removed because of fear of controversy. The power struggle was renewed during the memorial design process, which eventually was handed over to "experts."

How much of the citizen participants' contribution will characterize the buildings and the memorial that eventually will replace the World Trade Center remains to be seen. It is clear that more is at stake for both sides of this struggle than the design itself. The key factor in determining the outcome of this struggle seems likely to be the staying power of large numbers of those who thus far have expressed a deep commitment to the public participation process but whose patience has been sorely tested by delay and rejection. Moreover, their focus has been distracted by an adverse economy and the Iraq War, which was passionately rejected in advance by a large percentage of New Yorkers.

Nonetheless, these experiences show that, like "formal" sites of "second-strand" citizen participation within government, all of these "informal" sites—the courts, nongovernmental organizations, democratic mass movements, and issue-focused gatherings of scholars and other citizen-thinkers—can play valuable roles in shaping local and global futures, and they can become even more effective if they are consciously and creatively interwoven. I do not offer these particular examples as universal models for effecting democratic institutional and cultural change in all other countries or even in all of the regions of the United States. Thomas Jefferson wrote: "Every people have their own particular habits, ways of thinking, manners, etc., which have grown up with them from their infancy, are become a part of their nature, and to which the regulations which are to make them happy must be accommodated. . . . The excellence of every government is its adaptation to the state of those to be governed by it" (quoted in Dewey, "Introducing Thomas Jefferson," 215). However, contextually differing yet interrelated examples can be found in every part of the world, offering the beginnings of a global general "fund" of city-focused experience of citizen participation in processes of deepening democracy. Drawing on such experiences, citizens of various nations are learning from the "best practices" of citizens of other nations.[31]

Through the process of participating in such "urban schools" of second-strand, Jeffersonian democracy while working to achieve what Dewey called "continuously planning societies," citizen-thinkers are educating themselves in skills, knowledge, habits, and lifeways for deepening democracy in diverse global contexts. In the process, they may profoundly influence our future—though we can have no advance certainty that their efforts will be effective and no way to know what their benefits and costs to the individuals in question may be. Thus, the question remains: is "second-strand" democratic participation a wise choice for individual citizens in diverse global contexts, especially in places where it may involve great risks? This is the question for this book's final chapter.

Chapter 7

The Hope of Democratic Living
Choosing Active Citizen Participation for Preferable Global Futures

---

In truths dependent on our personal actions, then, faith based
on desire is certainly a lawful and possibly an indispensable
thing.

—William James, "The Will to Believe"

Democracy as a personal, an individual, way of life involves
nothing fundamentally new. But when applied it puts a new
practical meaning in old ideas. Put into effect it signifies that
powerful present enemies of democracy can be successfully
met only by the creation of personal attitudes in individual
human beings; that we must get over our tendency to think
that its defense can be found in any external means whatever, whether military or civil, if they are separated from
individual attitudes so deep-seated as to constitute personal
character . . .

—John Dewey, "Creative Democracy—The Task Before Us"

What matters is to make the best of any given situation.
"The best," however, is that which in Latin is called *opti-
mum*—hence the reason I speak of a tragic optimism, that
is, an optimism in the face of tragedy and in view of the human potential which at its best always allows for: (1) turning
suffering into a human achievement and accomplishment;
(2) deriving from guilt the opportunity to change oneself
for the better; and (3) deriving from life's transitoriness an
incentive to take responsible action.

—Viktor Frankl, "The Case for a Tragic Optimism"

Living with Hope, Faith, and Tragic Meliorism in the
Twenty-first Century

In these early years of the twenty-first century, the names of cities—Seattle, Washington, Lima, Prague, Belgrade, Quebec, Genoa, New York City, London, Paris, Berlin, Jerusalem, Beijing, Baghdad—have come to signify fears, tragedies, and a hopeful but still fragile rebirth of democratic citizen participation in shaping preferable global futures. The great practical and existential questions democratic theorists and democracy-minded citizens worldwide face now focus on how to frame their continuing hopes and life choices in the wake of the great and terrible events these city names evoke. Can democratic citizen participation effectively influence the course of future events on a global scale? Are there any sites of official citizen powers to participate directly and continuously in determining public policy? Can existing participatory democratic opportunities and processes fully develop the democratic future-vision and the practical capacities that citizen-activists will need in order to raise up, inform, and lead broader democratic "publics" that can resist and correct the overwhelming influence of cultural and economic elites, multinational corporations, and "democratic realists" on experienced constitutional democracies and the world's many nondemocratic regimes? If not, how shall we live: are there "postdemocratic" stories that can help us to frame lives that are interesting, or at least tolerable, in the absence of any meaningful influence as citizens in the shaping of world futures—or must we organize ourselves into supportive but ultimately futile cells of nostalgic democratic defiance as a therapeutic alternative to depression and despair?

Reflecting on William James's insight that the truths we most need to know sometimes cannot be warranted in advance of taking an active hypothetical belief stance concerning them, and on John Dewey's hope for a worldwide rebirth of faith in democratic living, and on Viktor Frankl's Holocaust-born insights about how to live a meaningful, even joyful life during tragic times, I advance here a threefold, "tragically melioristic" thesis. First, recent events show that there is at least a possibility that active citizen participation in efforts to deepen democracy can influence global affairs, perhaps because many citizens' recent determinations to take up wider responsibilities have been provoked by anticipated and actual tragedies that have revealed life's complex preciousness and simple fragility, stimulating feelings of anger and guilt for contributing to or somehow failing to prevent great suffering, and provoked as well by hopes for a global future in which more deeply democratic visions and values prevail. Second, the development during the past thirty-five years of many urban sites for direct citizen participation in American government at all levels, as discussed in the previous chapter, shows that broadly inclusive, locally contextualized, democratic participatory cultures can emerge and help to build democratic citizen skills and capacities with translocal implications. Third, actively nurturing these systemic possibilities, deep emotions, and emerging capabilities into more significant, future-forging influence will require more effective institutions of communication, education, mutual support, and cooperation at all levels, which in turn will require countless individuals to adopt a "hypothetical faith" that citizen participation can deepen democracy in global contexts.

The Rebirth of Democratic Citizen Participation: A Global Story, a Working Hypothesis

In the two years preceding September 11, diverse democratic mass movements converged to create enormous gatherings of energized, change-focused ordinary citizens in various urban locations worldwide who came together to express their fears about recent trends and their hopes for more deeply democratic ways of living. Each of these events taught lessons and flowed into the next as citizen-activists corrected and expanded limited initial reports in globally interlinked mass communications media, sharing insider accounts and framing localized plans for future events via Web sites and e-mail and through older yet still potent personal communications media of telephone calls, letters, and face-to-face conversations. These loosely organized mass movements of democracy-minded citizen-activists faced powerful opposition and subversion from the beginning, eventually resulting in the loss of lives, but the imperative quality of their individual members' motivation and the rapid growth of their practical knowledge and communal self-understanding has allowed them to persist and even expand their sphere of influence.

However, September 11 and its aftermath revealed more clearly how powerful the opposing forces really are and how far they are willing to go to block the expansion and deepening of local, regional, national, and global movements for democratic citizen participation. Thus, to continue my story in the direction suggested by these movement participants' deeply felt democratic imperative, to enable them to resist the mental as well as the practical

impacts of such powerful opposition, and to effectively stabilize their ongoing influence within the world's future-shaping process, a critical mass of
these individuals will need to form or to join more stable organizations committed to active citizen participation in democratic decision making. They
will need to build or to enhance reliable coalitions among like-minded organizations, while creating or taking up existing opportunities for direct, real,
and ongoing democratic citizen participation, both in culture-shaping institutions and in all levels of government.

The rebirth of active, widespread faith in democratic citizen participation
emerged into public view in November 1999, when global economic power
brokers gathered on the Pacific Rim in the apparently serene, "New Age"
city of Seattle to decide how the World Trade Organization would direct the
process of economic globalization. The world was startled when these meetings were disrupted by a well-organized, nonviolent outpouring of more than
forty thousand citizen-activists representing converging American democratic
movements, including labor unions, democracy-minded students and professors, environmentalists, Native Americans, and church groups—all of them
motivated by ancient but still radical conceptions of social justice that require
more equal and humane sharing of the world's wealth, care for the Earth, and
respect for the right of members of diverse cultures to semiautonomously
express their life-framing values within more deeply democratic processes of
shaping global futures. Moments later, however, their peaceful protest was
disrupted by a violent police riot aiming to suppress a small group of "cop-
baiting," window-smashing, graffiti-spraying anarchists who communicated
a very different vision of global futures and who employed very different
methods of attaining it. Perhaps these Pacific Rim anarchists were acting out
a nineteenth-century European transformative political vision. Perhaps they
were following in the footsteps of a small number of America's own Students for a Democratic Society, highly visible antiwar activists in the 1960s
who valued participatory democracy but never figured out how to theorize
it practically, and thus "sacrificed [it] to an existentialist politics of (often
violent) self-assertion in the streets" (Westbrook, *John Dewey and American
Democracy*, 549).

In the following months, without knowing *why* these anarchists had sto-
len the communicative moment in Seattle, yet both chastened and energized
by this experience, citizen-activists who identified with similar, converging,
democracy-minded movements gathered for related mass protests in other

major cities worldwide. More than 100,000 citizen-activists associated with the Seattle set of converging, grassroots, American democratic movements gathered nonviolently in April 2000 in Washington, D.C., to protest an international gathering of decision makers of the International Monetary Fund and the World Bank and to call once again for democratic citizen participation in the process of shaping global futures. A few months later, when those same global power brokers gathered in Prague, even more protesters from closely linked European movements turned out to express the same message. In April 2001, citizen-activists from various nations in the Western Hemisphere gathered in Quebec to express this message again to their countries' leaders, who were meeting there to discuss creating a "hemispheric free trade zone" that would allow the forces of economic globalization to operate more freely in the Americas at the same high costs to the environment, union workers, indigenous cultures, and the poor. Later that summer, citizen-activists from all the European countries and many other nations gathered in Genoa to express the same nonviolent message; again as in Seattle, the nonviolent message of this communicative event was distorted by a small number of anarchists' destructive self-assertions against urban property and against the police, this time leading to a violent death.

Meanwhile, hundreds of thousands of citizen-activists marched nonviolently in Lima before and after a hotly contested national election to protest the corruption of their country's nascent democratic process by President Alberto Fujimori, who used the courts, the secret police, and a constitutional amendment in his failed attempt to retain control. Eventually, the efforts of these citizen-activists forced Fujimori to decamp and brought the democratically elected candidate Alejandro Toledo, a world-class economist of Native American ancestry, to Peru's presidency. These courageous, otherwise ordinary Peruvian citizen-activists thereby influenced both their country's future and the democratic transformation efforts of citizens of other countries worldwide, though enormous problems remain before them due to a long history of injustices, the human frailties of their leaders, and the pressures and practical limits linked to globalization.

Among those directly influenced must be counted the students and other democracy-minded citizens of cities throughout Yugoslavia who effectively employed both well-coordinated nonviolent tactics and carefully planned, controlled violence in the streets of Belgrade to reject the attempted theft of their first democratic election by the postcommunist dictator Slobodan

Milosevic, who had made their nation infamous for violent "ethnic cleansing" of non-Serbians from the body politic during a disastrous civil war and who had successfully resisted both concerted international diplomacy and military pressure for democratization in its aftermath. In spite of the eventual success of their grassroots efforts to give power to their democratically elected presidential candidate, these Yugoslav citizen-democrats nonetheless faced an uncertain future. NATO bombing had destroyed much of their urban infrastructure and key industrial facilities in an unsuccessful effort to force institutional democratization externally. They continued to face enormous international economic and political pressures. They, like the other post-totalitarian nations of Central and Eastern Europe, lacked both the experienced democratic leaders and the postrevolutionary citizen capacities and expectations that are necessary resources for building a democratic participatory culture. Two years after their great day of victory, corrupt high-level officials in the new government and powerful organized gangs contrived the assassination of their hope-inspiring new president, revealing that their path to a deeper, more stable democracy would continue to be troubled and unclear. Nonetheless, ordinary citizens' courageous and successful struggle to bring down Slobodan Milosovic, to bring him to trial before the World Court, and to give democratic governance a chance in badly damaged, history-scarred Yugoslavia had already enhanced the prospects for future democratic citizen participation in shaping preferable global futures, there and elsewhere.

Even during the days I have remembered here, however, it was clear that unless citizen participants in these and other world-influencing events were able to develop deeper democratic roots and more enduring participatory stakes within their governments and within culture-shaping institutions and reliable coalitions of organization-based social movements that could sustain and expand their effectiveness, these achievements were likely to be washed away or "adversely subsumed" within the dialectical process of future forging that is still dominated by the power brokers against whom they scored these partial victories. As John Dewey warned in 1939, we must deepen citizen participation in shaping global futures beyond the minimal democratic requirements of the franchise and beyond heroic demonstrations of the importance of freedom of speech and assembly in megaprotests and individual acts of civil disobedience. Otherwise, each hopeful, small achievement may succumb to hope-defeating reinforcements of the world's currently dominant processes of determining global futures by wealth-stacked market processes, profit-oriented mass-media spin, habitual use of overwhelming high-tech military force, and decision making by "experts" within national and international institutions who are committed to the ideological tenets of "democratic realism," which leave no roles for the rest of us except those of workers, consumers, and obedient citizens—as "ballast" for the unchanging course of our ship of state, as Henry David Thoreau put it.

The historical antecedents of our contemporary "democratic realists" have argued since the beginning of the modern era that direct and ongoing citizen participation in government is neither desirable nor feasible; they have claimed that direct democracy is incompatible with representative democracy and that this is as much democracy as we can realistically hope to achieve. During the twentieth century and the early years of the twenty-first, opponents of "participatory democracy" have included some very odd bedfellows. Dewey's contemporary Walter Lippman lost faith in citizens' democratic capacities, which eventually led him to promote "democratic" governance by experts. The libertarian economist Friedrich von Hayek eventually argued that democracy is incompatible with individual liberty. The Trilateral Commission's conservative institutional analyst, Samuel P. Huntington, wrote in an influential 1975 report that citizen participation creates destabilizing expectations that democracies cannot fulfill. The "neopragmatist" liberal philosopher Richard Rorty, a self-described "red diaper anti-communist baby," praised Dewey's wisdom while arguing that participatory democracy, like the end of capitalism, is an unrealizable ideal, one that "nobody is yet able to imagine being actualized," functioning within a "politically useless unconscious" that America's "cultural Left" helped to create in the years after the Vietnam War. Most recently, a network of neoconservative "democratic realists" who gained influence in policy formation within the post–September 11 Bush White House have used the president's "formal" democratic authority to scale back Americans' civil liberties, unplug compensatory mechanisms to redress harms created by earlier generations' denials of basic civil and human rights, justify two wars of invasion that violated our country's international treaty obligations, and select justices who agree with them for lifetime appointments to the United States Supreme Court.[1]

As I write this story, the meanings of recent events for the world's future are unclear and filled with conflicting potentials, as are their lessons for citizen-activists whose more deeply democratic vision was ignored by the "democratic realists" who persuaded President Bush to launch the 2003 Iraq

War and who failed so profoundly in predicting its costs and consequences. These events' future meanings and potentials depend in part on what we and others do. Thus, we must live and act without advance assurance, with faith in the democratic ideal and in hope that our efforts can help to actualize it—and also on the basis of the best evidence we can obtain about the forces and currents operating within the world today, and with the best insights we can muster about our own needs and powers for living the kinds of lives that can motivate and sustain us during these unpredictable times of crisis and struggle. These are times in which we need the experience-born wisdom of James, Dewey, and Frankl, who told us that tragedy and grief are deeply woven into human life, and that we must struggle against our feelings of guilt and despair, as well as against our external opponents, if we are to re-found hope, to achieve something valuable over the course of our lives, and perhaps to weave some better, fairer pattern into the future lengths of our nation's and our world's history.

Educating for Dewey's Personal Democracy: Conflict Resolution and Citizen Voice

In many respects, our present era echoes the bleak days in the depths of the Great Depression, as the Nazis prepared to seize Europe, when John Dewey battled that era's influential proponents of a limited, "formal" democracy. Then, as now, "democratic realists" claimed that it is neither feasible nor desirable to involve citizens more actively and directly in the daily operation of democratic institutions and processes. Now, as then, advocates for democracy's "first," representative strand treat the constitutional principles and formal institutions that arose during the Age of Revolutions in America and Western Europe as solely definitive of democracy, even though the practical capacities of ordinary citizens to collaboratively direct their affairs in which Jefferson placed his hopes for a "second," deeper strand of democracy have grown enormously since that time. At present, however, actual capabilities for democratic citizen participation are being undermined in their emergence and in their influence by expert-guided global institutions and transnational economic, political, and military processes controlled by a small group of supremely powerful actors who seek to make client states of almost all of the world's countries and who see no value in preserving diverse cultures, species, and aspirations for the future.

Against popular and intellectual mainstreams of his own time, Dewey argued that American democracy's constitutional principles and institutions derive their justification and their efficacy from citizens' democratic values, habits, and daily involvements in self-governance. Lacking these, formally democratic principles and institutions are ungrounded, hollow, and readily subvertible by powerful antidemocratic forces.[2] In "Creative Democracy—The Task Before Us," his 1939 speech for a celebration in honor of his eightieth birthday, Dewey wrote:

> The depth of the present crisis is due in considerable part to the fact that for a long period we acted as if our democracy were something that perpetuated itself automatically; as if our ancestors had succeeded in setting up a machine that solved the problem of perpetual motion in politics. We acted as if democracy were something that took place mainly at Washington and Albany—or some other state capital—under the impetus of what happened when men and women went to the polls once a year or so—which is a somewhat extreme way of saying that we have had the habit of thinking of democracy as a kind of political mechanism that will work as long as citizens were reasonably faithful in performing political duties.
>
> (225)

Dewey argued that representative democracy needs to be balanced by what I have called "second strand," actively participatory democracy—by democracy as "a way of life"—and then he argued that even this analysis does not go deep enough. "Of late years we have heard more and more frequently that this is not enough: that democracy is a way of life. This saying gets down to hard pan. But I am not sure that something of the externality of the old idea does not cling to the new and better statement" (225). Dewey's deeper point was this: democracy's future depends upon individual persons joining Jefferson and his transgenerational inheritors in continuing to make personal commitments of time and energy that have real "opportunity costs" and that depend for their efficacy on a critical mass of others making well-timed, convergent commitments even amid uncertainty and danger.

In fact, the efficacy of democratic personal commitments in times of crisis depends upon their pervasiveness throughout the habits and relations of daily living; this must be our ultimate focus.

In any case, we can escape from this external way of thinking only as we realize in thought and act that democracy is a *personal* way of individual life; that it signifies the possession and continual use of certain attitudes, forming personal character and determining desire and purpose in all the relations of life. Instead of thinking of our own dispositions and habits as accommodated to certain institutions we have to learn to think of the latter as expressions, projections and extensions of habitually dominant personal attitudes.

(226)

Dewey's point was that the democratic quality of institutions ultimately depends on the dispositions, habits, and experiences in self-governance of the individual persons they serve and should reflect.

Though he greatly valued America's democratic heritage, Dewey believed that Americans' mid-twentieth-century cultural outlook and social practices had become overly reliant on the *forms* of our traditional institutions, giving insufficient attention to *democratic culture*—to actively nurturing the kinds of *dispositions and habits of daily living* that underlie the actual functioning of these institutions and that are indivisible elements of the democratic ideal. Moreover, he argued, such deeply democratic habits are necessary to the effective functioning of our American democratic institutions or any alternative institutional forms that can actualize the democratic ideal. Absent widespread "personal" democracy, understood as a habitual reliance on one's own and one's fellow citizens' developable capacities for cooperative self-governance, we have no effective way to resist the very real antidemocratic forces of Dewey's era or our own. "Democracy is a way of personal life controlled not merely by faith in human nature in general but by faith in the capacity of human beings for intelligent judgment and action *if proper conditions are furnished*" (227). In conditions of adequate freedom and sufficiently open communication, Dewey argued, we can nurture in individual members of our society the effective capacities for cooperative employment of intelligence in inquiry and action to meet pressing problems and to promote mutual flourishing—but developing such capacities requires actual experiences of actively employing intelligence in cooperative decision and action amid real differences in values and outlooks.

As William R. Caspary has emphasized in *Dewey on Democracy*, Dewey did not believe that effective democratic cooperation among individuals who have developed these requisite capacities depends upon perfect agreement among them. In fact, predictable differences in their perspectives and in their proposals can positively enhance the prospects for their effective collaborative response to the challenges and opportunities in their shared situation—*if* they can learn to resolve their conflicts constructively.

> Democracy as a way of life is controlled by personal faith in personal day-by-day working together with others. Democracy is the belief that even when needs and ends or consequences are different for each individual, the habit of amicable cooperation—which may include, as in sport, rivalry and competition—is itself a priceless addition to life. To take as far as possible every conflict which arises—and they are bound to arise—out of the atmosphere and medium of force, of violence as a means of settlement into that of discussion and of intelligence is to treat those who disagree—even profoundly—with us as those from whom we may learn, and in so far, as friends.
>
> (Dewey, "Creative Democracy," 228)

Building on Dewey's insight here, William Caspary, Noelle McAfee, Lawrence Susskind, and a diverse network of contemporary theorists from various disciplines are working to develop models and methods of democratic conflict resolution and of effective citizen participation in public policy decisions that go beyond Rawls's and Habermas's liberal constitutionalist approach to deliberative democracy in emphasizing the importance of structures and processes that teach and support habits of real dialogue.[3]

A significant obstacle these theorists seek to overcome is American culture's tendency to substitute dismissal, ridicule, and even shouting down others' ideas for democratic dialogue of the kind that would actually allow people to listen to and learn from one another. Our culture fosters these shared bad habits through political talk shows that too often turn into shouting matches, political "debates" in which participants merely repeat "sound bites" and insult one another instead of proposing serious public policies, real-life events and reality-based dramas in which firms and families rely on the courts and adversarial attorneys to resolve their differences instead of talking with one another, and a pervasive popular culture motif in music, television, and movies of treating a willingness to resort to physical violence as the meaning of strength and personal resolve. These undemocratic daily habits block the way to peace at intrapersonal, interpersonal, and international levels, now as in Dewey's time. If we would have peace, we must change them.

A genuinely democratic faith in peace is faith in the possibility of conducting disputes, controversies and conflicts as cooperative undertakings in which both parties learn by giving the other a chance to express itself, instead of having one party conquer by forceful suppression of the other—a suppression which is none the less one of violence when it takes place by psychological means of ridicule, abuse, intimidation, instead of by overt imprisonment or in concentration camps.

(228)

The anger-management classes that some of our most violent central-city schools and prisons have begun to institute in recent years are just a beginning—we need to teach these skills more widely, as increasing incidents of "road rage," domestic violence, suicide, depression, and substance abuse show that our cultural habits of dismissal, disrespect, and exclusion are taking a toll on even our relatively fortunate families.

However, we must do more than learn to manage our anger if we hope to experience democracy's deeper gift in our personal lives and in the future history of our nation; we must learn to positively value, listen to, and learn from others. "To cooperate by giving differences a chance to show themselves because of the belief that the expression of difference is not only a right of the other person but is a means of enriching one's own life-experience, is inherent in the democratic personal way of life" (228). Shaping these practices and habits of democratic living must become the shared task of all of our "schools," from prekindergarten through the educative institutions of adult living: workplaces, churches, clubs, civil organizations, and the wide range of opportunities for citizen participation in government, civic improvement, and culture development.[4] The practical challenge in cooperatively harvesting the benefits of individual and group-linked differences for democracy in the various arenas of our lives is twofold. Individuals must learn to appreciate such differences among themselves and among the groups of which they are members; in addition, they must gain access to processes of democratic citizen participation that allow such differences to actively interplay and effectively influence their shared social futures.

In Dewey's terms, citizens must have opportunities to participate in continuously planning their communities' futures that allow them to learn from one another transactionally. At the same time, we must revise our public decision processes in ways that give greater weight to insights from diverse citizens' differing experiences and evaluative frameworks than these are given when they are reductively aggregated in voting mechanisms, especially "first-past-the-post" and "winner-takes-all" systems like those generally used in Great Britain and the United States today. This developmental requirement is not met adequately by the very limited opportunities most Americans and citizens of other "experienced democracies" actually have to learn about the activities, beliefs, and values of their government representatives—and the even more limited opportunities most of these citizens have to learn from each other and then to educate their representatives directly through ongoing cooperative interactions. Painful and protracted as America's 2000 presidential election process was, it taught our nation and the world valuable lessons about the impact of every vote and the importance of the rule of law. However, it also showed how very little ongoing interaction American citizens from different regions, races, classes, religious beliefs, and evaluative perspectives currently have with one another and how little education we have had in listening respectfully across our differences with the expectation of learning something that may be of value to ourselves and to our shared communities. Our nation's deep divisions over the Iraq War may have worsened this cultural tendency to dismiss and demonize those who dissent from the majority's view. Adversarial political professionals with seemingly unlimited funds at their disposal certainly worked hard during America's 2002 congressional election and our 2004 presidential election to fan such habits of disdain and distrust of those with whom we differ. It was a hopeful sign for the future of our democratic culture, however, that in 2006, many citizens who were interviewed as they exited polling places indicated that they had had enough of this politics of manufactured dissention—that they wanted our Congress to effectively address important domestic issues and to end the Iraq War. Above all, they expressed a determination to reclaim a more active role in democratic self-governance. The tasks before us as public philosophers today are to educate our fellow citizens about existing opportunities for ongoing democratic participation and to create new ones to meet their needs, our country's, and our world's.

This is why Dewey called democracy "radical"—not because it had never been proposed or tried before, but because it had not then and still has not yet achieved full actualization through ongoing citizen participation in continuous social planning processes, in America or anywhere else in the world. In order to develop and employ effectively the citizen habits and capacities that

Dewey argued the democratic ideal implies as its justification and requires for its stable and successful operation, our communities, nations, and international organizations must develop opportunities for citizens to participate in continuous social planning at all levels, in matters small and great, to complement and correct the work of elected representatives and the "experts" they employ. What guidance does Dewey's work offer us about how to create such opportunities in twenty-first-century contexts and conditions? Robert Westbrook has suggested that the best answer is, "not enough." We must consider why he says this and what is to be done.

Dewey on Deepening Democracy Through Citizen Participation: A Helpful Guide?

John Dewey took citizen participation in continuous social planning very seriously, regarding "the freest possible play of intelligence through the widest cooperative form of give-and-take" as necessary both to the discovery of a society's most promising ways forward and to avoiding future shaping by violence (Dewey, "Creative Democracy," 321–322). However, Robert Westbrook argued in *John Dewey and American Democracy*, a carefully researched, thoughtful, and valuable contribution to the revitalization of participatory democratic theory, that Dewey's analysis of "second-strand" democracy is flawed by his failure to answer the key question of *how* to transform or supplement our existing, formally democratic institutions and social practices to achieve the kind of deeper, more personal, continuously planning democracy he rightly recognized as our only hope for defeating the powerful antidemocratic forces of his time and our own. Most crucial among Dewey's theoretical omissions, in Westbrook's view, is his failure to explain what "continuous social planning" entails and how the right kinds of participatory democratic roles and opportunities for citizens are to be created, so that we can achieve participatory democracy's dual benefits of individual development and cooperation-enhanced effectiveness in promoting the general welfare.

Westbrook cited *The Public and Its Problems* and many other books, essays, journal articles, and speeches from Dewey's last years to demonstrate that he regarded voting as an insufficient participatory role for citizens of a democracy. Rather, "the logic of Dewey's political theory and ethics pointed to a government that would include, indeed maximize, agencies of direct democracy" as "essential to self-realization," in combination with similar roles in directing all the other institutions of adult life (Westbrook, *John Dewey and American Democracy*, 317). Direct citizen participation in shared governance is one aspect of creating the kind of society in which each citizen would fulfill what Dewey described as "a responsible share according to capacity in forming and directing the activities of the groups to which one belongs and in participating according to need in the values which the groups sustain" (Dewey, *The Public and Its Problems*, 327–328). Therefore, Westbrook argued, we might reasonably expect Dewey to have offered some guidance about how to create such roles. Instead, Dewey "fudged" on the difficulties of decentralizing power, just as he did by "asserting the easy interdependence of local communities with the Great Community, difficulties inherent in any effort to preserve a measure of direct democracy in a large nation state. . . . For a philosopher who put democratic ideals at the center of his thinking, Dewey had surprisingly little to say about democratic citizenship" (Westbrook, *John Dewey and American Democracy*, 317).

This omission or incompleteness within Dewey's creative contribution to democratic theory is a serious failing, in Westbrook's view, because of Dewey's emphasis on the inseparability of theory from practice and of insightful critique from transformative proposals for reconstruction. The problem is not just one of inconsistency, in Westbrook's view; rather, as Dewey himself argued, unless we attend to *the means* by which the goals that focus our aspirations are to be achieved, they remain fantasies that substitute wishing for action. At the same time, our own contemporary "democratic realists," such as Dewey's rival Walter Lippman, are hard at work creating obstacles to citizen access to governance while formulating and pressing "expert" opinions very different from those ordinary citizens would be likely to support (Westbrook, *John Dewey and American Democracy*, 456). Ideal goals like deep democracy can guide our "working ends" only when we carefully study actual conditions and discover what transformative processes actually are available to us. However, Westbrook argues, Dewey failed to offer a systematic account of how to create participatory roles for citizens that would deepen their personal democracy, coordinate their efforts into "publics," and thereby multiply their power to transform actual social institutions and processes.

Therefore, although Dewey's journal articles and speeches during his late years insightfully addressed many topical issues, Westbrook charged that his failure to delineate transformative means for actualizing the participatory democratic ideal allowed it to remain a wish fantasy without power to effectively oppose the democratic realists. Westbrook softened this criticism somewhat with the comment that "this reluctance to think abstractly about politics is, I suppose, as it should be for a philosopher who insisted that ideas arose in the context of particular, concrete, and problematic situations" (317–318). In addition, Westbrook acknowledged that Dewey's activist practice and topical writings are parts of his philosophical legacy that have continuing value for those in our own era who aspire toward a deeper, more personal kind of participatory democracy.

Westbrook clearly is correct in his assessment that Dewey addressed only part of his own agenda for a complete democratic theory. However, Westbrook is wrong to suggest that Dewey or any other single democratic theorist might reasonably be expected to complete such a comprehensive agenda singlehandedly. This is beyond the scope of any individual's time, capacities, and life experience. Moreover, if we take seriously Dewey's frequent allusions in various contexts to the practice of science as a guide to improving the interdisciplinary project of democratic theory and practice, an important aspect of their relevance here is the insight that both must be understood as collaborative undertakings with an empirical dimension within an ongoing time process, projects that can best be advanced when consciously so understood.

From this perspective, Dewey's contributions to the interdisciplinary, intercultural field of democratic theory and practice rightly focused on those aspects of the whole project that his own gifts and interests especially fitted him to address, as these emerged in interaction with others in their cooperative response to the urgent needs of their times, a process he outlined in "Time and Individuality." Though Dewey framed his own contributions in light of his awareness of many other developments in this enormous intellectual and practical field, they were never intended to be comprehensive in their own right, much less final. Such an aim would have been fundamentally—even metaphysically—inappropriate to a necessarily cooperative activity within a processively developing world. Rather, Dewey stands as a great contributor to deepening democracy, whose work and life model invite democratic theorists and transformative practitioners of our own era to interactively develop our capacities and to cooperatively contribute our best efforts to this still urgent, never final project.

In this spirit, we must respond to Dewey's and Westbrook's call for more theoretical work linked to practical experimentation in developing appropriate roles for "citizen-thinkers" within those continuous social planning processes that both Dewey and Westbrook rightly regard as necessary elements of democratic individuation, desirable cultural revitalization, and effective cooperative self-governance. As I discussed in the previous chapter, a wide range of recent "second-strand" democratic theory and a variety of ongoing experiments show that citizen participation is desirable for moral, political, ontological, and epistemological reasons:

- it can teach respect for fellow citizens and shared responsibility for the future;
- it can forge cooperative solutions instead of NIMBY ("not in my backyard") opposition;
- it can break down ignorance-based barriers between social groups while allowing citizens to contribute widely dispersed local knowledge and life-born wisdom to each others' continuing education, as well as to the process of democratic governance;
- it can bring into active being practical intelligence as well as valuable individual gifts and skills that otherwise would remain only potentials.[5]

Moreover, as Berry, Portney, and Thomson argued in *The Rebirth of Urban Democracy* (5–6), which I discussed at length in chapter 6, participatory democracy is "redemptive" because it encourages the democratic spirit in individuals; it builds community while encouraging values like compassion, tolerance, and equality; and it transforms institutions to make them "more effective instruments of democracy."

A Conclusion and a Hypothesis for Living: Risking Our Hopes on Citizen Participation

In spite of many challenges to its desirability from critics and to its feasibility from worried friends, Jeffersonian direct citizen participation beyond the voting booth is already a well-established practice in many areas of public policymaking at all levels in the United States, especially in our cities. Overcoming successive waves of opposition from generations of "democratic realists" as well as from powerful antidemocratic interests, various formal and informal opportunities for citizen participation in democratic self-governance have emerged piecemeal during the past thirty-five years. More active citizen roles have emerged as possible and as necessary in response to the manifest limitations of representative government to govern wisely and equitably in its absence, and also to rising expectations and associated participatory capacities of an increasingly well-educated and well-informed citizenry, in America and in many other parts of the world.

In concert with these trends, participation in voting, the most basic and still most important citizen role and responsibility, had rebounded in recent years, including near-record turnouts of all age and income groups in America's 2006 elections, when the Iraq War was the main issue that decided voters' choices for Congress, and record levels of financial contributions and voting in the 2008 presidential primaries, in which economic pain joined war in motivating citizen involvement. Voter participation had decreased dramatically prior to the American presidential election of 2000, both in most "experienced democracies" and in many "new democracies" of Central and Eastern Europe. Perhaps the international cable television networks' thirty-six-day global seminar on the rule of law and the importance of every vote during the *Bush v. Gore* presidential vote recount struggle in 2000 positively influenced many citizens' likelihood of voting in subsequent elections, especially once-cynical young people who had shrugged off the opportunity to vote as meaningless. During our 2004 presidential elections, millions responded to charismatic presidential candidate Howard Dean's call for their Web-linked participation in change processes, returning to mainstream political activism in great numbers and with a movementlike spirit that many have carried over into community service, expressing an increasingly widespread hunger for creative new ways to connect with others in common causes that are both local and global.[6]

The continuing global communications revolution has speeded up the pace and vastly extended the resources for citizens' education in the meaning and preconditions of democracy worldwide, helping to increase the numbers of people who cross the divide between ignorance and knowledge about the importance of citizen participation through and beyond the voting booth. Even in the years of declining voter participation, however, many citizens were willingly taking up an expanding array of opportunities for direct participation in government decision making throughout the United States and in many other parts of the world. Nongovernmental organizations and community-based coalitions dug in, attracting the involvement of citizen-activists who were committed to and increasingly effective in making small gains within long-term struggles to change the actual conditions in which humans and other species live at local and global levels. Many citizens have taken great risks to assert their democratic influence on global futures outside government institutional frameworks, drawing on the protest traditions of Mohandas Gandhi, Martin Luther King Jr., Malcolm X. Shabazz, Saul Alinsky, Nelson Mandela, and the great movements for social justice they led—and at the same time, following in the footsteps of citizen predecessors in other cities only weeks or months earlier.

Responding affirmatively and effectively to this desirable and expanding hunger for experiences of deep, participatory democracy will require a far-reaching educational campaign about the existence and importance of already available opportunities for direct citizen participation in government, and why we need more of these. It will require federating local, community-based democratic citizen organizations into effective regional, national, and global "virtual communities" of information, innovation, and mutual support. In addition to ongoing formal participatory roles within government and ongoing informal roles within community-based nongovernmental organizations, fostering more deeply democratic ideal possibilities in our real world of the twenty-first century will continue to require occasional citizen participation in mass movements and protest events against unacceptable conditions and government proposals, especially in times of crisis, and will also require participation in issue-focused colloquies that can harvest citizens' widely dispersed reconstructive insights about how to build preferable global futures. In close combination with petitioning the courts and employing the full resources of the representative processes of constitutional democracies, these four additional forms of direct citizen participation, if embraced with commitment and persistence by a critical mass of world citizens, may be able to carry forward the processes of democratic transformations in diverse cultures and in the emergence of a deeply democratic global cosmopolitanism, as they have been doing since World War II. These are the inner "evolution" processes underlying the worldwide emergence of that desirable democratic cosmopolitanism Seyla Benhabib has so ably documented—processes that lack the historical inevitability she has attributed to them in part because their opponents are more powerful and better organized than she has acknowledged.[7]

When considering whether expanding all of these kinds of opportunities for direct citizen participation is desirable, whether they are capable of having a significant positive influence even though opposed by powerful forces, and in particular, whether *we ourselves* should take the plunge into one or more of these modes of democratic citizen-activism, we might be wise to follow

John Dewey's lead: we should interrelate our thinking about their *desirability* (would it be good for us to get involved) with their *feasibility* (can we make a positive difference if we do), considering both of these aspects of our decision in relationship to our actual context and the likely consequences of our alternative choices. The various city-based events and developments discussed above show that an increasing number of people in America and throughout the world in fact *do* desire a deeper democracy. They want a new way of living that heightens the experience of community, that includes but goes deeper than the institutions of representative self-governance, and that makes provision for ongoing, cooperative, difference-valuing, mutually educational processes of direct citizen participation in shaping the terms of our increasingly globally interconnected lives. Moreover, the multiplicity of opportunities for "real" citizen participation that has emerged in the last half-century because of determined citizen advocacy in the face of powerful opposition shows that both the will and the basic capabilities for this "second strand" of democracy already exist, in America and in many other parts of the world.

We cannot reasonably expect that we will ever have decisive evidence of the scope of potential transformative efficacy of democratic citizen participation, much less a proof so powerful that it would make one's brain explode if one refused to accept it, as Robert Nozick humorously suggested in his *Philosophical Explanations*, concerning another matter. This does not mean, however, that fallibilistic knowledge about this key question and about other important historical issues is impossible, as Richard Rorty argued. Nor does it mean that acknowledging ourselves to be permanently truth free in this domain would be liberatory, because it would make room for "joyous social hope" grounded only in "poetic imagination." This is no time for ungrounded life choices that are *merely* self-expressive, because there is a great deal at stake for all of us in this question. Terrorists have already shown in New York City, Jerusalem, Baghdad, and in many other great cities that they can and will stand up to the greatest concentrations of power the world has ever known and that they can and will frustrate power's smooth administration, even if the cost of doing so is loss of these antidemocratic activists' lives. The great question before us here is whether "second-strand" democratic citizen activism of the kinds whose rebirth I have chronicled here can constitute a counterpower of significant influence in shaping global futures and in shaping our individual lives.

As James argued in "The Will to Believe," when the choice between two hypotheses is a "genuine option"—living, forced, and momentous for us in the difference it will make in our lives—we should consider the best evidence available in order to make our choice as reasonable as possible. If this evidence is inconclusive, we should act with the guidance of our deepest sensibilities to choose that hypothesis that, *if it is borne out by experience*, seems most likely to make our lives meaningful and satisfying by leading to new experiences that can expand our understanding of the important question at issue, even if these eventually require us to modify or give up our hypothesis. Only by acting on such a fallible hypothesis will we be able to gain the additional experiences that will tell us whether it was the right one, the wrong one, or, as John Dewey suggested, a partially insightful one that may need to be modified in certain ways to more fruitfully guide future experience. James's insight about our epistemological "right" to adopt such a provisional hypothesis in the case of such a "genuine option," as well as the impossibility of avoiding a choice one way or the other, is as relevant to the question of whether and how to engage in democratic citizen participation as it is to the religious and scientific questions that originally motivated James's analysis.[8]

The "tragically melioristic" hypothesis about the transformative potential of democratic citizen participation for which I have argued and offered evidence in this book is not a simpleminded, silver lining–seeking, "glass is always half full" denial of the dangers we are in and the dreadful losses we have already sustained. Critics of James and Dewey often read their work as such "cock-eyed optimism," and those of us who find insight and inspiration in their work are sometimes dismissed with a similarly airy misreading. However, the existential stance and philosophical commitment James and Dewey actually shared was "meliorism," based on the Latin term for "the better." Their philosophical claim was that in spite of our limited human understanding about the most important matters and our limited power to do good, and in the face of the great evils and tragedies we must contend with at many key junctures in living, there are always experientially warranted distinctions to be made between the worse and the better—in hypotheses and beliefs, in historical interpretations, in values, in words, in public policies, in actions, and in life choices. Their existential commitment and advice was to always choose and act for "the better" in a particular context, based on a reasonable interpretation of the evidence available to us at the time, even if "the best" is unclear or apparently unachievable. Then we must pay attention and learn from what happens in acting upon that particular hypothesis, so we can more effectively recognize and achieve "the better" on future occasions.

In spite of a difference in language, Viktor Frankl's "tragic optimism" (from the Latin term for "the best") is very close in spirit James and Dewey's "meliorism." In the face of tragedy, Frankl argued, we must existentially claim and actively employ our human potential to reshape the meaning of events, starting within ourselves in the attitude we take and the choices we make to fulfill *"the best" that is possible for us in those circumstances*. We must take our own and others' suffering as a spur to action, take our sense of guilt as evidence that we must change our habits in living, and take the rude shock of human mortality that hits us in times of great loss as a wake-up call to live responsibly in time, Frankl urged us, so as to make our own lives count for something more ideal (Frankl, *Man's Search for Meaning*, 162).

If we combine these two strands of wise guidance, the challenge of acting on my "tragically melioristic" existential and practical hypothesis is that it goes against much of the "common sense" of our age and requires us to form new habits of living that are countercultural in many ways. This may be doubly difficult for us as citizens of the twenty-first century because we are so "busy" just maintaining ourselves in our current cultural contexts, and because many regard efforts to change our life contexts as futile, or even dangerous, and thus tend to scorn and to actively oppose efforts to do so. The history of our century, though young, is already woven through with symbolic and practical patterns of terror, insecurity, grief, anger, and loss of that sense of partial control over circumstances we humans need in order to feel open to and hopeful about the future. These dreadful new patterns have emerged within a deeper, continuing fabric of twentieth-century globalization, in which a small number of "elite" decision makers who wield enormous and unprecedented economic, diplomatic, and military powers are committed to democracy only to the extent that their "democratic realism" means that they employ the flexible formal structures of constitutional democracies to make, legitimate, and enforce their decisions. In light of fresh patterns of grief and loss as well as this continuing background fabric of busy-ness and anxiety in our present lives, we might ask ourselves why we as individuals would even want to invest our time and our hopes in *seemingly irrational* efforts to sustain and expand opportunities for direct citizen participation in democratic self-governance.

My answer is this: *there is a deeper rationality of the human spirit* than the economic, political, and military models elite decision makers employ in wielding global power—an existential rationality that demands meaning,

hope, and lasting relationships with persons and with places and that can neither be silenced nor satisfied with a life of limited opportunity and limitless
insecurity in which all we care most about can be swept away in a moment,
not by an "act of God" but by another human person's decision, in whose
calculus our dreams have no place. It is this deeper rationality of the human
spirit that drives what Viktor Frankl calls "man's quest for meaning," that
motivates Dewey's imperative toward the conditions of our own and others'
growth within mutual relationships of depth that endure, and that justifies
James's will to believe, at least hypothetically, when the weight of our own
dreams of a life that matters is added to all the other forms of evidence that
careful inquiry makes available to us. All three of these wise ancestors had
experienced the deep marks of tragedy in their lives. James grappled with
the brutality of the American Civil War, which scarred his family and contributed for a time to his own emotional paralysis. Dewey lost two children
and his beloved first wife to early deaths, and he struggled against the rise of
fascism that was sweeping away global hopes for democratic living. Frankl
was marked at Auschwitz, and, even before that, when he parted from his
wife and other members of his family who would perish with so many of
the best in the Holocaust, which he wrote about as many small moments in
which people made decisions and acted from the values and the habits they
had become—moments more like than unlike other times in human history
and in ordinary people's lives. The lessons Frankl learned from observing
himself and others enduring those tragedy-laden days became the basis of
his teachings about "logotherapy." This was his innovative, influential, and
widely effective approach to aiding people who are living with a loss of hope,
of purpose, of health, and of loved ones to find new meaning and value in
their lives in one of three ways: through commitment to achieve some work
or some deed they feel is important, through love for someone or something
who has touched them, or through determination to be worthy of their suffering by finding a way to "say Yes to Life."

How effective citizens can become in more deeply democratizing current
globalization processes remains to be seen, but the examples I have discussed
in this book show that we have some good evidence on which to base shared
social hope that active citizen participation can have significant transformative influence, so that the actual scope of its effectiveness may depend upon a
critical mass of citizens claiming what William James called a "will to believe"
in deepening democracy. Not only the historical and contemporary evidence

from its proponents, but even the vigorous and continuing efforts of its opponents suggest that democratic citizen participation can be powerful, even
world changing, in its significance. Otherwise, as John Stuart Mill argued
on behalf of women's rights, why would so many try so hard to suppress
opportunities that they believe we could not in any case employ effectively?
Neither side's evidence is conclusive—nor should we expect it to be, given
the dynamic, context-dependent plasticity of our human capabilities and the
complexity of the social forces at work in shaping them. Nonetheless, the
evidence from several hundred years of American experience and from the
recent global events and the wide-ranging studies discussed above, suggests
five things:

- that active experiences of "second-strand" democratic citizen participation
  can foster the development of highly desirable individual potentials within
  active lives that satisfy deep human needs for meaning and for an active role
  in future forging;
- that these kinds of collaborative opportunities *can* bring together in com-
  mon-cause coalitions of people who have sometimes regarded each other as
  adversaries in the past;
- that cross-difference citizen participation in efforts to shape preferable local
  and global futures *can* give rise to new knowledge;
- that it *can* stimulate mutual, peace-making changes in citizens' values, view-
  points, goals, and practical powers;
- that it can eventually influence their countries' cultures, institutions, and
  public-policy decisions.

Thus, "hypothetically" choosing active citizen participation in the hope
of deepening democracy in global contexts can satisfy the evidence requirements for James's "will to believe." It can help us and others to grow into our
highest and best selves through our transactions with one another in common cause, as Dewey explained. Moreover, the "tragically melioristic" choice
to become actively involved in new or existing forms of active democratic
citizen participation can be Frankl's kind of meaning-infusing work, a tribute
to those who have touched us, and a fitting expression of our appreciation of
life. Drawing on a "deeper rationality of the human spirit," we can choose to
work with diverse "public philosophers" and citizen-thinkers worldwide to
create a balanced wellspring of shared human knowledge illuminated by our

stories from the journeys that have brought us this far. From this wellspring we can draw the guiding visions we will need to expand existing opportunities for our country's and our world's citizens to participate in achieving preferable futures, local and global.

Such a process of experimenting, learning from others' experience, and evolving truth- and justice-based transformative visions already has begun, as witness those host cities in all parts of the world in which citizens have gathered for large-scale democratic protests and those "continuously planning cities" on which I have focused my readers' attention in this book. Increasingly hard-to-limit, citizen-to-citizen communication about the results of democratic citizen participation efforts—within government; within nongovernmental organizations; within gatherings of scholars and other citizen-thinkers to inquire together, to tell their stories, and to seek guiding visions for our local and global futures; and within mass protests and reconstructive movements focused on peace, economic and social justice, democratic cultural inclusiveness, and environmental sustainability—already is forging a worldwide "Beloved Community" of shared concern, mutual education, growing cooperative intelligence, and collaborative struggle. How this story will end depends on what we do, what we learn, and who we become as each of us manifests and continuously reframes our social hopes in thought and action, responding to the great needs and events of our times.

NOTES

Introduction. Pragmatism and Social Hope

1. See Huntington, *The Clash of Civilizations*, 20.
2. See Jane Addams, *Newer Ideals of Peace*. For more of my own views about what we can learn from Jane Addams that is important for us now, see my forthcoming "Social Democracy, Cosmopolitan Hospitality, and Inter-Civilizational Peace: Lessons from Jane Addams."
3. Huntington, *The Clash of Civilizations*, 318, drawing on Walzer, *Thick and Thin*, 1–11.
4. On this last point, also see Huntington, *Who Are We?*
5. On the impossibility of pure cultures, see Locke, *Race Contacts and Interracial Relations*.
6. On recent processes of cultural change in response to external influences, including a stage of thoughtful affirmation and a later stage of more automatic performance, see Berger's introduction to *Many Globalizations*.
7. See Barber, *Jihad vs. McWorld*.
8. See Robert Dahl's insightful analysis of democracy's international scope and prospects for progress in the twenty-first century, *On Democracy*.
9. On the distinction between "formal democracy" and "deep democracy," see my *Deep Democracy: Community, Diversity, and Transformation*; Dahl, *On Democracy*; and Fung and Wright, *Deepening Democracy*. Barber marks a similar contrast in arguing for "strong" democracy; see his *Strong Democracy*, *Jihad vs. McWorld*, *A Passion for Democracy*, and *Fear's Empire*.
10. The panel on "Theoretical Cultures Across the Disciplines" at the American Sociological Association's annual meetings on August 17, 2004, from which I quote here, was organized and chaired by Michelle Lamont, and also included Don Brenneis and Hazel Markus.
11. Rorty offered more details about his various philosophical views that converge in *Achieving Our Country* (1998) in earlier and later books, including *Philosophy and the Mirror of Nature*, *Contingency, Irony, and Solidarity*, *Philosophy and Social Hope*, *The Future of Religion*, *Philosophy as Cultural Politics*, and *What's the Use of Truth*, and in various widely collected essays, including "Solidarity or Objectivity?" His replies to critics are also very interesting. See Saatkamp, *Rorty and Pragmatism*, which includes Rorty's essay "The Future of Philosophy," in addition to responses to each

critic; and Brandom, *Rorty and His Critics*, which includes Rorty's "Universality and Truth" and responses to each critic.

12. The French social theorist Alexis de Tocqueville visited all of the regions of the United States during 1833 and 1834, observing and talking with people from all walks of life in their homes and community organizations and taking extensive notes. After his return to France, he published an insightful two-volume work, *Democracy in America* (1835 and 1840), which has been read by thinkers worldwide ever since. One hundred and fifty years later, Tocqueville's concept and phrase "habits of the heart" became the main title of an important interdisciplinary study of how Americans were living during the last decades of the twentieth century. See Bellah et al., *Habits of the Heart*.

13. See Cornel West's best-selling philosophical meditation on our times, *Race Matters*, and its successor, *Democracy Matters*.

I. Achieving Our Country, Achieving Our World

1. I have written more about these civic responses to September 11, including the candlelight vigils, the interfaith prayer meetings, the tearful singing of "God Bless America" at baseball games, and the huge gatherings of citizens determined to express their values and visions for rebuilding lower Manhattan in my essay "Building a Cosmopolitan World Future Through Pragmatist Mutual Hospitality," in Koch and Lawson, *Pragmatism and the Problem of Race*.

2. The Conference of American Catholic Bishops published an important and insightful letter criticizing the invasion of Iraq as incompatible with the long-established requirements for a "just war," posting it on the Internet and circulating it to the news media. However, their credibility was greatly undermined during the period by the tidal wave of adverse publicity connected with the priest pedophilia scandal. In any case, many of the bishops were and continue to be much more active in opposing abortion than in opposing war. Those who did work hard to get the "just war" letter out to a wider public found very little news media interest.

3. See McGary and Lawson, *Between Slavery and Freedom*, especially McGary's chapter 6, "Forgiveness and Slavery." See also McGary, *Race and Social Justice*.

4. For more information about the multiplicity of American slave revolts and the fear they caused in the South, see Franklin and Moss, *From Slavery to Freedom*.

5. The international movement seeking reparations for the families of those who were held in chattel slavery from the national governments whose laws and use of armed force made this possible continues—as does slavery in twenty-first-century forms, including sex trafficking.

6. The concept of "family resemblances" comes from Wittgenstein's *Philosophical Investigations* (1953), which points out that many concepts, like the concept of

"games," cover diverse instances that lack any single set of necessary and sufficient conditions shared by all of their occurrences but that gain a certain unity from overlapping patterns of resemblance shared by overlapping subgroups within the whole, as various members of a family may share the family nose, or the family eyes, or the family hands, but not all of them. My suggestion here is that there have been such overlapping patterns of experiences, needs, and responsive strategies among diverse, overlapping oppressed groups with "the American family" and that the resemblances among these in contrast to those of the power wielders may have made a bipolar black-white racial logic seem to have broader inclusiveness to both Baldwin and King than solely in reference to their own African American struggle against European Americans.

7. See Huntington, *Who Are We?*

8. For Rorty's more detailed explanation of why we should take Freud so seriously, see his *Contingency, Irony, and Solidarity.*

9. For more autobiographical reflections on how Rorty came to hold his political and philosophical views, see his poignant essay "Trotsky and the Wild Orchids," in *Philosophy and Social Hope,* from which this book's title derives, as well as Knobe, "A Talent for Bricolage—An Interview with Richard Rorty." For a complete bibliography of Rorty's writings, see the Stanford Encyclopedia of Philosophy Web site.

10. See Bell, *Faces at the Bottom of the Well;* and Bell, *Gospel Choirs.*

11. See also Dewey's earlier essay "The Need for a Recovery of Philosophy" (1917), in which he called for a refocusing of attention from "the problems of philosophy" to "the problems of men."

12. For a persuasive argument that readings of the influential French "postmodernists" by their American disciples and their American critics have generally been insufficiently careful, see Stuhr, *Genealogical Pragmatism.*

13. See Glazer, *We Are All Multiculturalists Now.*

14. Two years before he gave the lectures that became *Achieving Our Country,* in 1997, Rorty used the words "cosmopolitan" and "bridge" to describe the utopian efforts by philosophers he recommended in his essay "The Future of Philosophy," while stating flatly that philosophers are no good at telling stories: "We philosophers are good at building bridges between nations, at cosmopolitan initiatives, but not at telling stories. When we do tell stories, they tend to be bad ones, like the stories that Hegel and Heidegger told the Germans about themselves—stories about the superior relation in which a certain country stands to some supernational power." See Saatkamp, *Rorty and Pragmatism,* 203. How amusing to consider what might have led to this about-face!

15. "Cosmopolitan" is used in two importantly different ways in contemporary American philosophy. Rorty and Hill use the term to reflect an assumed, transnational placelessness, which worries Rorty for the reasons noted here but which seems like a good thing to Hill because he thinks it allows one to step outside one's own

culture's narrowness, racism, sexism, and heterosexism. See Hill's *Becoming A Cosmopolitan*. A very different kind of "rooted cosmopolitanism" is one that I and other contemporary thinkers have learned from reading Alain Locke's critical pragmatism from the first half of the twentieth century, which treats human individuals as always members of the particular cultures that formed them, but not uncritically so, and as fully capable of also learning from widely differing cultures and capable of forming deep solidarities with some of their members. See my *Deep Democracy*, especially chapter 4, "Cosmopolitan Unity Amidst Valued Diversity: Alain Locke's Vision of Deeply Democratic Transformation." See also Harris, *The Critical Pragmatism of Alain Locke*.

2. American Dreaming

1. John Stuhr makes a persuasive case that such a misreading of the "postmodernists" occurred widely among American philosophers; see Stuhr's *Genealogical Pragmatism* and *Pragmatism, Postmodernism, and the Future of Philosophy*.

2. See the *New York Times* nine-part series on "Class Matters," May–June 2005.

3. See Heilbroner, "The Triumph of Capitalism" (1989), which originally appeared in the *New Yorker* shortly after the fall of the Berlin Wall and has since been widely anthologized. See also Derrida, *Specters of Marx*.

4. See Rorty's frank and moving autobiographical essay, "Trotsky and the Wild Orchids," in his *Philosophy and Social Hope*.

5. In his influential, widely anthologized 1988 presidential address to the American Sociological Association, "Sociology in America," Herbert Gans called for the emergence of "Public Sociology" as a highly respected, socially engaged branch of the discipline that would correct the social claims of journalists, engage in cultural criticism, and undertake studies of issues of our times important to the American public, using extended interviews and other qualitative methods and written in accessible, engaging language for a wide readership. Though most of the discipline's practitioners continue to work according to the old model, and those who pursue Public Sociology as their calling may have trouble finding an audience for their work and have difficulty getting tenure, several of the most successful—including William Julius Wilson, Patricia Hill Collins, and Gans himself—have made important contributions to public policy and cross-disciplinary research, including my own. I include them among the contributors to the work of "Public Philosophy" as I broadly described it in the introduction to this book.

6. For a better understanding of Addams's life, work, and continuing philosophical insightfulness, see Charlene Haddock Seigfried's excellent book, *Pragmatism and Feminism*.

7. I have written more about what I think Jane Addams can teach us about deepening democracy in global contexts in my forthcoming "Social Democracy, Cosmopolitan Hospitality, and Intercivilizational Peace."

8. See Huntington's *The Clash of Civilizations* and *Who Are We?*

9. Here Rorty quotes from Dewey's "Maeterlinck's Philosophy of Life" (1911), available in *The Middle Works of John Dewey*, 6:135. For Rawls's argument that we can do political philosophy without metaphysics, including adequately addressing moral issues of justice, see his 1985 essay "Justice as Fairness," his "Reply to Habermas," and his fuller development of these ideas in *Political Liberalism*.

10. See Huntington's *The Clash of Civilizations*, Rawls's "Justice as Fairness" and *Political Liberalism*, and Benhabib's *Another Cosmopolitanism*.

11. See, for example, Seigfried's "Ghosts Walking Underground," "Pragmatist Metaphysics?" and "Experience, Anyone?

12. At the inaugural conference of the Köln University Center for Dewey Studies, hosted by Kersten Reich and Stefan Neubert, I presented "Dr. Dewey's Deeply Democratic Metaphysical Therapeutic for America's Post-9/11 Democratic Disease," which expands these reflections on the purposes, characteristics, and ongoing collaborative reconstruction of a pragmatist metaphysics. This paper and others from the conference are forthcoming in Garrison, *Reconstructing Democracy, Recontextualizing Dewey*.

13. Larry Hickman was responding orally to an earlier version of the paper I presented at the inaugural conference of the Köln University Center for Dewey Studies; see note 12, above.

14. As I argued above, rather than broad, stable ideological orientations, messy complexity has always characterized American political life, with multiple lines of affiliation and overlapping coalitions reflecting piecemeal political visions built up from issue orientations.

15. On Dewey's cautious, contingent hope for a more deeply democratic future, see, among other works, Dewey's *The Public and Its Problems* and my own *Deep Democracy*, especially chapter 3, "The Deeply Democratic Community: Reconstructing Dewey's Transformative Ideal," which quotes and critically discusses many passages from various works in which Dewey suggests the preconditions for a deeper democracy and how these may be developed actively by citizens consciously working to transform existing social structures and "habits of the heart."

16. For Rorty's characteristically language-focused definition of "irony," see his *Contingency, Irony, and Solidarity*, 73–74.

17. For more on this, see Rorty's *Philosophy as Cultural Politics*, 4–5, 28–29.

18. See Rorty and Vattimo, *The Future of Religion*, 33.

19. Based on his experience as a Wall Street ethical compliance consultant, David McClean has presented many of these promising suggestions in a series of papers

at Annual Meetings of the Society for the Advancement of American Philosophy. I hope he will soon publish them.

20. See Greene, *The Elegant Universe*. See also Peat, *Blackfoot Physics*.

3. Hope's Progress

1. For a partial expression of James's view that moral emotions like hope are "embodied feelings," see his essay "What Is Emotion?" (1895), with the understanding that this essay is by itself incomplete and must be read in relation to his more developed works on psychology.

2. For an influential discussion of "ontological security," see Giddens, *Modernity and Self-Identity*. I am grateful to John Lachs for reminding me that not everyone longs for peace, or so it seems—some long for holy war, or war that will be good for their business profits, or a war that will allow boys to become men by fighting for their lives, or a civil war like America's as necessary to end chattel slavery or some other intolerable harm, or a revolutionary war as necessary to end colonialism or unresponsive government, or war for land, for natural resources, or for countless other reasons. Yet there is a peace on the other side of war for which antagonists long, when some great good will have been achieved, or the enemy will have been destroyed, or both. There is good social science that tends to support my hunch that longing for war per se is pathological, a confusion of means with ends like miserliness with money, or perhaps just a profound character disorder. I hold this belief hypothetically, as James advised in "The Will to Believe," prepared to be corrected by evidence and experience, yet clear about the necessity of taking a position on such a "living" issue if the evidence for or against it is ever to come forth through active participation in a great "inquiry."

3. For Dewey's very helpful analyses of how the individuation process develops over time, within actively collaborative social relations and within a specific cultural and historical context, see his "Time and Individuality" and his *Freedom and Culture*.

4. On the characteristics and social formation processes of this shared social sense of the normal and the right, see George Herbert Mead on the development of "the social self" in Aboulafia's "A (neo) American in Paris" and Bourdieu on "*habitus*" in *Distinctions*. A helpful collection of essays that draws on and explains the work of both theorists is Shusterman, *Bourdieu: A Critical Reader*. I am grateful to David Woods for bringing all of these texts to my attention in this connection.

5. For a discussion of the grounds for "ethnocentrism," see Rorty's widely anthologized essay "Objectivity or Solidarity?"

6. See Rorty's and Engel's critical interchange in *What's the Use of Truth?*

7. For an insightful discussion of the sojourner's valuable role in knitting together cross-difference inquiries toward a common pursuit of justice, see Collins, "Searching for Sojourner Truth."

8. There are countless valuable books in which various critics offer detailed, carefully critical analyses of Rorty's view and in which his replies simply dismiss their concerns while expanding the range and scope of his "ethnocentric" view. One of the first of these collections of critical essays was the one in which the version "Solidarity or Objectivity?" quoted here first appeared: Rajchman and West, *Post-Analytic Philosophy*. Subsequent ones have featured exchanges with feminists, critical theorists, and fellow postmodernist philosophers. Two of the most recent feature exchanges with contemporary pragmatists in the classical American stream and with contemporary analytic philosophers: Saatkamp, *Rorty and Pragmatism*; and Brandom, *Rorty and His Critics*, respectively.

9. Though Dewey thought more often in terms of other categories earlier in his life, in some of his last works the concept of "culture" plays a leading role, and his comments are still insightful, both critically and transformatively. See, for example, his foreword to the twenty-fifth anniversary edition of *Reconstruction in Philosophy*; his draft introduction to a proposed revision of his most metaphysical work, *Experience and Nature*, in which he thought of using the term "culture" in replacement for the much-misunderstood term "nature"; and last but not least, his *Freedom and Culture*.

10. Dewey's conception of truth had already been loyally and cheerfully misrepresented with the best possible intentions by William James in the much-misunderstood essay on that subject that made pragmatism's conception of truth infamous. Like Rorty, James in his originality often misrepresented his friends as well as his opponents. James had so greatly misrepresented his dear friend Charles Sanders Peirce's significantly different pragmatist conception of truth in an earlier essay that Peirce renamed his position "pragmaticism" in order to dissociate himself from the school of thought increasingly associated with James's own views. James's own pragmatist conception of truth, as this emerged in his texts over time, is well worth reconsideration. The important point here is that Dewey's conception of truth was neither that attributed to him by James nor that attributed to him by Rorty.

11. Peirce and James called this world process of generating emergent newness "tychism."

12. For insightful and beautifully expressed discussions of the characteristics and needs we more evolved humans share with our ancient forebears and would be wise to recognize and to find satisfying and sustainable ways to fulfill, see Wilshire's *The Primal Roots of American Philosophy* and Dunsmore's *Earth's Mind*.

13. Dewey argued for an immanent impulse within history toward conditions of mutual human flourishing as a well-warranted key premise in so many places that it is difficult to know where to begin in citing them, but they include *Reconstruction in Philosophy*, *Experience and Nature*, *The Public and Its Problems*, *The Quest for Certainty*, *Individualism Old and New*, *Art as Experience*, and *Theory of Valuation*.

4. Choosing Our History, Choosing Our Hopes

1. For excellent insights about how such a Deweyan pragmatist conflict resolution process might proceed, see Caspary's excellent book *Dewey on Democracy*.

2. See Huntington's *The Clash of Civilizations* and *Who Are We?* For more reasons why I think Huntington is wrong on these issues, see the introduction and chapter 1 of this book; for reasons why I think he was wrong earlier, in the study he authored with Michael Crozier and Joji Watanuki, *The Crisis of Democracy*, see chapter 5.

3. I explain briefly in the introduction what I think Rorty means by calling himself an "ironist" and why I think this was a mistake. For Rorty's fuller explanation, see his *Contingency, Irony, and Solidarity*.

4. However, in *Contingency, Irony, and Solidarity* and in other places, Rorty specifically argued that there really is no such thing as "common sense," because we humans are all unique beings who do not share a common human nature (his "nominalism") and because we are confined to our particular times and places in history (his "historicism"). I say a little more about these ideas, how they interrelate, and why I think they must be wrong in the introduction to this book.

5. Following Nietzsche, Rorty did not think that everyone is or could become a "strong poet"—his way of referring to an exemplary human being with the strength of mind and character as well as the gifts with language to create a new self-image and a new world vision and to move others to accept these through "persuasive rhetoric." However, contra Nietzsche, Rorty's democratic utopianism is expressed in the hope that others will learn to appreciate and to willingly emulate their nation's "strong poets." Again, see his *Contingency, Irony, and Solidarity*.

6. Pragmatists and some others often use a capital T when writing the word "truth" to suggest what I call a Super Truth—an important proposition that is or could be known with certainty, that could not be unseated by any future inquiry, that would be acknowledged by any reasonable person who understood it, and that fruitfully determines and regulates many other beliefs we could reasonably hold. It is not clear whether Charles Sanders Peirce, one of the founding pragmatists who later distinguished his own views from theirs as "pragmaticism," believed that communities of inquirers are actually fated to arrive at Super Truths some day if they adhere strictly to the intellectual virtues he highlighted, or whether this was a regulatory ideal for him that directs effective inquiry. Other pragmatists agree that, in any case, we need to strive for interim, revisable, falliblistic "truths" that mark our advance over past beliefs or theories that were harmfully vague or downright wrong and that guide our efforts to do better in the future. Rorty disagreed with using the word "truth" to refer to such beliefs, propositions, or theories—his texts are unclear about whether this was because he thought the word itself is misleading when used in this way or because he thought the activity of searching for "truths" is not a fruitful way to think about the past and prepare for the future.

7. To see what John Dewey actually has to say about why and how democracy emerged out of feudalism and why its structures and social processes better satisfy the deep needs and aspirations of modern peoples, see his *The Public and Its Problems* and various passages in *Individualism Old and New, The Quest for Certainty, Liberalism and Social Action*, and *Freedom and Culture* (1939), among other works.

8. Thomas Kuhn's blockbuster, *The Structure of Scientific Revolutions*, influentially drew on cross-era historical evidence that should have violated the principles of "Rorty the historicist" to show that science does not proceed in a progressive, linear fashion, with everyone in a particular field in basic agreement about what they are doing, which theories are closest to right, and what evidence matters for settling any unresolved issues, but rather that there are rival research programs even within times of "normal science," and that occasionally a new "paradigm" emerges that people either accept or reject for complex reasons, but not because the evidence somehow "forces" them to do so. The "ethical emotivists" were a prominent school of thought in English-language philosophy during the 1950s who claimed that there can never be the right kind of (scientific) evidence for or against ethical beliefs, judgments, and "arguments," but that they rest on "emotional" grounds alone and amount to no more than cheering and booing.

9. In the *Republic* and other works, Plato claimed that it is possible to fully grasp a detailed understanding of ideal Super Truths in moments of insight, and thereafter we can work to conform our behavior and the world to them by stages of progress toward getting it right, or "successive approximations."

10. I think the view of truth I sketched here is very close to Pascal Engel's in his exchange with Richard Rorty, *What's the Use of Truth?* While Engel distances himself from the pragmatist conception of truth that Bertrand Russell attributed to William James, this is not the same as distancing himself from James's and Dewey's actual view, which Engel understands through Russell's distorting lens. As unfortunately was often the case, Rorty was no help in explaining James's and Dewey's actual views, being more interested in using them as a foil for advancing his own views, including his view that there are no true interpretations of works of literature and philosophy and thus no false ones. I disagree—there may be multiple true pragmatist interpretations, and there clearly are countless false ones. More on this at a later time.

11. See Wittgenstein's *Philosophical Investigations*.

12. I am grateful to Msgr. Howard Calkins for an illuminating explanation of what is involved in ritual remembering in Jewish and Christian religious contexts and also for emphasizing the importance of reconciliation in creating personal and social conditions for fulfilling one's moral resolve to live differently and better after one has done great harm. He is not responsible for unorthodox aspects of my pragmatist use of these and other religious ideas throughout this discussion, though I hope he will find them fruitful.

13. See Delbanco, *The Death of Satan*, 175–176.

14. See my forthcoming "Social Democracy, Cosmopolitan Hospitality, and Inter-Civilizational Peace."

15. See James, "The Moral Philosopher and the Moral Life," which has been widely reprinted and anthologized.

16. Vagueness is not necessarily a bad thing, in James's view—some of our most important ideals and insights are vague, and always will be, though they help to guide our living as well as our inquiry, and, over time and with care, we may learn to understand them better. Democracy, justice, love, truth, knowledge, and world peace are all vague in this way and yet fruitful. For helpful insights in this, see Gavin's beautifully written book *William James and the Reinstatement of the Vague*.

17. See James, "The Will to Believe." This is an important essay, and it requires careful reading to avoid misinterpreting it.

18. See Royce, *The Problem of Christianity*.

19. See Harris's *The Philosophy of Alain Locke* and *The Critical Pragmatism of Alain Locke*.

20. See King's last monograph, *Where Do We Go from Here*, and his related writings, in Washington, *Testament of Hope*.

21. Democratically tolerable Lockean "functional variants" in cultural practices that express "common human values" may include some important differences in marriage customs, such as practices of arranged marriages and perhaps even polygamy and polyandry that are not culturally acceptable or even legal in many Western romantic love–oriented, ideally monogamous countries, provided that the partners give full and free consent as adults, provided that the terms of marriage do not prevent the partners' full and free public participation and overall growth as human persons, and provided that they assure positive social environments for children, older people, and other family members who may be intimately affected by such marriage arrangements. Of course, the same provisos of democratic tolerability apply to the West's romantic love–oriented, "ideally monogamous" marriage practices.

22. See my essay "Deepening Democratic Transformation." See also Nussbaum's list of basic human capabilities that require social support for their development in chapter 1 of her *Sex and Social Justice*, and Sen's related discussion of human development in his *Development as Freedom*. While these are not pragmatist analyses of human capabilities and the contextual requisites for their development, they are suggestive in their specifics, which do not hinge on methodological issues where my view differs from theirs.

23. In *A Theory of Justice*, Rawls explained the ideal of "lexical" ordering among his two main principles of justice. Lexical ordering, as he used the concept there and I use it here, means that second principles did not come into play in ways that undercut a primary one—the idea is not to bring them into some kind of a "balance"

or even what Rawls call a "wide reflective equilibrium" but rather to protect the first principle and to work out how to fulfill it using the second one.

24. Martha Nussbaum and several other speakers made this argument at a session on the politics of globalization at the 2002 Eastern Division Meetings of the American Philosophical Association, in Philadelphia.

25. I draw here upon Addams's thinking about mutual transformation within democratic processes of working together across differences to meet basic human needs in her discussion of "Charitable Effort" in *Democracy and Social Ethics*, and upon Seigfried's meditations on Addams's example in her *Pragmatism and Feminism* and her edited collection *Feminist Interpretations of John Dewey*.

26. Such a process draws on Benhabib's many practical insights on recent events in *Another Cosmopolitanism* without entangling us in Kantian claims about already shared universal, cross-cultural rationality or in her surprising attributions of evolutionary powers to human-rights claims themselves, instead of to our thinking as those of us culturally located cosmopolitan humans who come to understand and to advance them.

5. Trying Deeper Democracy

I must acknowledge my debt here to David W. Woods, AICP, who is a member of the board of directors of the American Planning Association; my fellow principal of our urban planning firm, GreenWoods Associates; and my primary teacher about urban planning, as well as my spouse and traveling companion to other parts of the world where we have heard stories from colleagues and strangers that have expanded and corrected my earlier versions of our American story. This life-expanding educational process continues.

1. See Rorty's nightmare essay, "Looking Backwards from the Year 2096," in his *Philosophy and Social Hope*, and the passages I quoted earlier from *Achieving Our Country*.

2. In *Another Cosmopolitanism*, Seyla Benhabib shared imagination-stretching stories of struggles to deepen democracy in France ("the scarf affair") and Germany (the successful effort to gain voting rights for resident aliens in local elections) in support of her argument that a now unstoppable human-rights sensibility is evolving intranationally and internationally, as if from its own ideal energies, so that it is just a matter of time until the whole world will embrace Kantian practices of hospitality to the displaced and recognition of universal human rights in every country's laws. I think her stories and her analyses of them are invaluable, though I do not share her optimism about the ease of attaining democratic recognitions of universal human rights in our own country's laws and those of others, nor do I think she has rightly focused her account of who and what needs to evolve in

order to make this so. For my more detailed argument on this subject, see my essay "Cultivating Cosmopolitan Pluralism: Democratic Community Amidst Diversity After Huntington and Benhabib," forthcoming in Green and Reich, *Democracy and Diversity in the Pragmatic Tradition.*

3. As a faculty member at Fordham University, New York City's Jesuit university, "subsidiarity" is familiar to me as a Jesuit concept that calls for assigning responsibility at the lowest competent level rather than attempting to organize and control an institution's or a society's discernment process and active engagements in a "top-down," hierarchical manner. See Wills, *Inventing America*; and Dewey, "Presenting Thomas Jefferson."

4. See Pratt, *Native Pragmatism*; and Green, "Equality."

5. See Emerson, "Nature" and "The American Scholar."

6. I am indebted to David Woods for this reminder of the continuing importance of Burnham's legacy as a trailblazing urban planner, in Chicago and in many other American cities.

7. See Westbrook, *John Dewey and American Democracy*, and Cristi, "Hayek on Liberalism and Democracy."

8. For a more detailed analysis of how the civil rights movement advanced its culture-transforming goals through "second-strand" democratic citizen participation during these years, and what we can learn from their effective efforts, see my essay "King's Civil Rights Act Turns Forty."

9. I am indebted to David Woods for the reminder that Sherry Arnstein's "ladder of participation," ranging from "manipulation" to "citizen control," served as the standard framework for imagining and assessing forms and scopes of citizen participation during the Model Cities Program era. See Arnstein's "The Ladder of Citizen Participation," which she developed as one of President Johnson's coordinators of the Model Cities Program for use by citizen-activists .

10. For an excellent discussion of SDS's strengths and weaknesses as a democratic change organization, see Polletta, *Freedom Is an Endless Meeting.*

11. See Evans, *Personal Politics.*

12. See Miklaszewska, *Democracy in Central Europe, 1989–1999.*

13. Part 2 of this chapter is a revised and expanded version of an essay with this same title that appeared in a special issue of *The Journal of Speculative Philosophy* on "Pragmatism and Deliberative Politics." For some of my related thoughts on deliberative politics, see my essay "Pluralism and Deliberative Democracy."

14. Barack Obama issued a related invitation in *The Audacity of Hope* and in his campaign for the American presidency. The passionate response to him shows how hungry for a deeper democracy many Americans now are.

15. See Moses, *Revolution of Conscience.*

16. See Lerner, *The Grimke Sisters from South Carolina.*

17. See James, "The Will to Believe."

6. The Continuously Planning City

1. See Sandel, *Democracy's Discontent*; and Barber, *Jihad vs. McWorld*.

2. In her much-used model of the "Ladder of Participation," Sherry Arnstein contrasted significant, future-influencing citizen participatory roles of various scopes with "manipulation," time- and energy-wasting ways to appear to involve citizens while actually preventing them from organizing and being heard as Deweyan "publics." See Arnstein, "The Ladder of Citizen Participation," which she developed for citizen use during her time as one of President Johnson's leading commissioners in his American "War on Poverty" in the 1960s.

3. For preliminary analyses of citizen demands to participate in planning for the "Sixteen Acres" of lower Manhattan where the World Trade Center stood until 9/11, see Paul Goldberger's *Up from Zero*, Daniel Libeskind's *Breaking Ground*, and my own "Building a Cosmopolitan World Future Through Pragmatist Mutual Hospitality." David Woods is currently developing what promises to be the most in-depth sociological analysis of citizen participation in the rebuilding of lower Manhattan through processes developed by an alliance of civic organizations that formed shortly after September 11, which he served as a professional urban planner and participant-observer; see his forthcoming *Rebuilding Lower Manhattan*.

4. See my *Deep Democracy*, especially chapter 6, "Transforming World Capitalisms Through Radical Pragmatism: Economy, Law, and Democracy."

5. See, for example, works listed in this book's bibliography by Michael Sandel, Benjamin Barber, Howard McGary, Daniel Kemmis, Jim Wallis, Michael Lerner, Harry C. Boyte, Sara M. Evans, Alain Touraine, Eric Olin Wright, Archon Fung, Carmen Siriani, Louis Friedland, Theda Skocpol, Robert D. Putnam, Amatai Etzioni, and Jeffrey C. Alexander.

6. See, for example, works listed in this book's bibliography by Richard Rorty, Richard Bernstein, Hilary Putnam, Cornel West, Stephen Rockefeller, Robert Westbrook, Hans Joas, William R. Caspary, John J. McDermott, Beth J. Singer, R. W. Sleeper, Bruce Wilshire, Larry A. Hickman, Vincent Colapietro, Jacqueline Ann Kegley, Thomas M. Alexander, John J. Stuhr, Michael Eldridge, Mitchell Aboulafia, Pierre Bordieu, Richard Shusterman, Joseph Margolis, Charlene Haddock Seigfried, Jim Garrison, Donald Koch and Bill E. Lawson, Shannon L. Sullivan, Scott L. Pratt, Erin McKenna, Leonard Harris, Noelle McAfee, Robert B. Talisse, John Shook, John Stuhr, Ruth Anna Putnam, Morris Dickstein, Patrick Shade, Naoko Saito, Sor-Hoon Tan, Roudy William Hildreth, and Louis Menand, whose best-selling study *The Metaphysical Club* won the Pulitzer Prize and attracted a wide public audience to thinking about the merits of classical American pragmatism.

7. See, for example, works listed in this book's bibliography by Jürgen Habermas, John Forester, Seyla Benhabib, Nancy Fraser, James L. Marsh, Martin Matustik, and Jorge M. Valadez.

8. See, for example, works listed in this book's bibliography by Dorothy Smith, Carol Gilligan, Sara Ruddick, Alison Jaggar, Iris Marion Young, Martha Nussbaum, Nel Noddings, Karen M. Warren, Julia Kristeva, Linda Martin Alcoff, Patricia J. Huntington, Patricia Hill Collins, bell hooks, Charlene Haddock Seigfied, Marjorie Miller, Erin McKenna, Catherine Eschele, and Robin Morgan. An extensive bibliography, grouped according to schools of feminist thought, is included in Tong, *Feminist Thought*. My own work also contributes to feminist theory and transformative practice.

9. See, for example, works listed in this book's bibliography by Benjamin Barber, Robert Dahl, Archon Fung, Jürgen Habermas, John Rawls, Joshua Cohen, Amy Gutmann and Dennis Thompson, Stephen Macedo, James Bohman, and John Dryzek.

10. See, for example, works listed in this book's bibliography Andreas Duany and Elizabeth Plater-Zybark, Anton C. Nelessen, Anthony Downs, and Peter Calthorpe. See also excellent work from various members of the Congress of New Urbanism, a network of urban planning scholars and practitioners, founded in 1995.

11. See Aldo Leopold's now classic "The Land Ethic," which is widely reprinted, including in May et al., *Applied Ethics*.

12. On real versus pseudoparticipation, see Carole Pateman's brief, clear, and enormously helpful work, *Participation and Democratic Theory*.

13. See Alexis de Tocqueville's *Democracy in America* (first published in 1835 and 1840), his two-part analysis of his observations of American patterns of social living during his nine-month visit from May 1831 to February 1832, during which he visited various northern and southern cities and states that then composed the United States of America, all of them in the eastern part of what is now a much larger, more urbanized, and even more diverse country.

14. On "ontological insecurity," which is my post-9/11 reconstruction of Anthony Giddens's concept of "ontological security," see chapter 3 (above) and his *Modernity and Self-Identity*.

15. Martin Luther King Jr. theorized and worked to heighten creative tensions in his approach to citizen participation in democratic transformation; see his "Letter from Birmingham Jail," which is widely anthologized, including in Washington, *A Testament of Hope*. William R. Caspary outlines and analyzes a pragmatist approach to conflict resolution in his *Dewey on Democracy*.

16. Dewey theorized such a growth process of leaders in his "Time and Individuality." In *The Souls of Black Folk*, W. E. B. Du Bois showed how America's Black churches emerged as such democratic-participatory institutions, providing for basic needs and offering social support to their pressured members while also functioning as schools of democracy that built members' citizen participation skills. Taylor Branch documents how King and the Southern Christian Leadership Conference used Black churches as such schools for democracy in his *Parting the Waters*. James H. Cone's analysis in *Martin and Malcolm and America* explores how King's efficacy and that of Malcolm X. Shabazz depended upon the ability of their core group of

valued activists to create wider, change-minded organizations that could function as schools of democracy that prepared a wider constituency of citizens for democratic participation in shaping America's future. In her *Pragmatism and Feminism*, Charlene Haddock Seigfried explored how Jane Addams and the women of Chicago's Hull House created such a school of democracy for new immigrants to America at the turn of the twentieth century and what we might learn from their example. For a recent analysis of how such an approach might empower women, including those struggling with poverty and illiteracy in less developed countries, see my "Deepening Democratic Transformation."

17. See Polletta, *Freedom Is an Endless Meeting*; Cone, *Malcolm and Martin and America*; Evans, *Personal Politics*; Johnston, *Sexual Politics*; and Dryzek, *Deliberative Democracy and Beyond*, especially his discussion of the worldwide environmental movement.

18. In responding to my essay "Participatory Democracy," John Dryzek commented that it would be a mistake for issue-focused nongovernmental organizations and activist movements to make gaining a formal seat at the table where government decisions are made their primary goal, or even an aspiration, because they play a valuable outsider role in organizing pressure that allows them to express a clear message. I take his point seriously; my point here is that it is sometimes desirable and possible for some members of a coalition to become insiders with formal roles in government, while their colleagues remain the kind of valuable outsiders Dryzek described.

19. See DeGrove, *Land Growth and Politics*.

20. I am grateful to David W. Woods for this information.

21. For additional studies and "best-practices" analyses of democratic citizen participation efforts in cities throughout America and in some other parts of the world, see Fung and Wright, *Deepening Democracy*; Fung, *Empowered Participation*; Siriani and Friedland, *Civic Innovation in America*; and Woods, *Rebuilding Lower Manhattan*.

22. After reaching out to 7,500 leaders of citizen participation efforts in various parts of the United States, and supplementing their responses with information from the data bank at the Lincoln Filene Center for Citizenship and Public Affairs at Tufts University, the three authors and their large team of research assistants chose 415 programs for further study, reviewed scholarly studies and other literature about them, and interviewed program administrators by telephone as needed. Having narrowed their list to fifteen exemplary programs, they chose their focal five cities because they are geographically dispersed, have socioeconomically diverse populations of more than 100,000 people, and display "an impressive commitment to the idea of participatory democracy," as expressed in neighborhood associations that are open to and run by average citizens and that have a formal role in government concerning planning, zoning, city services, and proposed developments. See Berry et al., *The Rebirth of Urban Democracy*, 1. In 1986 and 1987, the researchers

surveyed approximately 1,100 citizens representing all of the officially recognized neighborhoods of these cities, then reinterviewed them eighteen months later (contacting a total of ten survey groups, with approximately 66 percent of the participants being included in both surveys). An eleventh control group of 1,500 people was interviewed once, having been chosen in groups of approximately 150 from ten comparison cities, two groups for each focal city drawn from other cities that matched it in size and socioeconomic characteristics but that did not have extensive citizen participation efforts. In addition, the researchers conducted field interviews with city administrators, city council members, and citizen participation program officials, and citizen group leaders, as well as with focus groups of activists in some neighborhood associations.

23. See sociologist Mark R. Warren's study of San Antonio's Communities Organized for Public Service (COPS) and the Industrial Areas Foundation (IAF) organizational network of which it is a part, *Dry Bones Rattling*. See also Wilson, *The Bridge Over the Racial Divide*.

24. See Alinsky's *Reveille for Radicals* and *Rules for Radicals*, and Boyte's *CommonWealth*.

25. See Wilson, *The Bridge Over the Racial Divide*.

26. For a few more details on our experiences with the King County Organizing Project in the mid-1990s, see the final chapter of my *Deep Democracy*, "Deepening Democracy: Rebuilding the Public Square."

27. One of the two books that complete this three-part meditation on deepening democracy will include a chapter on "Democratizing the Universities."

28. For thoughtful discussions of ways in which the presence and absence of democratic virtues shows up in American public life, see Kemmis, *Community and the Politics of Place*. On the nature of such democratic virtues and how they might be cultivated, see Talisse, *Democracy After Liberalism*.

29. See the *New York Times*, April 14, 2001.

30. I am indebted to David Woods for "insider knowledge" about the development of the Civic Alliance and its post-9/11 citizen participation events; see his forthcoming *Rebuilding Lower Manhattan* for fuller details and insights about how well this process has worked.

31. For example, fifty-six countries are now attempting to transform poverty at the grassroots level by experimenting with localized variants of Prof. Mohammed Yunus's Grameen Bank, which has had real effectiveness in improving the lives of millions of poor people in Bangladesh by funding microloans to small entrepreneurs supported by networks of other microborrowers (Green, *Deep Democracy*, chap. 6). These other countries' experiences already constitute a fund of experience with alternative strategies and techniques upon which Prof. Muhammed Yunus and Bangladesh can draw in increasing the Grameen Bank's reconstructive effectiveness.

7. The Hope of Democratic Living

1. On Walter Lippman, see Boisvert, *John Dewey*; and Savage, *John Dewey's Liberalism*. On Hayek's final view, see Cristi, "Hayek on Liberalism and Democracy." For Huntington's views, see Huntington et al., *The Crisis of Democracy*, as well as his more recent books. For a balanced evaluation of these views, see Pharr and Putnam, *Disaffected Democracies*. For Rorty's self-description as a "red-diaper anti-communist baby," see his *Philosophy and Social Hope*, 102. For a balanced treatment of "neoconservatives," see Halper and Clarke, *America Alone*.

2. For my fuller Deweyan critique of "formal" democratic institutions, see my *Deep Democracy*.

3. See my essay "Pluralism and Deliberative Democracy." See also Caspary, *Dewey on Democracy*; Dryzek, *Deliberative Democracy and Beyond*; McAfee, "Three Models of Democratic Deliberation"; and Susskind et al., *Transboundary Environmental Negotiation*.

4. See Dewey's discussion of the importance of the educative institutions of adult living in *Reconstruction in Philosophy* and in passages from many of his other works, some of which I quoted and commented on in chapter 3 of my *Deep Democracy*.

5. See my *Deep Democracy* and Woods's "Lynnwood Legacy" and "Collaborative Planning for the Lynnwood Legacy."

6. My students have found Loeb's *Soul of a Citizen* a great help in thinking through their own existential decisions about whether to risk their time and their hopes on some form of active citizen participation in local and global future shaping.

7. See Benhabib, *Another Cosmopolitanism*.

8. James's assertion of this epistemological "right" was framed in terms of an ethics of belief that he broadly shared with his main opponent in the controversy, William Clifford, as well as many other scientists and philosophers of the late nineteenth century. That is, James acknowledged that our thought-in-action draws upon and influences the future of a shared fund of truths that make a difference for the practical security and the meaningfulness of human existence. Thus, he argued, we must take seriously our reliance and our influence upon others in making our own belief commitments, and we must make them in such a way as to be open to future evidence one way or the other. Nonetheless, James argued, if our goal is not just to avoid error but to know and to benefit from the truth about something that greatly matters to us and that requires a provisional decision *now*—in this case, the "moral truth" about how much democracy is possible and desirable in our times—we must risk the possibility of being wrong and all that goes with it by adopting one belief or the other. Thus, in the case of a "genuine option," having considered the available evidence carefully, we have the "right" to adopt a hypothesis and to actively seek to know whether experience will confirm or falsify it.

BIBLIOGRAPHY

Aboulafia, Mitchell. "A (neo)American in Paris: Bourdieu, Mead, and Pragmatism." In *Bourdieu: A Critical Reader*, edited by Richard Shusterman. Malden: Blackwell, 1999.

——. *The Cosmopolitan Self: George Herbert Mead and Continental Philosophy*. Urbana: University of Illinois Press, 2001.

Addams, Jane. *Democracy and Social Ethics*. New York: The Macmillan Press, 1902.

——. *Newer Ideals of Peace*. New York: Macmillan, 1907.

——. *Twenty Years at Hull-House*. New York: Macmillan, 1910.

Alcoff, Linda Martin. *Visible Identities: Race, Gender, and the Self*. Oxford: Oxford University Press, 2005.

Alexander, Jeffrey C. *The Civil Sphere*. Oxford: Oxford University Press, 2006.

Alexander, Thomas M. *John Dewey's Theory of Art, Experience, and Nature*. Albany: State University of New York Press, 1987.

——. "The Fourth World of American Philosophy: The Philosophical Significance of Native American Culture." *Transactions of the Charles S. Peirce Society* 32, no. 3 (1996).

Alinsky, Saul. *Reveille for Radicals*. New York: Random House, 1946, 1969.

——. *Rules for Radicals: A Pragmatic Primer for Realistic Radicals*. New York: Random House, 1971.

Arnstein, Sherry. "The Ladder of Citizen Participation." *Journal of the American Institute of Planners* 35 (1969): 216–224.

Baldwin, James. *The Fire Next Time*. New York: Vintage Books, 1963.

Barber, Benjamin R. *Strong Democracy: Participatory Politics for a New Age*. Berkeley: University of California Press, 1984.

——. *Jihad vs. McWorld: How Globalism and Tribalism Are Reshaping the World*. New York: Ballantine Books, 1995.

——. *A Passion for Democracy: American Essays*. Princeton, N.J.: Princeton University Press, 1998.

——. *Fear's Empire: War, Terrorism, and Democracy*. New York: W. W. Norton & Company, 2005.

Bell, Derek. *Faces at the Bottom of the Well: The Permanence of Racism*. New York: Basic Books, 1992.

——. *Gospel Choirs: Psalms of Survival in an Alien Land Called Home*. New York: Basic Books, 1996.

Bellah, Robert N., Richard Madsen, William M. Sullivan, and Anne Swidler. *Habits of the Heart: Individualism and Commitment in American Life*. Berkeley: University of California Press, 1985.

Benhabib, Seyla, ed. *Democracy and Difference: Contesting the Boundaries of the Political*. Princeton, N.J.: Princeton University Press, 1996.

——. *The Claims of Culture: Equality and Diversity in the Global Era*. Princeton, N.J.: Princeton University Press, 2002.

——. *Another Cosmopolitanism*. Oxford: Oxford University Press, 2006.

Berger, Peter L., and Samuel P. Huntington. *Many Globalizations: Cultural Diversity in the Contemporary World*. Oxford: Oxford University Press, 2002.

Bernstein, Richard. *Praxis and Action: Contemporary Philosophies of Human Activity*. Philadelphia: University of Pennsylvania Press, 1971, 1999.

——. "The Resurgence of Pragmatism." *Social Research* 4 (1982): 813–840.

——. "Community in the Pragmatic Tradition." In *The Renewal of Pragmatism*, edited by Morris Dickstein. Durham, N.C.: Duke University Press, 1998.

Berry, Jeffrey M., Kent E. Portney, and Ken Thomson. *The Rebirth of Urban Democracy*. Washington, D.C.: Brookings Institute Press, 1993.

Bohman, James. *Public Deliberation; Pluralism, Complexity, and Democracy*. Cambridge, Mass.: The MIT Press, 1996.

——. "Realizing Deliberative Democracy as a Mode of Inquiry: Pragmatism, Social Facts, and Normative Theory." *Journal of Speculative Philosophy* 18, no. 1 (2004).

Boisvert, Raymond D. *John Dewey: Rethinking Our Time*. Albany: State University of New York Press, 1998.

Bourdieu, Pierre. *Distinctions: A Social Critique of the Judgment of Taste*. Translated by Richard Nice. Cambridge, Mass.: Harvard University Press, 1984.

Boyte, Harry C. *CommonWealth: A Return to Citizen Politics*. New York: The Free Press, 1989.

——. *Everyday Politics: Reconnecting Citizens and Public Life*. Philadelphia: University of Pennsylvania Press, 2004.

Branch, Taylor. *Parting the Waters: America in the King Years, 1954–63*. New York: Simon & Schuster, 1988.

Brandom, Robert B., ed. *Rorty and His Critics*. Oxford: Blackwell, 2000.

Brown, Joseph Epes, and Emily Cousins. *Teaching Spirits: Understanding Native American Religious Traditions*. New York: Oxford University Press, 2001.

Bunge, Robert. *An American Urphilosophie: An American Philosophy BP (Before Pragmatism)*. Lanham, Md.: University Press of America, 1984.

Butler, Judith. *Gender Trouble: Feminism and the Subversion of Identity*. New York: Routledge, 1991, 1999.

——. "Performativity's Social Magic." In *Bourdieu: A Critical Reader*, edited by Richard Shusterman. Oxford: Blackwell, 1999.

——. "Theoretical Cultures Across the Disciplines." Paper presented at the annual meeting of the American Sociological Association, San Francisco, California, August 17, 2005.

Calthorpe, Peter. *The Next American Metropolis: Ecology, Community, and the American Dream*. Princeton, N.J.: Princeton Architectural Press, 1993.

Caspary, William R. *Dewey on Democracy*. Ithaca, N.Y.: Cornell University Press, 2000.

Cohen, Joshua. *Association and Democracy in the Modern World*. New York: Verso, 1995.

——. "Procedure and Substance in Deliberative Democracy." In *Deliberative Politics: Essays on Democracy and Disagreement*, edited by Stephen Macedo. Oxford: Oxford University Press, 1999.

Cohen, Roger. "Who Really Brought Down Milosevic?" *New York Times*, November 26, 2000.

Colapietro, Vincent. *Peirce's Approach to the Self: A Semiotic Perspective on Human Subjectivity*. Albany: State University of New York Press, 1989.

Collins, Patricia Hill. "Searching for Sojourner Truth: Toward an Epistemology of Empowerment." In *Fighting Words: Black Women and the Search for Justice*. Minneapolis: University of Minnesota Press, 1998.

——. *Black Feminist Thought: Knowledge, Consciousness, and the Politics of Empowerment*. New York: Routledge, 1991.

——. *Black Sexual Politics: African Americans, Gender, and the New Racism*. New York: Routledge, 2004.

Cone, James H. *Martin and Malcolm and America: A Dream or a Nightmare?* Maryknoll: Orbis Books, 1991.

Cristi, Renato. "Hayek on Liberalism and Democracy." In *Democracy in Central Europe*, edited by Justyna Miklaszewska. Krakow: Meritum, 1999.

Dahl, Robert. *Democracy and Its Critics*. New Haven, Conn.: Yale University Press, 1989.

——. *On Democracy*. New Haven, Conn.: Yale University Press, 1998.

DeGrove, John M. *Land Growth and Politics*. Chicago: Planners Press, 1984.

Delbanco, Andrew. *The Death of Satan: How Americans Have Lost the Sense of Evil*. New York: Farrar, Straus and Giroux, 1995.

Derrida, Jacques. *Spectres of Marx: The State of the Debt, The Work of Mourning, and the New International*. Translated by Peggy Kamuf. New York: Routledge, 1994.

Dewey, John. "Maeterlinck's Philosophy of Life." *The Middle Works of John Dewey: 1899–1924*, vol. 6, edited by Jo Ann Boydston. Carbondale: Southern Illinois University Press, 1978. Originally published in 1911.

——. *Democracy and Education*. In *The Middle Works of John Dewey: 1899–1924*, vol. 9, edited by Jo Ann Boydston. Carbondale: Southern Illinois University Press, 1980. Originally published in 1916.

——. "The Need for a Recovery of Philosophy." In *The Middle Works of John Dewey: 1899–1924*, vol. 10, edited by Jo Ann Boydston. Carbondale: Southern Illinois University Press, 1980. Originally published in 1917.

——. *Reconstruction in Philosophy*. In *The Middle Works of John Dewey: 1899–1924*, vol. 12. Edited by Jo Ann Boydston. Carbondale: Southern Illinois University Press, 1982. Originally published in 1920.

——. *Experience and Nature*. In *The Later Works of John Dewey: 1925–1953*, vol. 1, edited by Jo Ann Boydston. Carbondale: Southern Illinois University Press, 1981. Originally published in 1925.

——. *The Public and Its Problems*. In *The Later Works of John Dewey: 1925–1953*, vol. 2, edited by Jo Ann Boydston. Carbondale: Southern Illinois University Press, 1984. Originally published in 1927.

——. *The Quest for Certainty*. In *The Later Works of John Dewey: 1925–1953*, vol. 4, edited by Jo Ann Boydston. Carbondale: Southern Illinois University Press, 1984. Originally published in 1929.

——. *Individualism Old and New*. In *The Later Works of John Dewey: 1925–1953*, vol. 5, edited by Jo Ann Boydston. Carbondale: Southern Illinois University Press, 1984. Originally published in 1930.

——. *Art as Experience*. In *The Later Works of John Dewey: 1925–1953*, vol. 10, edited by Jo Ann Boydston. Carbondale: Southern Illinois University Press, 1987. Originally published in 1934.

——. *Liberalism and Social Action*. In *The Later Works of John Dewey: 1925–1953*, vol. 11, edited by Jo Ann Boydston. Carbondale: Southern Illinois University Press, 1987. Originally published in 1935.

——. "Democracy Is Radical." In *The Later Works of John Dewey: 1925–1953*, vol. 11, edited by Jo Ann Boydston. Carbondale: Southern Illinois University Press, 1987. Originally published in 1937.

——. *Logic: The Theory of Inquiry*. In *The Later Works of John Dewey: 1925–1953*, vol. 12, edited by Jo Ann Boydston. Carbondale: Southern Illinois University Press, 1986. Originally published in 1938.

——. *Experience and Education*. In *The Later Works of John Dewey: 1925–1953*, vol. 13, edited by Jo Ann Boydston. Carbondale: Southern Illinois University Press, 1988. Originally published in 1939.

——. *Freedom and Culture*. In *The Later Works of John Dewey: 1925–1953*, vol. 13, edited by Jo Ann Boydston. Carbondale: Southern Illinois University Press, 1988. Originally published in 1939.

——. *Theory of Valuation*. In *The Later Works of John Dewey: 1925–1953*, vol. 13, edited by Jo Ann Boydston. Carbondale: Southern Illinois University Press, 1988. Originally published in 1939.

——. "Creative Democracy—The Task Before Us." In *The Later Works of John Dewey: 1925–1953*, vol. 13, edited by Jo Ann Boydston. Carbondale: Southern Illinois University Press, 1988. Originally published in 1939.

——. "Time and Individuality." In *The Later Works of John Dewey: 1925–1953*, vol. 14, edited by Jo Ann Boydston. Carbondale: Southern Illinois University Press. Originally published in 1940.

——. "Presenting Thomas Jefferson." In *The Later Works of John Dewey: 1925–1953*, vol. 14, edited by Jo Ann Boydston. Carbondale: Southern Illinois University Press. Originally published in 1940.

Dewey, John, and James H. Tufts. *Ethics, Revised Edition*. In *The Later Works of John Dewey: 1925–1953*, vol. 7, edited by Jo Ann Boydston. Carbondale: Southern Illinois University Press, 1985. Originally published in 1932.

Dickstein, Morris, ed. *The Revival of Pragmatism: New Essays on Social Thought, Law, and Culture*. Durham, N.C.: Duke University Press, 1998.

Downs, Anthony. *New Visions for Metropolitan America*. Washington, D.C.: The Brookings Institution and Lincoln Institute of Land Policy, 1994.

Dryzek, John. *Discursive Democracy: Politics, Policy, Political Science*. Cambridge: Cambridge University Press, 1990.

——. *Deliberative Democracy and Beyond*. Oxford: Oxford University Press, 2000.

——. "Pragmatism and Democracy: In Search of Deliberative Politics." *Journal of Speculative Philosophy* 18, no. 1 (2004).

Du Bois, W. E. B. *The Souls of Black Folk*. New York: Bantam Books, 1969. Originally published in 1903.

Duany, Andreas, and Elizabeth Plater-Zybark. *Towns and Town-Making Principles*. New York: Rizzoli Press, 1991.

Dunsmore, Roger. *Earth's Mind: Essays in Native Literature*. Albuquerque: University of New Mexico Press, 1997.

Eldridge, Michael. *Transforming Experience: John Dewey's Cultural Instrumentalism*. Nashville, Tenn.: Vanderbilt University Press, 1998.

Emerson, Ralph Waldo. "Nature." In *The Portable Emerson*, edited by Carl Bode in collaboration with Malcolm Cowley. New York: Penguin, 1981. Originally published in 1836.

——. "The American Scholar." In *The Portable Emerson*, edited by Carl Bode in collaboration with Malcolm Cowley. New York: Penguin, 1981. Originally published in 1837.

Erlanger, Steven. "From a Summons to a Slap: How the Fight in Yugoslavia Was Won." *New York Times*, October 15, 2000.

Eschele, Catherine. *Global Democracy, Social Movements, and Feminism*. Boulder, Colo.: Westview Press, 2001.

Etzioni, Amatai. *The Spirit of Community: Rights, Responsibilities, and the Communitarian Agenda*. New York: Crown Publishers, 1993.

——. *The New Golden Rule: Community and Morality in a Democratic Society*. New York: Basic Books, 1996.

——. *From Empire to Community: A New Approach to International Relations*. New York: Palgrave Macmillan, 2004.

Evans, Karen G. "Reclaiming John Dewey: Democratic Inquiry, Pragmatism, and Public Management." *Administration and Society* 32, no. 3 (2000).

Evans, Sara M. *Personal Politics: The Roots of Women's Liberation in the Civil Rights Movement and the New Left*. New York: Random House, 1979.

——. *Tidal Wave: How Women Changed America at Century's End*. New York: The Free Press, 2003.

Evans, Sara M., and Harry C. Boyte. *Free Spaces: The Sources of Democratic Change in America*. Chicago: University of Chicago Press, 1986, 1992.

Fishkin, James S. *Democracy and Deliberation: New Directions for Democratic Reform*. New Haven, Conn.: Yale University Press, 1991.

Forester, John. *The Deliberative Practitioner: Encouraging Participatory Planning Processes*. Cambridge, Mass.: The MIT Press, 1999.

Frankl, Viktor. *Man's Search for Meaning*. New York: Pocket Books, 1984.

Franklin, John Hope, and Alfred A. Moss Jr. *From Slavery to Freedom: A History of Negro Americans*. 6th ed. New York: Alfred A. Knopf, 1988.

Fraser, Nancy. *Unruly Practices*. Minneapolis: University of Minnesota Press, 1989.

——. *Justice Interruptus: Critical Reflections on the "Postsocialist Condition."* New York: Routledge, 1997.

Fung, Archon. *Empowered Participation: Reinventing Urban Democracy*. Princeton, N.J.: Princeton University Press, 2004.

Fung, Archon, and Eric Olin Wright, eds. *Deepening Democracy: Institutional Innovations in Empowered Participatory Governance*. New York: Verso, 2003.

Gans, Herbert. "Sociology in America: The Discipline and the Public." *American Sociological Review* 54 (1989).

Garrison, Jim. *Dewey and Eros: Wisdom and Desire in the Art of Teaching*. New York: Teachers College Press, 1997.

——, ed. *Reconstructing Democracy, Recontextualizing Dewey*. Albany: State University of New York Press, 2008.

Gavin, William J. *William James and the Reinstatement of the Vague*. Philadelphia: Temple University Press, 1992.

Giddens, Anthony. *Modernity and Self-Identity: Self and Society in the Late Modern Age*. Stanford, Calif.: Stanford University Press, 1991.

Gilligan, Carol. *In a Different Voice: Psychological Theory and Women's Development*. Cambridge, Mass.: Harvard University Press, 1982.

Glaude, Eddie S., Jr. *In a Shade of Blue: Pragmatism and the Politics of Black America.* Chicago: University of Chicago Press, 2007.

Glazer, Nathan. *We Are All Multiculturalists Now.* Cambridge, Mass.: Harvard University Press, 1997.

Goldberger, Paul. *Up from Zero: Politics, Architecture, and the Rebuilding of New York.* New York: Random House, 2004.

Goodwin, Jeff, James M. Jasper, and Francesca Polletta, eds. *Passionate Politics: Emotions and Social Movements.* Chicago: University of Chicago Press, 2001.

Grange, Joseph. *The City: An Urban Cosmology.* Albany: State University of New York Press, 1999.

Green, Judith M. *Deep Democracy: Community, Diversity, and Transformation.* Lanham, Md.: Rowman & Littlefield, 1999.

——. "Alain Locke's Multicultural Philosophy of Value: A Transformative Guide for the Twenty-First Century." In *The Critical Pragmatism of Alain Locke: A Reader on Value Theory, Aesthetics, Community, Culture, Race, and Education*, edited by Leonard Harris. Lanham: Rowman & Littlefield, 1999.

——. "Deepening Democracy in Central Europe: A Radical Pragmatist Perspective from the American Experience." In *Democracy in Central Europe, 1989–1999: Comparative and Historical Perspectives*, edited by Justyna Miklaszewska. Krakow: Meritum/Jagiellonian University Printing House, 2000.

——. "Deepening Democratic Transformation: Deweyan Individuation and Pragmatist Feminism." In *Feminist Interpretations of John Dewey*, edited by Charlene Haddock Seigfried. University Park: The Pennsylvania State University Press, 2002.

——. "Philosophical Windows on Native American Spiritualities." *Chicago Studies* 42, no. 3 (2003).

——. "Participatory Democracy: Movements, Campaigns, and Democratic Living." *The Journal of Speculative Philosophy* 18, no. 1 (2004).

——. "Building a Cosmopolitan World Future Through Pragmatist Mutual Hospitality." In *Pragmatism and The Problem of Race*, edited by Donald Koch and Bill E. Lawson. Bloomington: Indiana University Press, 2004.

——. "Guiding Post-Totalitarian Economic Democratization Through Deweyan Radical Pragmatism." In *Democracy and the Post-Totalitarian Experience*, edited by Leszek Koczanowicz and Beth J. Singer. Amsterdam: Rodopi, 2005.

——. "King's Civil Rights Act Turns Forty: Leading the Beloved Community in the Twenty-First Century." *The Journal of Social Philosophy* (Summer 2005).

——. "Pluralism and Deliberative Democracy." In *A Companion to Pragmatism*, edited by John Shook and Joseph Margolis. New York: Blackwell, 2006.

——. "Equality." In *The Encyclopedia of American Philosophy*, edited by John Lachs and Robert Talisse. New York: Routledge, 2007.

——. "Friendship." In *The Encyclopedia of American Philosophy*, edited by John Lachs and Robert Talisse. New York: Routledge, 2007.

——. "Growth." In *The Encyclopedia of American Philosophy*, edited by John Lachs and Robert Talisse. New York: Routledge, 2007.

——. "On the Passing of Richard Rorty and the Future of American Philosophy." *Contemporary Pragmatism* 4, no. 2 (December 2007).

——. "Dr. Dewey's Metaphysical Therapeutic for America's Post-9/11 Democratic Disease: Toward Cultural Revitalization and Political Reinhabitation." In *Reconstructing Democracy, Recontextualizing Dewey*, edited by Jim Garrison. Albany: State University of New York Press, 2008.

——. "Social Democracy, Cosmopolitan Hospitality, and Inter-Civilizational Peace: Lessons from Jane Addams." In *Feminist Interpretations of Jane Addams*, edited by Maurice Hamington. University Park: Penn State University Press, 2008.

——. "Cultivating Cosmopolitan Pluralism: Democratic Community Amidst Diversity After Huntington and Benhabib." In *Democracy and Diversity in the Pragmatic Tradition*, edited by Judith Green and Kersten Reich, forthcoming.

——. "Deeply Democratic Education for Whole Persons in Twenty-First-Century Global Contexts." In *Reconstructing Democracy for a New World*, edited by Larry A. Hickman and Giuseppe Spadafora, forthcoming.

Greene, Brian. *The Elegant Universe: Superstrings, Hidden Dimensions, and the Quest for the Ultimate Theory*. New York: Random House, 1999.

Gutmann, Amy, and Dennis Thompson. *Democracy and Disagreement*. Cambridge, Mass.: Harvard University Press, 1996.

Habermas, Jürgen. "A Reply to My Critics." In *Habermas: Critical Debates*, edited by John Thompson and David Held. Cambridge, Mass.: The MIT Press, 1982.

——. *The Theory of Communicative Action*. Translated by Thomas McCarthy. Boston: Beacon Press, 1984, 1987.

——. *Postmetaphysical Thinking: Philosophical Essays*. Cambridge, Mass.: The MIT Press, 1992.

——. *Between Facts and Norms: Contributions to a Discourse Theory of Law and Democracy*. Cambridge, Mass.: The MIT Press, 1996.

——. "Three Normative Models of Democracy." In *Democracy and Difference: Contesting the Boundaries of the Political*, edited by Seyla Benhabib. Princeton, N.J.: Princeton University Press, 1996.

Halper, Stefan, and Jonathan Clarke. *America Alone: The Neo-Conservatives and the Global Order*. Cambridge: Cambridge University Press, 2004.

Harris, Leonard, ed. *The Philosophy of Alain Locke: Harlem Renaissance and Beyond*. 1989.

——, ed. *The Critical Pragmatism of Alain Locke: A Reader on Value Theory, Aesthetics, Community, Culture, Race, and Education*. Lanham, Md.: Rowman & Littlefield, 1999.

——, ed. *Racism: Key Concepts in Critical Theory*. Amherst, Mass.: Humanities Books, 1999.

Heilbroner, Robert. "Reflections on the Triumph of Capitalism." *The New Yorker* 64 (January 23, 1989). Reprinted in *Moral Issues in Business*, 5th ed., edited by William H. Shaw and Vincent Barry. Belmont, Calif.: Wadsworth Publishing Company, 1992.

Hickman, Larry A. *John Dewey's Pragmatic Technology*. Bloomington: Indiana University Press, 1990.

——, ed. *Reading Dewey: Interpretations for a Postmodern Generation*. Bloomington: Indiana University Press, 1998.

Hildreth, Roudy William. *Living Citizenship: John Dewey and the Renewal of American Democratic Life*. Forthcoming.

Hill, Jason. *Becoming A Cosmopolitan*. Lanham, Md.: Rowman & Littlefield, 2000.

hooks, bell. *Feminist Theory: From Margin to Center*. Boston: South End Press, 1984.

——. *Where We Stand: Class Matters*. New York: Routledge, 2000.

——. *Teaching Community: A Pedagogy of Hope*. New York: Routledge, 2003.

Howe, Irving. *A Margin of Hope: An Intellectual Autobiography*. 1982.

Huntington, Patricia J. *Ecstatic Subjects, Utopia, and Recognition: Kristeva, Heidegger, Irigaray*. Albany: State University of New York Press, 1998.

Huntington, Samuel. *American Politics: The Promise of Disharmony*. Cambridge, Mass.: Harvard University Press, 1981.

——. *The Third Wave: Democratization in the Late Twentieth Century*. Norman: University of Oklahoma Press, 1991.

——. *The Clash of Civilizations and the Remaking of World Order*. New York: Touchstone, 1996.

——. *Who Are We? Challenges to America's National Identity*. New York: Simon & Schuster, 2004.

——, and Peter L. Berger, ed. *Many Globalizations: Cultural Diversity in the Contemporary World*. Oxford: Oxford University Press.

——, Michel Crozier, and Joji Watanuki. *The Crisis of Democracy: Report on the Governability of Democracies to the Trilateral Commission*. New York: New York University Press, 1975.

Jaggar, Alison. *Feminist Politics and Human Nature*. Lanham, Md.: Rowman & Littlefield, 1984, 1988.

James, William. "What Is an Emotion?" *Mind* 9 (1884): 188–205. Reprinted in *Collected Essays and Reviews*. New York: Longmans, Green & Co., 1920. Also in *The Works of William James*, edited by Frederick H. Burghardt. Cambridge, Mass.: Harvard University Press, 1975.

——. "The Moral Philosopher and the Moral Life." *International Journal of Ethics* 1 (1891). Reprinted in *The Will to Believe and Other Essays in Popular Philosophy*. New York: Longmans, Green & Co., 1911. Also in *The Works of William James*, edited by Frederick H. Burghardt. Cambridge, Mass.: Harvard University Press, 1975.

——. "The Will to Believe." In *The Will to Believe and Other Essays in Popular Philosophy*. New York and London: Longmans, Green & Co., 1911. Also in *The Works of William James*, edited by Frederick H. Burghardt. Cambridge, Mass.: Harvard University Press, 1975.

——. "The Ph.D. Octopus." *Harvard Monthly* 36 (1903). Reprinted in *Memories and Studies*. New York: Longmans, Green & Co., 1911. Also in *The Works of William James*, edited by Frederick H. Burghardt. Cambridge, Mass.: Harvard University Press, 1975.

——. "The Social Value of the College Bred." *McClure's Magazine* 30 (1908). Reprinted in *Memories and Studies*. New York: Longmans, Green & Co., 1911. Also in *The Works of William James*, edited by Frederick H. Burghardt. Cambridge, Mass.: Harvard University Press, 1975.

Joas, Hans. *Pragmatism and Social Theory*. Chicago: University of Chicago Press, 1993.

Johnston, Carolyn. *Sexual Politics: Feminism and the Family in America*. Tuscaloosa: University of Alabama Press, 1992.

Kegley, Jacqueline Ann. *Genuine Individuals and Genuine Communities: A Roycean Public Philosophy*. Nashville, Tenn.: Vanderbilt University Press, 1997.

Kemmis, Daniel. *Community and the Politics of Place*. Norman: University of Oklahoma Press, 1990.

——. *This Sovereign Land: A New Vision for Governing the West*. Washington, D.C.: Island Press, 2001.

King, Martin Luther, Jr. "Letter from A Birmingham Jail." In *A Testament of Hope: The Essential Writings and Speeches of Martin Luther King, Jr.*, edited by James Melvin Washington. San Francisco: HarperSanFrancisco, 1986. Originally published in 1963.

——. *Where Do We Go From Here: Chaos or Community?* New York: Harper and Row, 1967.

Knobe, Joshua. "A Talent for Bricolage—An Interview with Richard Rorty," *The Dualist* 2 (1995).

Koch, Donald, and Bill E. Lawson, ed. *Pragmatism and the Problem of Race*. Bloomington: Indiana University Press, 2004.

Koczanowicz, Leszek, and Beth J. Singer, ed. *Democracy and the Post-Totalitarian Experience*. Amsterdam: Rodopi, 2005.

Kristeva, Julia. *Intimate Revolt: The Powers and Limits of Psychoanalysis*. New York: Columbia University Press, 2002.

——. *Murder in Byzantium, a Novel*. Translated by C. Jon Delogu. New York: Columbia University Press, 2004, 2006.

Kuhn, Thomas. *The Structure of Scientific Revolutions*. Chicago: University of Chicago Press, 1962.

Lachman, Beth E. *Linking Sustainable Community Activities to Pollution Prevention: A Sourcebook*. Santa Monica, Calif.: RAND Corporation, Critical Technologies Institute, 1997.

Lackey, Douglas. "Just War Theory." In *Applied Ethics: A Multicultural Approach*, 3rd ed., edited by Larry May, Shari Collins-Chobanian, and Kai Wong. Upper Saddle River, N.J.: Prentice Hall, 2002.

Leopold, Aldo. "The Land Ethic." In *Applied Ethics: A Multicultural Approach*, 3rd ed., edited by Larry May, Shari Collins-Chobanian, and Kai Wong. Upper Saddle River, N.J.: Prentice Hall, 2002. Originally published in 1948.

Lerner, Gerda. *The Grimke Sisters from South Carolina: Pioneers for Woman's Rights and Abolition*. New York: Schocken Books, 1967.

Lerner, Michael. *Spirit Matters*. Charlottesville, Va.: Hampton Roads Publishing Company, 2000.

Libeskind, Daniel. *Breaking Ground: Adventures in Life and Architecture*. New York: Riverhead Books, 2004.

Locke, Alain L. *Race Contacts and Interracial Relations*. Edited by Jeffrey C. Stewart. Washington, D.C.: Howard University Press, 1917, 1992.

——. "Values and Imperatives." In *The Philosophy of Alain Locke: Harlem Renaissance and Beyond*, edited by Leonard Harris. Philadelphia: Temple University Press, 1989. Originally published in 1935.

Loeb, Paul Rogat. *Soul of a Citizen: Living with Conviction in a Cynical Time*. New York: St. Martin's Griffin, 1999.

Macedo, Stephen, ed. *Deliberative Politics: Essays on Democracy and Disagreement*. Oxford: Oxford University Press, 1999.

Margolis, Joseph. *Life Without Principles: Reconciling Theory and Practice*. Malden, Mass.: Blackwell, 1996.

——. *Reinventing Pragmatism: American Philosophy at the End of the Twentieth Century*. Ithaca, N.Y.: Cornell University Press, 2002.

Marsh, James L. *Critique, Action, and Liberation*. Albany: State University of New York Press, 1995.

——. *Process, Praxis, and Transcendence*. Albany: State University of New York Press, 1999.

——. *Unjust Legality: A Critique of Habermas's Philosophy of Law*. Lanham, Md.: Rowman & Littlefield, 2001.

Matustik, Martin J. Beck. *Specters of Liberation: Great Refusals in the New World Order*. Albany: State University of New York Press, 1998.

McAfee, Noelle. "Three Models of Democratic Deliberation." *The Journal of Speculative Philosophy* 18, no. 1 (2004).

McCarthy, E. Doyle. "Toward a Sociology of the Physical World: George Herbert Mead on Physical Objects." *Studies in Symbolic Interaction* 5 (1984): 105–121.

———. *Knowledge As Culture: The New Sociology of Knowledge.* New York: Routledge, 1996.

McDermott, John J. *The Culture of Experience: Philosophical Essays in the American Grain.* New York: New York University Press, 1976.

———. ed. *The Writings of William James: A Comprehensive Edition.* University of Chicago Press, 1977.

———. *Streams of Experience: Reflections on the History and Philosophy of American Culture.* Amherst: University of Massachusetts Press, 1987.

———. *Experience as Philosophy.* Edited by James Campbell and Richard Hart. New York: Fordham University Press, 2007.

McGary, Howard. *Race and Social Justice.* New York: Blackwell, 1998.

McGary, Howard, and Bill E. Lawson. *Between Slavery and Freedom: Philosophy and American Slavery.* Bloomington: Indiana University Press, 1992.

McKenna, Erin. *The Task of Utopia: A Pragmatist and Feminist Perspective.* Lanham, Md.: Rowman & Littlefield, 2001.

Menand, Louis, ed. *Pragmatism: A Reader.* New York: Random House, 1997.

———. *The Metaphysical Club: A Story of Ideas in America.* New York: Farrar, Straus and Giroux, 2001.

Miklaszewska, Justyna, ed. *Democracy in Central Europe, 1989–1999: Comparative and Historical Perspectives.* Krakow: Meritum/Jagiellonian University Printing House, 2000.

Momaday, N. Scott. *The Man Made of Words.* New York: St. Martin's Griffin, 1997.

Moses, Greg. *Revolution of Conscience: Martin Luther King, Jr., and the Philosophy of Nonviolence.* New York: The Guilford Press, 1997.

Moynihan, Daniel Patrick. *Maximum Feasible Misunderstanding.* New York: The Free Press, 1970.

Narayan, Uma. *Dislocating Cultures: Identities, Traditions, and Third World Feminism.* New York: Routledge, 1997.

Nelessen, Anton C. *Visions for a New American Dream: Process, Principles, and an Ordinance to Plan and Design Small Communities.* Chicago: American Planning Association Press, 1994.

Noddings, Nel. *Caring: A Feminine Approach to Ethics and Moral Education.* 2nd ed. Berkeley: University of California Press, 1984, 2003.

Nozick, Robert. *Philosophical Explanations.* Cambridge, Mass.: Harvard University Press, 1981.

Nussbaum, Martha C. *Sex and Social Justice.* Oxford: Oxford University Press, 1999.

———. *Women and Human Development: The Capabilities Approach.* Cambridge: Cambridge University Press, 2000.

Obama, Barack. *The Audacity of Hope: Thoughts on Reclaiming the American Dream.* New York: Crown, 2006.

Pateman, Carole. *Participation and Democratic Theory.* Cambridge: Cambridge University Press, 1970.

Peat, F. David. *Blackfoot Physics.* York Beach: Phanes Press, 2002.

Pharr, Susan, and Robert D. Putnam, ed. *Disaffected Democracies: What's Troubling the Trilateral Countries?* Princeton, N.J.: Princeton University Press, 2000.

Polletta, Francesca. *Freedom Is an Endless Meeting: Democracy in Social Movements from Pacifism to the Present.* Chicago: University of Chicago Press, 2002.

Pratt, Scott L. *Native Pragmatism: Rethinking the Roots of American Philosophy.* Bloomington: Indiana University Press, 2002.

Putnam, Hilary. *Renewing Philosophy.* Cambridge, Mass.: Harvard University Press, 1992.

——. *Pragmatism: An Open Question.* Malden, Mass.: Blackwell, 1995.

——. *The Threefold Cord: Mind, Body, and World.* New York: Columbia University Press, 1999.

Putnam, Robert D. *Bowling Alone: The Collapse and Revival of American Community.* New York: Simon & Schuster, 2000.

Putnam, Ruth Anna, ed. *The Cambridge Companion to William James.* Cambridge: Cambridge University Press, 1997.

Rajchman, John, and Cornel West. *Post-Analytic Philosophy.* New York: Columbia University Press, 1985.

Randall, John Herman, Jr. "Dewey's Interpretation of the History of Philosophy." In *Library of Living Philosophers*, edited by Paul Arthus Schilpp and Lewis Edwin Hahn. Chicago: Open Court, 1939.

Rawls, John. *A Theory of Justice.* Cambridge, Mass.: Harvard University Press, 1971.

——. "Justice as Fairness: Political Not Metaphysical." *Philosophy and Public Affairs* 14 (1985): 223–252.

——. "The Idea of an Overlapping Consensus." *Oxford Journal of Legal Studies* 7 (1987).

——. "The Domain of the Political and Overlapping Consensus." *New York University Law Review* 64 (1989).

——. "Reply to Habermas." *The Journal of Philosophy* 92, no. 3 (1995): 132–180.

——. *Political Liberalism.* New York: Columbia University Press, 1996.

——. "The Ideal of Public Reason Revisited." *University of Chicago Law Review* 94 (1997).

Rockefeller, Stephen C. *John Dewey: Religious Faith and Democratic Humanism.* New York: Columbia University Press, 1991.

Rorty, Richard. *Philosophy and the Mirror of Nature.* Princeton, N.J.: Princeton University Press, 1979.

——. *Consequences of Pragmatism*. Minneapolis: University of Minnesota Press, 1982.

——. "Solidarity or Objectivity?" In *Post-Analytic Philosophy*, edited by John Rajchman and Cornel West, 3–19. New York: Columbia University Press, 1985.

——. *Contingency, Irony, and Solidarity*. Cambridge: Cambridge University Press, 1989.

——. "The Banality of Pragmatism and the Poetry of Justice." In *Pragmatism in Law and Society*, edited by Michael Brint and William Weaver. Boulder: Westview Press, 1991.

——. "The Future of Philosophy." In *Rorty and Pragmatism: The Philosopher Responds to His Critics*, edited by Herman J. Saatkamp Jr. Nashville, Tenn.: Vanderbilt University Press, 1995.

——. *Achieving Our Country: Leftist Thought in Twentieth Century America*. Cambridge, Mass.: Harvard University Press, 1998.

——. *Philosophy and Social Hope*. New York: Penguin Books, 1999.

——. "Universality and Truth." In *Rorty and His Critics*, edited by Robert B. Brandom. Oxford: Blackwell Publishing, 2000.

——. "Philosophical Geniuses and Professional Philosophers." Panel presentation on the topic "Theoretical Cultures Across the Disciplines," at the annual meeting of the American Sociological Association, San Francisco, California, August 17, 2005.

——. *Philosophy as Cultural Politics*. Cambridge: Cambridge University Press, 2007.

Rorty, Richard, and Pascal Engel. *What's the Use of Truth?* New York: Columbia University Press, 2007.

Rorty, Richard, and Gianni Vattimo. *The Future of Religion*. New York: Columbia University Press, 2005.

Roy, Arundhati. *An Ordinary Person's Guide to Empire*. Cambridge: South End Press, 2004.

Royce, Josiah. *The Philosophy of Loyalty*. Nashville, Tenn.: Vanderbilt University Press, 1995. Originally published in 1908.

——. *The Problem of Christianity*. Chicago: University of Chicago Press, 1967. Originally published in 1916.

Ruddick, Sara. *Maternal Thinking: Toward a Politics of Peace*. Boston: Beacon Press, 1995.

Saatkamp, Herman, ed. *Rorty and Pragmatism: The Philosopher Responds to His Critics*. Nashville, Tenn.: Vanderbilt University Press, 1995.

Saito, Naoko. *The Gleam of Light: Moral Perfectionism and Education in Dewey and Emerson*. New York: Fordham University Press, 2005.

Sandel, Michael. *Democracy's Discontent: America in Search of a Public Philosophy*. Cambridge, Mass.: Harvard University Press, 1996.

Savage, Daniel. *John Dewey's Liberalism: Individual, Community, and Self-Development*. Carbondale: Southern Illinois University Press, 2002.

Seigfried, Charlene Haddock. *Pragmatism and Feminism: Reweaving the Social Fabric.* Chicago: University of Chicago Press, 1996.

——. "Experience, Anyone? Why Pragmatists Should Get Over the Realism/Anti-Realism Debate." *Intellectual History Newsletter* 20 (1998).

——. "Pragmatist Metaphysics? Why Terminology Matters." *Transactions of the Charles S. Peirce Society* 37, no. 1 (2001).

——, ed. *Feminist Interpretations of John Dewey.* University Park: The Pennsylvania State University Press, 2002.

——. "Ghosts Walking Underground: Dewey's Vanishing Metaphysics." *Transactions of the Charles S. Peirce Society* 40, no. 1 (2004).

Sen, Amartya. *Development as Freedom.* New York: Alfred A. Knopf, 1999.

Serageldin, Ismail. "The Environment and Development: Strange Bedfellows?" Speech at Reuters Forum at Columbia University, April 30, 1997.

Shade, Patrick. *Habits of Hope: A Pragmatic Theory.* Nashville, Tenn.: Vanderbilt University Press, 2001.

Shook, John R., and Joseph Margolis, ed. *A Companion to Pragmatism.* New York: Blackwell, 2006.

Shusterman, Richard. *Practicing Philosophy: Pragmatism and the Philosophical Life.* New York: Routledge, 1997.

——, ed. *Bourdieu: A Critical Reader.* Malden, Mass.: Blackwell, 1999.

Singer, Beth J. *Operative Rights.* Albany: State University of New York Press, 1993.

——. *Pragmatism, Rights, and Democracy.* New York: Fordham University Press, 1999.

Siriani, Carmen, and Lewis Friedland. *Civic Innovation in America: Community Empowerment, Public Policy, and the Movement for Civic Renewal.* Berkeley: University of California Press, 2001.

Skocpol, Theda. *Diminished Democracy: From Membership to Management in American Civic Life.* Norman: University of Oklahoma Press, 2003.

Sleeper, R. W. *The Necessity of Pragmatism: John Dewey's Conception of Philosophy.* Urbana: University of Illinois Press, 2001.

Smith, Dorothy. *The Everyday World as Problematic: A Feminist Sociology.* Boston: Northeastern University Press, 1987.

——. *The Conceptual Practices of Power: A New Feminist Sociology of Knowledge.* Boston: Northeastern University Press, 1990.

Stanton, Elizabeth Cady. *The Woman's Bible.* New York: European Publishing Company, 1895.

Stewart, Jeffrey C., ed. *Alain L. Locke's Race Contacts and Interracial Relations.* Washington, D.C.: Howard University Press, 1992.

Stikkers, Kenneth W. "Instrumental Relativism and Cultivated Pluralism: Alain Locke and Philosophy's Quest for a Common World." In *The Critical Pragmatism of Alain Locke: A Reader on Value Theory, Aesthetics, Community, Culture, Race, and Education*, edited by Leonard Harris. Lanham, Md.: Rowman & Littlefield, 1999.

Stuhr, John J. *Genealogical Pragmatism: Philosophy, Experience, and Community.* Albany: State University of New York Press, 1997.

——. *Pragmatism, Postmodernism, and the Future of Philosophy.* New York: Routledge, 2002.

Sullivan, Shannon L. *Living Across and Through Skins: Transactional Bodies, Pragmatism, and Feminism.* Bloomington: Indiana University Press, 2002.

Susskind, Lawrence, et al. *Transboundary Environmental Negotiation: New Approaches to Global Cooperation.* San Francisco: Jossey-Bass, 2002.

——. *Democracy After Liberalism: Pragmatism and Deliberative Politics.* New York: Routledge, 2005.

Tan, Sor-Hoon. *Confucian Democracy: A Deweyan Reconstruction.* Albany: State University of New York Press, 2004.

Tocqueville, Alexis de. *Democracy in America.* Edited by J. P. Mayer. Translated by George Lawrence. New York: Harper and Row, 1969. Originally published in 1835 and 1840.

Tong, Rosemarie Putnam. *Feminist Thought: A More Comprehensive Introduction.* 2nd ed. Boulder, Colo.: Westview Press, 1998.

Touraine, Alain. *What Is Democracy?* Translated by David Macey. Boulder, Colo.: Westview Press, 1998.

Tyler, Patrick E. "There's a New Enemy in Iraq: The Nasty Surprise." *New York Times,* June 1, 2003.

Valadez, Jorge M. *Deliberative Democracy, Political Legitimacy, and Self-Determination in Multicultural Societies.* Boulder, Colo.: Westview Press, 2001.

Wallis, Jim. *The Soul of Politics.* New York: The New Press and Orbis Books, 1994.

Walzer, Michael. *Thick and Thin: Moral Arguments at Home and Abroad.* Notre Dame, Ind.: University of Notre Dame Press, 1994.

Warren, Karen M. *Ecofeminism: Women, Culture, Nature.* Bloomington: Indiana University Press, 1997.

——. *Ecofeminist Philosophy: A Western Perspective on What It Is and Why It Matters.* Lanham, Md.: Rowman & Littlefield, 2002.

Warren, Mark R. *Dry Bones Rattling: Community Building to Revitalize American Democracy.* Princeton, N.J.: Princeton University Press, 2001.

West, Cornel. *The American Evasion of Philosophy.* Madison: University of Wisconsin Press, 1989.

——. *Race Matters.* New York: Vintage, 1994.

——. *Democracy Matters: Winning the Fight Against Imperialism.* New York: Vintage, 2004.

Westbrook, Robert. *John Dewey and American Democracy.* Ithaca, N.Y.: Cornell University Press, 1991.

———. *Democratic Hope: Pragmatism and the Politics of Truth*. Ithaca, N.Y.: Cornell University Press, 2005.

Whitman, Walt. *Song of Myself*. In *The Portable Walt Whitman*, edited by Mark Van Doren. New York: Penguin, 1973. Originally published in 1855.

———. 1865–66. "When Lilacs Last in the Dooryard Bloomed." In *The Portable Walt Whitman*, edited by Mark Van Doren. New York: Penguin, 1973. Originally published in 1865–1866.

———. 1865–66. "O Captain! My Captain!" In *The Portable Walt Whitman*, edited by Mark Van Doren. New York: Penguin, 1973. Originally published in 1865–1866.

———. 1871. *Democratic Vistas*. In *The Portable Walt Whitman*, edited by Mark Van Doren. New York: Penguin, 1973. Originally published in 1871.

Wiesel, Elie. "Only the Guilty Are Guilty, Not Their Sons." *New York Times*, May 5, 2001.

Wills, Garry. *Inventing America: Jefferson's Declaration of Independence*. New York: Random House, 1978.

Wilshire, Bruce. *The Primal Roots of American Philosophy: Pragmatism, Phenomenology, and Native American Thought*. University Park: Pennsylvania State University Press, 2000.

———. *Get 'Em All, Kill 'Em: Genocide, Terrorism, Righteous Communities*. Lanham, Md.: Lexington Books, 2004.

Wilson, William Julius. *The Bridge Over the Racial Divide: Rising Inequality and Coalition Politics*. Berkeley: University of California Press, 1999.

Wittgenstein, Ludwig. *Philosophical Investigations*. 3rd ed. Translated by G. E. M. Anscombe. New York: Macmillan, 1958.

Woods, David W. "Lynnwood Legacy: A Collaborative Planning Model for the 1990s." *Urban Design and Planning* (July 1993).

———. "Collaborative Planning for the Lynnwood Legacy: A Successful Alternative to 'Traditional' Planning." In *Compendium of Papers for the Fifteenth Annual International Bicycle and Pedestrian Conference*. Boulder: City of Boulder, 1994.

———. *Participatory Democracy, Civil Renewal: Rebuilding Lower Manhattan and the Question of Citizen Voice*. Forthcoming.

Young, Iris Marion. "Community and the Other: Beyond Deliberative Democracy." In *Democracy and Difference: Contesting the Boundaries of the Political*, edited by Seyla Benhabib. Princeton, N.J.: Princeton University Press, 1996.

———. *Inclusion and Democracy*. Oxford: Oxford University Press, 2000.

Yunus, Muhammad. *Creating a World Without Poetry: Social Business and the Future of Capitalism*. New York: Public Affairs, 2007.

INDEX